Published by Academica Group

**CANADIAN OFFICES**

131 Wharncliffe Road S.
London, ON N6J 2K4, CA

490 Adelaide St. W.
Toronto, ON M5V 1T2, CA

**U.S. OFFICES**

100 Cummings Center
Suite 207p, Beverly, MA 01915

1175 Revolution Mill Road, Suite 3
Greensboro, NC 27405

Electronic versions of this publication may be retrieved at no cost from www.academicagroup.ca. Print versions may be purchased from Academica Group by calling 519-433-8302 or online at www.academicagroup.ca.

Academica Group publishes its books and white papers in electronic formats. Some content that appears in print may not be available in electronic versions.

Printed in Canada
FIRST EDITION

# CONTENTS

# PREFACE

Strategic Enrolment Intelligence reflects the emergence of a discipline within Canadian higher education that is increasingly a staple of the business and planning practices of colleges and universities. Conceptually, the term is defined as "the use of actionable intelligence to inform enrolment strategies and practices and thus, position an institution strategically to achieve optimal enrolment results." In practical terms, strategic enrolment intelligence refers to doing the right things, at the right time, with the right people in order to achieve enrolment-related goals.

As you may be aware, the discipline of enrolment management has a relatively brief history. It began in the U.S. at Boston College in the mid-70s. The advent of enrolment management in Canada did not occur until recently—spurred by increased competition, demographic shifts, and in some provinces, government mandates related to growth expectations, funding levels, or changes to institutional missions. Still in its infancy in Canada, we believe that enrolment management will play a major role in the vitality of institutions for the foreseeable future. By applying enrolment management concepts and principles to a changing postsecondary education (PSE) landscape, institutions will more strategically position themselves for anticipated, external opportunities and threats as well as hone their internal strengths and mitigate weaknesses.

In the early days of its evolution, enrolment management was focused primarily on institutional marketing followed by student recruitment. Today, however, enrolment management has emerged as a holistic, "cradle to endowment" model for attracting, retaining, and graduating students and often, building loyalty among alums. At its core, enrolment management is about an integrated, data-driven approach to initiating and cultivating relationships with students throughout their life cycle with an institution. Fundamentally, enrolment management embraces both the strategic and tactical, leverages data for decision-making, works across organizational boundaries to engage the entire campus community, and focuses on the needs of students as learners and customers.

Based on the authors' collective experience, first as higher education practitioners and subsequently, as consultants, researchers, technology service providers for numerous colleges and universities throughout Canada and beyond, we have written chapters that bring to the forefront insightful observations that apply to any institutional type or setting. Moreover, the theory and recommendations in this book are grounded in the reality of our own experiences and the Canadian PSE environment. In this regard, Academica is best known for its research with hundreds of thousands of PSE applicants over the past fourteen years along with the *Top Ten*, a daily e-newsletter with over 5,000 Canadian PSE subscribers. The insights gained from surveying applicants and canvassing the PSE environment for emerging trends are infused into the content of this book.

As the first Canadian book on enrolment management, *Strategic Enrolment Intelligence* will serve as a valuable resource for your institution. We encourage you to share this book with other leaders on your campus. Host a book club or a Conversation Café around the implications of the book's conclusions for your institution. You also are invited to contact Academica to arrange a Webinar with one or more of the chapter authors.

## THE PURPOSE OF THE BOOK

*Strategic Enrolment Intelligence* is intended to create conversation around the enrolment issues facing executive leaders on college and university campuses. Our hope is that these conversations will lead to research, planning, action, and evaluation of enrolment efforts linked to institutional goals.

In addition to insights into the literature on enrolment management and other disciplines that inform enrolment practices, this book identifies the role of leaders in various aspects of the enrolment enterprise and provides practical strategies and leadership approaches. This is not a "how-to" book for enrolment practitioners. Instead, the book focuses on what leaders can and should do to ensure their institutions have high-performing enrolment organizations with the capacity and strategic intelligence necessary to execute goal-driven strategies to perfection. Throughout the book, authors advocate for continuous improvement as a means to sustaining competitive advantage.

## INTENDED AUDIENCE

The book is primarily written for those in leadership roles who can influence enrolment direction and strategies, organizational capacity, and institutional culture. On many campuses, "executive leaders" refers to individuals at the dean's level or above. While the book is targeted to this audience, the authors believe that leaders can and do come from many levels within the organizational structure. Hence, the book is recommended for anyone who has the ability to influence people and the organization.

## THE ORGANIZATION OF THE BOOK

The book is organized into two parts and nine chapters. Part One (Chapters One, Two, and Three) provides a high-level contextual overview of common enrolment issues, the Canadian PSE landscape, and the actionable intelligence required to inform enrolment strategy. In Part Two (Chapters Four through Eight), the focus shifts to key enrolment enablers and core strategy areas, including the organizational capacity necessary to effectively execute enrolment strategies and foster a strategic enrolment management (SEM) culture. The Conclusion conveys imperatives related to reputation, recruitment, and retention—describing practical actions institutional leaders should pursue.

## ACKNOWLEDGEMENTS

The chapter authors and staff of Academica deserve our thanks for sharing their expertise and valuable time. Their commitment to contributing to the literature of enrolment management has been exemplary.

# ABOUT THE AUTHORS

## DR. JIM BLACK

Dr. Black is the president and CEO of SEM Works, and an internationally recognized expert in enrolment management as well as in change management. He has published a monograph titled, *Navigating Change in the New Millennium: Strategies for Enrollment Leaders*, and three books, The *Strategic Enrollment Management Revolution*, considered to be a groundbreaking publication for the enrolment management profession; *Gen Xers Return to College*; and *Essentials of Enrollment Management: Cases in the Field*. Among his other published works are numerous articles and book chapters including a feature article in *College & University*, "Creating Customer Delight"; a chapter, "Creating a Student-Centered Culture," for a book on best practices in student services published by SCUP and sponsored by IBM; a chapter on enrolment management in a Jossey-Bass book on student academic services; as well as a bimonthly feature in *The Greentree Gazette*.

Black was honored as the recipient of the 2005 AACRAO Distinguished Service Award. He has been interviewed by publications such as *The Chronicle of Higher Education, Converge Magazine, The Enrollment Management Report, The Lawlor Review*, and was interviewed for AACRAO's Data Dispenser. Black also was featured in an international teleconference on enrolment management sponsored by The Center for the Freshman Year Experience at the University of South Carolina, and a PBS broadcast on "Blending High Tech and High Touch Student Services." Since 1999, Jim Black has been an IBM Best Practices Partner, one of only twenty-three in the world. He was invited by The College Board to Heidelberg, Germany, to evaluate the APIEL Exam and most recently was invited to lead conferences on enrolment management and student services in the United Kingdom and the Netherlands.

Dr. Black has served on the boards of several technology companies and has consulted with companies such as Microsoft, Blackboard, and the SAS Institute. Higher education clients have included over 300 two-year, four-year, public, and private institutions.

Jim earned a B.A. in English education and M.A. in higher education administration from the University of South Carolina, as well as a Ph.D. in higher education curriculum and teaching from The University of North Carolina at Greensboro. His doctoral experience provides our clients with unique perspectives into innovative pedagogical, curricular, and program opportunities that impact enrolment outcomes. Leveraging his educational background along with his many years as an associate provost, dean, and faculty member in a higher education environment, Dr. Black provides institutions with strategic insights that are grounded in theory and are actionable.

## PHILIP BLISS

Philip Bliss, a digital pioneer, has been at the forefront of digital media development for the past twenty-five years. He is an accomplished technology, marketing, and business strategist and entrepreneur with the hands-on ability to turn ideas into results. He has founded and grown three market-leading communications agencies: The Creative Marketing Network, x2idea Corporation, and Group Multimedia Network (GMN), Canada's fifth-largest privately owned agency at the time.

Philip's national and international track record includes many educational, nonprofit, American Indian, and corporate clients, including the Smithsonian Institution National Museum of the American Indian, Grant MacEwan University, Brock University, Tyndale University & Seminary, Confederation College, First Nations Oweesta Corporation, Georgian College, Bayshore Bank & Trust, Microsoft, ATI Technologies, NEC, Samsung, and Cisco Systems.

Since Academica Group acquired x2idea, Philip has led the technology practice of the company, which provides Web strategy, creative, and development services for medium to large scale Web projects in the higher education sector. Currently, Philip's team is also developing a new collaborative Enrolment Analytics Research Platform for Higher Education and has just released Version3 of Academica's Drupal-based HigherEdCMS Module.

Philip holds an Honours B.A. in English and Media Studies from the University of Stirling, Scotland.

## DR. BRYANT HUTSON

Dr. Bryant Hutson has over fifteen years of experience in higher education as an administrator, program evaluator, and faculty member, including coordinating first-year experience and retention programming and leading assessment efforts as Associate Director for Student Academic Services at The University of North Carolina at Greensboro (UNCG). He was also research associate at the Center for Educational Research and Evaluation at UNCG, where he participated in large-scale program evaluation projects and played a key role in developing instruments used in K–12 and higher education settings. He served as the technology and research coordinator for The College Foundation of North Carolina Resource Center when it was first established, and has been a faculty member at The University of North Carolina at Greensboro, Greensboro College, Rockingham Community College, and Guilford Technical Community College.

Hutson holds a Ph.D. in higher education administration with a concentration in educational research, measurement, and evaluation. His research focuses on the development and impact of first-year experience and retention programming on student success. He has been an active member of the National Academic Advising Association (NACADA), American Educational Research Association (AERA), and American Evaluation Association (AEA) and has made over fifty refereed presentations at national conferences. Collaborating with international colleagues, he has presented at international conferences and was an invited guest lecturer at Shanghai Normal University. His publications include a leading text on strengths-based academic advising, *The Appreciative Advising Revolution*; a chapter on organizational change for a NACADA research monograph; a chapter in *Gen Xers Return to College*; a section in the *Academic Advising Handbook*; and refereed articles in the *Journal of Applied Research in Higher Education* and the *Journal of College Student Retention.*

Hutson's work with SEM Works includes planning, conducting, and overseeing research projects; environmental scanning; conducting market opportunity analyses, academic program reviews, and application and retention enrolment decision studies; and developing program evaluation plans and instrumentation.

## ROD SKINKLE

Building upon his background in higher education student affairs research, Rod has led Academica Group to become a leading provider of higher education focused policy, consumer research, enrolment consulting, and technology innovation throughout North America. With Canadian corporate offices in London and Toronto, Academica Group has worked with most of Canada's leading universities and colleges coast-to-coast, and is growing rapidly in the U.S. with offices in Boston, Massachusetts and Greensboro, North Carolina.

Rod has pioneered the development of research tools and studies for North American institutions and is the founder of the largest ongoing syndicated study of higher education consumers in North America, the University & College Applicant Survey (UCAS™). This study has provided valuable insights into the motivations and aspirations of post-secondary students from 1996 to present. Rod presents research and position papers to a wide range of policy/government groups (e.g., Canada Millennium Scholarship Foundation, Higher Education Quality Council of Ontario, Council of Ontario Universities, Association of Community Colleges of Canada, Human Resources and Skills Development Canada) and has published numerous studies in scholarly journals, including *The Journal of College Student Development, Canadian Journal of Higher Education*, the *American Psychological Association, and Ivey School of Business Journal.*

Rod has been an invited guest expert addressing trends in higher education on Canada AM, Report on Business Television, CBC, Maclean's magazine, Marketing magazine, and was recently a featured interview guest with University Affairs magazine along with Academica Group cofounder, Ken Steele.

In addition to his overall leadership and executive responsibilities, Rod leads and is committed to maintaining a thriving social policy research division focused on higher education accessibility, student success, education, and career goal development.

Rod holds a Diploma in behavioural science, Loyalist College, an Honours Degree in psychology, The University of Waterloo, and a Master's degree in applied social research from the University of Saskatchewan.

## KEN STEELE

Steele is cofounder and Senior Vice-President of Academica Group, Inc., with Canadian corporate offices in London and Toronto. Academica Group has worked with most of Canada's leading universities and colleges coast-to-coast, and is growing rapidly in the U.S. with offices in Boston, Massachusetts and Greensboro, North Carolina. Ken's area of consulting practice is institutional brand strategy and recruitment marketing, and he has led major projects in recent years for Lethbridge College, the University of the Fraser Valley, Mount Royal University, and the University of Saskatchewan, among others.

Four years ago, as a service to Canada's higher education community, Ken founded a free daily news brief, Academica's *Top Ten*, which summarizes important events, emerging trends, research findings, and aspects of youth culture for more than 9,000 subscribers, including college and university presidents and senior executives, government policy analysts, faculty, high school guidance counselors, and national media editors. Ken has written numerous articles and white papers on institutional marketing and strategy, a syndicated column on graphic design, and a regular blog on higher education issues, and now manages a YouTube channel featuring notable higher education commercials.

Ken is a "recovering academic," who was an award-winning Ph.D. candidate in English Literature at the University of Toronto before leaving academia to found a regional advertising agency in 1990. Ken and his team developed branding, marketing, and advertising campaigns for dozens of corporate, nonprofit, and education-sector clients throughout the 1990s, before merging the agency to form Academica Group in 2005.

## LYNDA WALLACE-HULECKI

Lynda Wallace-Hulecki, SEM Works' Vice-President for Strategy, has extensive experience and a proven record of accomplishments in facilitating campus-wide strategic planning and transformative change in policies, systems, and practices within both a college and university context. Her higher education career spanned more than thirty years and encompassed successful senior leadership roles in directing an institutional research and planning office— a role she served for more than twenty-three years, followed by almost a decade in leading strategic change in enrolment management operations at both the undergraduate and graduate levels. A highlight of her professional career was receiving a staff-nominated "Distinguished Administrator Award" for which she was recognized for her contributions as a visionary leader of change who has a passion for excellence.

Regarded as a thought leader within the Canadian higher education system, Wallace-Hulecki served on provincial and federal task forces related to inter-provincial student mobility and higher education accountability. As an experienced enrolment management professional, she has authored numerous white papers and book chapters on the evolving field of strategic enrolment management (SEM) practice, and has served as past editor of a monthly enrolment management e-newsletter, *SEM Canada*. She also has been an active member of numerous professional associations, such as AACRAO, ARUCC, NASPA, AIR, SCUP, and EDUCAUSE.

Wallace-Hulecki is an experienced higher education consultant who specializes in facilitating an integrated approach to academic and enrolment planning. As a current doctoral candidate at the University of Nebraska, her graduate research has focused on the evolving field of SEM, and on the application of learned concepts in building organizational capacity for high enrolment performance. Wallace-Hulecki holds a B.Sc. in the mathematical sciences from the University of Manitoba, and an M.Ed. in higher education from the University of Nebraska. She is currently an Ed.D. candidate in educational leadership and higher education at the University of Nebraska.

# PART ONE

Enrolment Issues and Opportunities

Strategic Enrolment Issues Facing Higher Education Leaders

The Changing Canadian PSE Landscape

Actionable Intelligence: Research for SEM

# INTRODUCTION:
## ENROLMENT ISSUES AND OPPORTUNITIES

The Canadian higher education landscape is in the midst of significant change. We contend that most institutions will emerge from these tumultuous times definitively different. Whether or not they evolve as stronger entities depends largely on how strategic they are within the context of enrolment and reputational management. How effectively they use scarce institutional resources to enhance quality, maintain or increase enrolments, and improve their competitive position in the postsecondary market will determine their viability and relevance to those they serve.

We believe that colleges and universities that do not have a firm grasp of the implications of environmental factors and take measured steps to seize opportunities and mitigate threats will falter. Similarly, they must leverage data and research to target institutional responses to the enrolment issues and opportunities on the horizon. The days of learning through "trial and error" are over. In this PSE environment, organizational missteps or negligence will have profound consequences, and the recovery time will be much longer and more painful than ever before. Today's educational consumers are unforgiving.

The chapters in Part One provide a glimpse into the enrolment context for Canadian colleges and universities. Chapter One foreshadows key concepts described in detail in the chapters that follow. In particular, this chapter focuses on the use of strategic intelligence to inform decisions and strategy. Chapter Two reflects several years of actively monitoring PSE trends in Canada. The author shares trend data and institutional examples to illustrate the changing landscape. In Chapter Three, the core message of the book is conveyed—transforming research into actionable intelligence. Without this ingredient, an institution cannot be strategic. This chapter addresses the need for quality research as well as the best uses of research in SEM.

# CHAPTER ONE
## STRATEGIC ENROLMENT ISSUES FACING HIGHER EDUCATION LEADERS

**BY JIM BLACK**

In today's economic environment, institutional leaders are painfully aware of the need to manage costs and grow revenue streams. If leveraged properly, strategic enrolment management (SEM) is an invaluable tool for achieving both of these objectives. SEM is "a comprehensive process designed to achieve and maintain the optimum recruitment, retention, and attainment of students where optimum is defined within the academic context of the institution" (Dolence, 1993, 1997). Over the past decade and at an accelerated rate during the last five years, Canadian college and university leaders have increasingly developed an appetite for integrating enrolment management into institutional strategic planning, analyzing enrolment data, and investing in a resource hungry enrolment enterprise (Black, 2008a). However, many still struggle to (1) proactively exploit external opportunities and mitigate threats, (2) convert raw data into actionable intelligence, (3) utilize technology to enable enrolment strategies and practices, (4) position the institution effectively among competitors, (5) significantly impact student success and retention, (6) align enrolment efforts with the goals and capacity of the academic enterprise, and (7) build organizational capacity to sustain competitive advantage.

The remainder of this chapter is dedicated to introducing related issues and opportunities. Chapters that follow delve deeply into each—conveying the underlying theory and recommending strategies and models for institutional leaders to consider.

## THE BOILING FROG METAPHOR

You may recall the metaphor of the boiling frog. According to the metaphor, if a frog is placed in a pot of boiling water, it instinctively leaps out. However, if the water is room temperature and the heat is gradually ratcheted up, the frog will remain and eventually boil.

The lesson for higher education in this metaphor is not to fall prey to incremental shifts in the environment. As consultants for some 400 institutions across North America, we see this scenario repeated far too often. Usually, institutions at the most risk are those that have experienced consecutive years of enrolment success. They become comfortable—assuming that enrolment will continue to grow without intervention or further investments. Institutional paralysis sets in and leaders begin to overlook the obvious and their instincts betray them (Gladwell, 2005). Eventually, a tipping point is reached and enrolment begins to spiral downward.

To avoid this pitfall, you must begin by facing what Jim Collins (2001) calls the "brutal facts." Chapter Two addresses the emerging Canadian postsecondary education (PSE) landscape. While this chapter provides an excellent overview of trends and related PSE implications, it should be viewed as a starting point. Longer term, your institution should continuously monitor the environment for trends that may affect your enrolment positively or negatively. Trend spotting, environmental scanning, and situational analyses are but a few of the methodologies to consider. Aguilar (1967) described this process as the systematic collection and analysis of external information to (1) reduce the randomness of information flowing into an organization, and (2) provide decision-makers with early warnings of changing conditions that may impact the organization.

Regardless of the methodology you deploy, there are three critical success factors. First, there should be an individual or administrative unit charged with the task of collecting and analyzing environmental trends. At least annually, reports that include analysis and institutional implications should be presented to the executive team for discussion and action. Second, you must get in front of emerging trends. Reacting to them once they arrive at your doorstep produces minimal results. Your institution's strategic plan and enrolment plan should address trends directly with strategies. Frankly, what we most often observe are plans that are inwardly focused. Third, as a campus leader, you have opportunities to convey these trends to the masses. To guard against your message falling on deaf ears, you must articulate how these trends may impact the institution and why individuals at your campus should care. They need to hear specifically what they can do to assist the institution in capitalizing on opportunities or mitigating threats. If your message is primarily about looming threats, you should interject hope—a vision of a better college or university in the midst of environmental challenges. Most importantly, the executive team needs to have a consistent message and stay on message.

The aforementioned recommendations will cause the institution to focus on the right things. But, doing the right things is another matter. Desired strategies and behaviours follow only if the leadership possesses the will to act (Black, 2008b). In this context, the will to act refers to holding people accountable and letting go of less effective strategies and practices. Bridges (1993) asserts that "letting go" is one of the most difficult things for people and organizations to embrace. Our experience with most institutions supports this claim. Institutions are perhaps instinctively inclined to add new initiatives, programs, and services but are reluctant to cease or reduce existing activities. Clearly, this is not a sustainable practice and can effectively stall new initiatives designed to address emerging trends. Begin the process of "doing the right things" by identifying what you will discontinue, morph, or reduce in order to free up the organizational capacity to execute new strategies effectively.

## ANALYSIS WITHOUT PARALYSIS

Every campus we have visited has been engaged in a flurry of enrolment-related activity. However, the most telling question we ask (and one you should ask of your direct reports) is "what works?" Once we get past the "deer in the headlights" reaction, we commonly find that there has been minimal analysis of the effectiveness of strategies—even resource-intensive strategies. In Sun Tzu's *The Art of War* (Giles, 1910), there are many parallels to the business of enrolment management. Perhaps the most important tenet practiced by this ancient consultant of war is that of knowing what works in order to perfect strategy. Without knowing what works, there is no reliable means of "letting go" of less productive strategies, continuously improving existing strategies, or finding room for new strategies within existing capacity. In order to discern what works, you must not only evaluate strategies but you must know your students, your institution, and your competitors as well as create a culture of evidence.

Understanding your students as educational consumers is a basic tenet of marketing (Hayes, 2004). Chapter Three speaks directly to the imperative of knowing your students. Beyond the need to know basic demographic and academic information about students, the strategic insights required to manage enrolments include:

- Institutional awareness
- Institutional perceptions
- Decision factors in selecting your institution or a competitor
- Motivators and barriers to enrolling
- Motivators and barriers to persistence

- Underlying causation of attrition

- Experiential factors related to persistence

- Student satisfaction levels

- Course-taking patterns and preferences

- Learning modality preferences

- Learning style strengths

In addition to these mostly quantitative measures, we fervently believe that institutions should engage in ethnographic (the study of student cultures) and psychographic (the study of student values, beliefs, and behaviours) research. By combining quantitative and qualitative research methods, mere numbers become humanized. You will learn from their stories, rituals, artifacts, social norms, and behaviours.

Another, perhaps intuitive, necessary analysis is a study of institutional identity. In our consulting work with colleges and universities, we frequently find institutions grappling with the definitive identity question: "What are we to those we serve?" This seemingly simple question often perplexes executive leaders in the sense that an institution's identity must be unique, true to its mission, and must resonate with its constituents and stakeholders. Without this clarity, it is virtually impossible to market an institution effectively to the outside world. The reputational positioning described in Chapter Five becomes an elusive goal. Internally, a blurred identity leads to confusion around priorities, direction, strategy, and even day-to-day operations. As conveyed in Chapter Eight, organizational capacity building is hampered without this clarity of identity and purpose.

Equally as important is knowing as much as possible about your primary competitors (Kotler, 1999 & Whiteside, 2004). A competitor analysis should consist of comparisons of program array; program curriculum; co-curricular offers such as apprenticeships, internships, and co-ops; faculty expertise; class size; available learning options; job placement rates; transfer rates; and other program or institutional attributes. From an enrolment strategy perspective, a competitor analysis also should assess institutional image, cost, perceived value, marketing message, marketing and enrolment resources, inquiry response time, the quality and relevance of inquiry fulfillment and ongoing cultivation, the frequency of prospective student contacts, and tactics deployed to convert inquiries to applicants and admits to enrolled students. Armed with competitor comparisons, an institution can identify and secure a desired market position, especially as it relates to unclaimed market niches (Black, 2008c).

As alluded to in Chapter Eight, institutional leaders should foster a culture of evidence. For enrolment management purposes, a culture of evidence should focus on continuous improvement—primarily by evaluating return on investment (ROI). A simple return on investment formula is depicted below:

$$ROI = \frac{(\text{Gain from Investment - Cost of Investment})}{\text{Cost of Investment}}$$

However, this formula is far too limiting for higher education. You also should evaluate ROI on the basis of a strategy's capacity to benefit students, the community you serve, and the institution in non-financial terms (e.g., institutional reputation, academic quality, student diversity). By routinely evaluating ROI in a holistic manner and redeploying resources and effort accordingly, your institution will have the potential to sustain competitive advantage.

## OPTIMIZING TECHNOLOGY

Often technology is viewed as the proverbial "black hole." While the capital expense of technology is formidable, our experience suggests that the missed opportunity costs are even higher. Rarely do we find institutions that are fully optimizing the technology they own. In fact, too often we observe technology that is not functional or is functioning at sixty percent or less capacity. More often than not, the problem is not with the technology itself but rather with the lack of organizational capacity. This is a leadership issue.

So that you are not squandering institutional investments in technology, ensure that the capacity to implement and maintain the technology you acquire is in place before purchasing anything. Without the capacity to support technology, your institution will limp along and students, faculty, and staff will suffer the consequences. Specifics about the infrastructure to support technology adequately are outlined in Chapter Seven.

The other common mistake we see at colleges and universities is technology absent of or driving strategy. In point of fact, strategy should be clearly defined prior to the purchase of technology. Strategy should drive technology. A profound example of this miscalculation can be found in portal technology. A few years back, institutions were chasing portal systems that could streamline student services and aid in the recruitment of students. The Information Technology Division at most institutions assumed responsibility for portal projects. As a result, the portals evolved as technically sound systems devoid of strategy. There was no clear marketing, recruitment, or retention purpose, and no one charged with harvesting information daily and repurposing said information for the portal, so that it was fresh every time a student chose to visit. Other than completing required business transactions with institutions, the true potential has not been realized. But the story does not end with portals. Most institutions possess enterprise systems, customer relationship management systems, Web sites, and other applications that suffer from the same omission of strategy.

## IN SEARCH OF GAME CHANGING INSTITUTIONAL POSITIONING

Massa (2004) posits that "institutions must develop a position that conveys a promise to its internal and external audiences." The concept of a promise-oriented approach to positioning is explored in Chapter Five. In general, reputational positioning follows a tried-and-true formula. According to Sevier (2003), there are three steps to creating a competitive market position:

1. **Competitor identification**
2. **Development of points of difference**
3. **Communication of points of difference to key audiences**

While these tenets are sound, alone they are not game changers. To radically alter your institution's position you must search for what Kim and Mauborgne (2005) call a blue ocean strategy. Fundamentally, blue ocean strategies are those that allow you to leapfrog the competition. In the private sector, the recent introduction of the iPad has changed the electronic reader and entertainment industry forever. Apple did not seek to emulate best practices in the industry or marginally surpass competing products such as the Kindle or Sony's Digital Reader. Their goal was to become the dominant player in the market.

In our work with colleges and universities, we search for blue ocean strategies that are congruent with an institution's mission and its natural personality. Sometimes the game changer is a new creation, but it always builds on the institution's existing strengths. Rarely have we found one thing powerful enough to reposition an institution. Instead, the game changing position usually involves bundling existing strengths together with compelling and intuitive packaging.

We also have learned that timing is everything. The release of the right positioning strategy just at the time when the market is ready for it determines the strategy's success. For example, the University of Regina launched the UR Guarantee in the midst of an uncertain economy when student anxiety around future employment possibilities peaked. The UR Guarantee is a promise to students who engage in career exploration and preparation, student success support, and leadership and service activities while enrolled that they will be employed within six months of graduation or be eligible for up to thirty hours of additional undergraduate course work with no cost for tuition. This strategy proved to be a game changer—bringing the institution national recognition and contributing to a significant increase in admission applications.

## STUDENT SUCCESS ONE STUDENT AT A TIME

A premise developed more fully in Chapter Six suggests that retention programs and services targeting at-risk students tend to have a short-term effect on a relatively small number of individuals. Though important, such efforts do not possess the reach or sustained impact that creating a culture of student success can yield. Correcting deeply engrained learning behaviours or profound academic deficiencies require labour-intensive, proactive interventions over a protracted timeframe. Similarly, there are seldom easy remedies for complex psychological, emotional, or social problems. For this reason, institutions that are serious about improving student outcomes need a comprehensive, integrated approach to student retention that empowers faculty, staff, and administrators with the skills and resources necessary to address student warning signs as they surface, not a loosely federated array of services. More importantly, by ensuring the conditions for student success are in place campus-wide, an institution can prevent attrition before the situation reaches a tipping point.

The tipping point is different for each student. Contrary to the findings of most withdrawal surveys, there is usually no single event or problem that pushes a student past the tipping point—where the costs of staying exceed the benefits. More often, it is the cumulative effect of various pressure points over time that leads to a student's premature departure. Consequently, "there is no 'quick fix' or single intervention that yields a substantive and lasting change in a human being's capacity to learn or to persist" (Black, 2010). Following this logic, it is clear that one-size-fits-all interventions seldom address the root causes of attrition, which are often masked by the obvious symptom (e.g., poor grades, class absences, or a lack of social integration). Effective interventions are customized, directly related to the individual's attrition causation factors, and administered over a period of time.

Executive leaders are in a unique position to promote a culture of student success—an ethos of caring. That said there must be more than rhetoric. You must demonstrate through action that student success is among the highest priorities of the institution. The following actions are recommended:

- Identify a retention champion, who has the authority and clout necessary to influence employee behaviour, policies, procedures, and strategies.

- Consider the organizational alignment of retention programs and services under the retention champion.

- Have the retention champion develop an integrated retention plan.

- Resource the retention plan adequately.

- Provide training to campus personnel on retention theory and practice as well as available campus resources and referral protocols.

- Reward contributions to the retention effort (e.g., by funding linked enrolments, recognition in the promotion and tenure review process, inclusion of contributions to student success in performance evaluations, release time to lead retention efforts, related professional development).

- Cease the practice of unintentionally punishing those who support student success (e.g., assigning the best advisors more advisees).

- Allocate a research analyst position dedicated to analyzing attrition causation and the effectiveness of retention initiatives.

- Eliminate or scale back less effective retention initiatives and replace them with strategies with greater potential to impact student outcomes.

- Determine what the conditions for success are given the population of students you serve, and ensure the conditions exist or are created.

- Frontload student interaction with your best teachers and advisors at the very time they are most vulnerable—their first year.

## ACADEMIC-DRIVEN ENROLMENT STRATEGIES

An isolated focus on traditional enrolment functions such as marketing, recruitment, retention, and student services will not yield optimal results. Failure to examine the academic product reduces the probability that programs align with market demand, attract desired students, meet learner needs, or possess compelling benefits that increase student retention. Most program review processes that we examine on campuses lead to marginal changes in curriculum or simply justify a program's existence. They typically lack the rigor and often the data required to support enrolment objectives. Devoid of high quality, market-driven, learner-centred academic programs, traditional enrolment functions become muted. No institution can effectively market and recruit for programs that are tone deaf to the needs and expectations of external constituents.

To fully realize the synergistic power of enrolment management and ensure that academic programs are in tune to the needs of the market, an institution must create a SEM culture that is integrated with the academic enterprise. Our experience suggests that this is an evolutionary process that begins with sharing enrolment and academic information across organizational boundaries (e.g., enrolment and retention trend data, academic program and policy changes, environmental scan information). The second evolutionary stage involves communication regarding the shared information—cross-divisional and interschool/college discussions regarding related implications and needed action. In the third stage, there is collaboration between academic and enrolment leaders designed to implement identified action items.

The first three stages are often ad hoc in practice. It is not until the fourth developmental stage of a SEM culture, fusion, that joint efforts begin to become standard practice. For example, in a fused SEM culture, there would never be a new academic program launched without thorough market research at the concept phase of program development to identify and/or validate the market potential. Pre-launch, a marketing plan would be designed to support the program rollout with target audiences, key selling points, marketing channels, recruitment strategies, and promotional collateral. Furthermore, related policies, procedures, and supporting services would be determined before the program launch, so that all individuals and units responsible for the program's success are on the same page. In the final stage, fusion evolves to full integration of the enrolment and academic enterprises such that the two are functioning with a common purpose and are totally in synch.

Never before has an integrated SEM culture been more important than it is today. As of the writing of this chapter, many Canadian colleges and universities are experiencing dramatic enrolment growth. Few, however, are growing strategically. Strategic enrolment growth refers to targeting programs for expansion that have demonstrated untapped demand and unused capacity or capacity that can be developed at a relatively low cost. Growth for growth's sake can result in the dilution of the quality of the academic experience. While random, uncontrolled growth may serve the short-term revenue generation needs of an institution, the longer term impact can be detrimental to the institution's reputation and capacity to effectively serve students.

Henderson (2004) described a blueprint for enrolment management in which the institution's leadership must set an academic tone for enrolment management. Simply put—academic objectives should drive the enrolment direction. Executive leaders should clearly define academic priorities and the institution's enrolment plan should support identified priorities. Even though academic priorities are largely aspirational, they should incorporate business intelligence, institutional capacity, and external forces (e.g., government, oversight boards, and industry leaders) that influence enrolment expectations. Assuming academic priorities are established considering these factors, they will provide a solid foundation for strategic enrolment planning.

## ORGANIZATIONAL CAPACITY: YOUR ONLY SUSTAINABLE COMPETITIVE ADVANTAGE

Through our consulting engagements, we have witnessed numerous exceptional enrolment strategies that have failed due to poor execution. In most cases, these failed strategies were embraced by well-intentioned people who intuitively knew what needed to be done but lacked the capacity to implement. Frequently, capacity constraints were related to insufficient human resources—dedicated time to complete the task at hand. Less often, constraints were associated with financial resources, technology limitations, access to needed data, and space.

Providing these necessary antecedents for success is the role of senior leadership. To guide you in assessing what antecedents are essential, consider the following questions. What are the characteristics of a high performing SEM organization? What capacity conditions are required to attain optimal performance? Both questions are addressed in Chapter Eight with sufficient granularity.

The bottom line is that enrolment strategies "done off the side of the desk" seldom produce desired results and often demoralize the enrolment team. You are encouraged not to pursue a single enrolment strategy without the antecedents for success in place. Your institution will be better served by implementing fewer strategies well. Clearly, this assumes the strategies that matter most to achieving enrolment goals are pursued. Institutional leaders should require justifications and supporting data before approving strategies and follow up to determine the actual ROI. By doing so, you will increase the likelihood that the right strategies are in the mix.

Lastly, you should focus less on enrolment numbers and more on the capacity to produce enrolment results—your people. Invest in human capital. Staff learning and retention will directly affect your institution's ability to achieve enrolment outcomes. For example, it is common for recruiter positions to turn over every two to three years. With such attrition among your sales team, your institution will never develop relations with school counsellors, and your recruiters will never adequately learn your academic product. They leave your institution because they are underpaid, overworked, and have limited opportunities for advancement. You control these staff attrition factors.

## SUMMARY

The title of this book, *Strategic Enrolment Intelligence*, implies that being strategic is fundamental to creating and sustaining competitive advantage. Core elements of this chapter and the entire book demonstrate how executive leaders can position their institutions to increasingly be strategic in enrolment planning, execution, and assessment. The authors fervently believe that seeing what is on the horizon and proactively seizing anticipated opportunities and mitigating threats is a prerequisite for becoming strategic. Likewise, it is impossible to be strategic without leveraging available data and research as actionable intelligence.

Remaining core elements focus on strategic opportunities that, if supported by institutional leaders, can produce considerable results for your institution. By leveraging technology fully, you will enable your faculty and staff to effectively implement enrolment initiatives and serve students. Out-of-the-box reputational positioning will secure your competitive foothold in an increasingly saturated and aggressive higher education market. A student success culture will foster improved student performance and retention. And finally, congruence between the objectives of the academic enterprise and enrolment efforts will ensure that your institution is nimble and market responsive.

Of course, your success in pursuing these strategic opportunities is largely dependent upon building organizational capacity to support the attainment of priorities and goals that matter most to your institution. Only senior leaders are in a position to develop the necessary capacity for success. Bold leadership combined with a clearly articulated enrolment vision and the will to act are requirements to realize your enrolment and institutional aspirations.

## REFERENCES

Aguilar, F. (1967). *Scanning the business environment*. New York, NY: Macmillan.

Black, J. (2008a). *New directions in strategic enrollment management*. VA: Strategic Initiatives.

Black, J. (2008b, May). *Enrollment management: A systems approach*. [White paper]. Retrieved from http://www.semworks.net/white-papers.php

Black, J. (2008c, May). *Perfecting enrollment strategy*. [White paper]. Retrieved from http://www.semworks.net/white-papers.php

Black, J. (2010, May). *Creating a retention culture*. [White paper]. Retrieved from http://www.semworks.net/white-papers.php

Bridges, W. (1993). *Managing transitions: Making the most of change*. Reading, MA: Addison-Wesley Publishing Company.

Collins, J. (2001). *Good to great*. New York, NY: HarperCollins Publishers Inc.

Dolence, M. G. (1993, 1997). *Strategic enrollment management: A primer for campus administrators*. (2nd ed.). Washington, DC: American Association of Collegiate Registrars and Admissions Officers.

Giles, L. (Sun Tzu, trans. 1910). *The art of war*. English translation published by the U.S. Military. Washington, DC: Gutenberg Project.

Gladwell, M. (2005). *Blink*. New York, NY: Time Warner Book Group.

Hayes, T. (2004). *Acquiring and using marketing information for strategic decision-making*. In Whiteside, R. (Ed.), Student marketing for colleges and universities, 47–62. Washington, DC: American Association of Collegiate Registrars and Admissions Officers.

Henderson, S. E. (2004, November). *Refocusing enrollment management: Losing structure and finding the academic context*. Fourteenth Annual Enrollment Management Conference, Orlando, Florida.

Kim, W. C. & Mauborgne, R. (2005). *Blue ocean strategy*. Cambridge, MA: Harvard Business School Publishing Corporation.

Kotler, P. (1999). *Kotler on marketing: How to create and dominate markets*. New York, NY: The Free Press.

Massa, R. J. (2004). *Mission and vision in institutional marketing*. In Whiteside, R. (Ed.), Student marketing for colleges and universities, 19–28. Washington, DC: American Association of Collegiate Registrars and Admissions Officers.

Sevier, R. A. (2003). *An integrated marketing workbook for colleges and universities*. Hiawatha, Iowa: Strategy Publishing.

Whiteside, R. (Ed.), (2004). *Student marketing for colleges and universities*. Washington, DC: American Association of Collegiate Registrars and Admissions Officers.

# CHAPTER TWO
## THE CHANGING CANADIAN PSE LANDSCAPE

### BY KEN STEELE

### ACCELERATING EVOLUTION OF PSE—THE LONG VIEW

In the world today there are universities that have endured, largely unchanged, for almost a millennium: the Università di Bologna traces its origins to 1088 AD, the Université de Paris to 1150 AD, and the University of Oxford to 1167 AD. Canada's oldest academic institutions are Université Laval (founded as the Seminaire de Quebec in 1663), the University of New Brunswick (1785), and the University of King's College in Halifax (1789). Although six hundred years had passed, the structure, governance, and mechanics of higher education had changed very little by the time it took root in this country. Academic institutions were still primarily committed to preserving knowledge, from antiquity to the present day, in massive libraries impervious to the incidental shocks of plague, warfare, religious schism, or political upheaval. Young would-be scholars went to "read" in university libraries, tutored by professors and enlightened by lectures. For centuries, timelessness was a key virtue of the academic enterprise, and there was nothing particularly denigrating about being labeled an "ivory tower."

In the mid-twentieth century, however, the global environment surrounding higher education began to evolve, and North American institutions have faced a climate of exponentially accelerating change over the past sixty years. Religious foundations gradually gave way to secular funding, and government interest in academic research has steadily grown since the 1940s for military, and now economic, ends. In the 1950s, the post-war GI Bill sparked an unprecedented expansion and democratization of higher education in the U.S., and ultimately in Canada. In the 1960s, networks of hundreds of community colleges were established in both countries to provide career-oriented workforce training, and immense government investments were made in the expansion of university capacity as affluent baby boomers flooded campus gates. In Canada, at least, public tertiary education was increasingly being seen as a fundamental human right and an essential component of a functioning democracy, much like elementary and secondary education had been previously. Industrial and commercial research migrated from dedicated corporate research parks onto the campuses of public universities. Over the course of three decades, from 1940 to 1970, the external pressures of military research, workforce development, democratization, and commercialization had breached the ivory tower walls and begun to transform the academic world. Government was intimately, inextricably involved in the affairs of academe.

Yet in many ways, the evolution of higher education over the final thirty years of the twentieth century reflects diminishing dependency on government for the success of the academic enterprise. In the mid-1970s, just as female undergraduate enrolments began to surge, government funding cuts became acute for Canadian universities, who responded by increasing class sizes and faculty-student ratios, growing their fund-raising arms, and investing their endowment funds more aggressively. The "massification" of higher education had begun in earnest, and the coming years would see the growth of ever-larger lecture theatres, the proliferation of multiple-choice exams, and increasing use of adjunct faculty and teaching assistants. Faculty associations on campuses across Canada began acting more like labour unions in the 1980s and 1990s, and tuition fees began rising in most jurisdictions. Canadian universities and colleges started thinking seriously about international student recruitment as a source of revenue, and technology transfer offices started generating more and more royalty income through licensing agreements and spin-off companies. Students and their parents, faced with larger sticker prices for post-secondary education, began acting more like consumers—comparison shopping, demanding luxury features, and measuring likely career Return on Investment (calculated as primarily a financial ROI). From 1970 to 2000, Canada's universities, and to a lesser extent community colleges, became stretched to capacity, and more susceptible to labour disputes, tuition freezes, international competition, investment losses, and other forces of what was becoming, for the first time, a "marketplace" of postsecondary education.

Since 2000, the "boiling frog" scenario has become apparent to Canadian colleges and universities, who are no longer merely in a pot, but in a pressure cooker. Provincial operating grants have been increasingly tied to per-capita enrolment and key performance indicators (KPIs), creating desperation in regions of declining population, and heightening competition for students in major urban centres. Federal tri-council research funding has been tightened and focused on government priorities. Credential inflation has led to growing demand for degrees—particularly professional degrees, applied degrees, post-degree diplomas, and graduate programs—and led many observers to lament grade inflation in high schools and on post-secondary campuses (Cote & Allahar, 2007). Growing international student recruitment has created real financial and social benefits for Canada's institutions, but has also contributed to new strains on student support services, amplified faculty complaints about student academic preparedness, and perhaps set the stage for incidents of racial tension and conflict on campuses and in surrounding communities; Australia, the most successful importer of international students in recent years, has experienced significant social backlash leading to acts of violence against Indian students studying in the country (*Top Ten*).

In the twenty-first century, effective institutional strategy demands a far-reaching and continually updated understanding of the external environment—particularly for market-focused functions like institutional branding, enrolment management, and recruitment marketing. Some long-term trends are readily apparent in statistics and research conducted over several decades, although they can often be ignored because their effects are subtle and gradual, like the pot of boiling water. More abrupt changes in the competitive landscape, often resulting from international or private-sector forces, are harder to ignore but more difficult to predict—although in many cases early warning signs exist. Canadian higher education can often look to the American experience as a leading indicator of pressures and changes to come. This chapter will survey some of the most critical trends affecting Canadian colleges and universities, and their enrolment management efforts. (Obviously, it cannot replace ongoing intelligence gathering and institution-specific data.)

## FISCAL CRISES ON CAMPUS

Canadians were insulated for the better part of a year from the economic recession that struck American markets in late 2008, but by 2009 Canadians also saw house prices and stock markets lose significant value, endowments and pension funds shrink, unemployment rates skyrocket, and government tax and natural resource revenues plummet. In late 2008, several institutions reported early budget challenges: in October the cautious University of Waterloo was among the first to announce a six-month "postponement" of hiring and major spending, and in November the University of British Columbia reported $38 million in losses on $130 million invested in asset-backed commercial paper. By early 2009, budget cuts or shortfalls were being announced by dozens of Canadian PSE institutions, including $7.5 million at Brock University, $6.5 million at Fanshawe College, $10 million at the University of Lethbridge, $10 million at the University of New Brunswick, $10.6 million at Bishop's University, $13 million at McGill University, and $13 million at the University of

Manitoba. McMaster University balanced its 2009 budget through $20 million in deferred maintenance, hiring freezes, and transfers from reserves, but anticipated annual deficits of as much as $50 million going forward. In March 2009, the University of Western Ontario reported investment losses of more than $11 million, and projected a $41 million deficit by 2011 unless action was taken: they therefore announced 5.5% across-the-board budget cuts, a 4.5% tuition hike, the postponement of capital investments, and the elimination of 114 full-time positions. (*Top Ten*)

In May 2009, Lakehead University projected a $6.3 million deficit, which was projected to grow to as much as $50 million over the coming five years. Lakehead was facing significant demographic challenges in addition to economic pressures: in the past few years the regional school board had closed almost half of its high schools due to declining enrolment. Lakehead publicly considered a hiring freeze, and imposed a four-day mandatory unpaid furlough prior to Christmas 2009 (a first in Canada). At the time, Michael Pawlowski, Lakehead's VP for Administration and Finance, said to the media:

We've got to rethink the way we do business here at Lakehead. If we don't change the way we run our business, we'll be just like GM . . . The model just doesn't work under the current funding arrangements for a university to operate. (Kelly, 2009)

The fiscal impact of the recession was felt most rapidly on campuses with significant endowment funds, who were therefore most dependent on endowment incomes for their operating budgets: in April 2009, Queen's University announced 15% in budget cuts in response to an endowment loss of $152 million, and the University of Toronto announced a loss of $1.3 billion in endowments, which equated to a $62 million budget cut that year alone. In July, the University of Calgary announced that it had lost $78 million on its endowments, and would cut at least 200 jobs to save $14.3 million that year. The University of Alberta reported that it had lost $112 million on its investments as of April 2009, and anticipated a $59 million budget shortfall that year. St. Francis Xavier University in Nova Scotia, with a volunteer-administered endowment fund, faced the steepest loss in the country: a 43% loss on its investments, which were largely in the stock market. (*Top Ten*)

Pension fund losses caused major financial pressure on campuses with defined-benefits retirement plans: by June 2009, York University had lost 18% on its endowment funds and was facing a potential $250 million pension plan deficit over the next three years. In April 2010, the University of Guelph announced that in addition to a structural deficit totaling $46.2 million by 2012, it was facing a $280 million pension shortfall, which by Ontario regulations would need to be covered by funds from the institution's operating budget. At time of writing, the Ontario government is working on special legislation to soften the impact of pension solvency requirements for publicly owned institutions like universities and colleges. (*Top Ten*)

The economic recession has simultaneously reduced institutional endowments and government tax revenues, and increased enrolment demand from newly unemployed students. Enrolment demand has risen most abruptly at Canada's community colleges, but universities are also enjoying a pleasant surge in applications and many are allowing their undergraduate enrolments to rise somewhat. The loss of endowment income has reduced the availability of financial aid on many campuses, and increased pressure on enrolment managers to generate tuition revenue. The rise in unemployment is creating an artificial sense of enrolment success, and institutions need to be conscious that, when economic strength returns, there will be an adjustment downward in application and enrolment volumes.

## TIGHTENING GOVERNMENT PURSE STRINGS

Since 1980, most Canadian universities have had progressively fewer financial resources per full-time student: AUCC calculates a decline from $21,000 per FTE in 1980 to just $15,000 in 2007, using constant 2007 dollars (AUCC, 2007). Of that per-student budget, the government share has dropped from about $18,000 to just $10,000, while student fees net of scholarships have almost doubled (CAUT, 2010). Naturally, government grants and tuition fees per FTE vary considerably from province to province: institutions in Saskatchewan, the most generous province as of 2008, enjoy a government grant per FTE almost double that of Nova Scotia, the least generous on this measure (AUCC, 2007). In Ontario, provincial operating grants to universities dropped from 78% of total institutional budgets in 1988 to just 50% in 2008 (Snowdon, 2010). Between 1993 and 2007, overall government investment in postsecondary education (PSE) stayed virtually flat per FTE in Quebec and Manitoba, rose 35% per FTE in Alberta, 23% per FTE in Saskatchewan, 16% in Newfoundland & Labrador, 14% in Nova Scotia, and 13% in Ontario, but fell 15% in New Brunswick, 19% in Prince Edward Island, and 24% in British Columbia (CAUT, 2010). The resource-rich provinces of Alberta and Saskatchewan are reinvesting in PSE, as part of provincial strategies to diversify their economies before resource revenues plateau. Quebec and Manitoba are taking a riskier strategy by holding the status quo, while B.C. seems deliberate about cutting funding to higher education, perhaps anticipating immense burdens on its health care system as retirement demographics balloon in the province.

More seriously, the resources per student of Canadian universities have fallen precipitously compared to their American competitors: from a per-student funding advantage of $2,000 in 1980, to a per-student disadvantage of $8,000 by 2006 (AUCC, 2007). Competing in a global arena with American institutions that have vastly superior resources (largely due to higher tuition fees) is not likely sustainable for Canadian universities, nor is government likely to maintain funding at a level that will support artificially low tuition fees much longer.

The recession of 2008 has impacted provincial budgets differently across the country. Alberta, facing slowed production in the Athabasca Tar Sands and sharp declines in royalties on natural gas, froze postsecondary budgets in 2009 after years of steady growth. (With cost-of-living increases enshrined in collective agreements, this meant Alberta colleges and universities faced budget cuts in real terms.) Ontario, facing massive tax losses because of its hard-hit manufacturing sector, projected a $50 billion deficit for 2010. Provincial budget cuts are likely to persist well after economic recovery buoys the private sector: the same taxation lag that insulated public institutions from the onset of the recession, will postpone the beneficial effects of the economic recovery, if and when it arrives. Furthermore, in the longer term, as baby boomers age and provincial governments face steadily more pressure on their health care budgets, it seems unlikely that provincial higher education budgets will grow more generous.

The federal government's response to the economic crisis of 2008 meant both good news and bad news for Canadian colleges and universities. In March 2009, tri-council research funding was cut by almost $120 million: $8.2 million for SSHRC, $40 million for CIHR, and $70 million for NSERC. At almost the same time, Ottawa announced a $2 billion Knowledge Infrastructure Program to benefit campuses across the country. KIP-funded construction and renovation announcements rolled out steadily, province by province, throughout 2009 (*Top Ten*). In effect, the federal government was reducing its support of researcher salaries, but increasing its commitment to the more visible bricks and mortar on university and college campuses. Academic leaders expressed concerns about the ongoing operational costs of the new infrastructure, but many focused on "shovel-ready" construction projects that were already planned, allowing institutions to shuffle funds back to their operating budgets.

## CAMPUSES RESPOND TO FISCAL PRESSURES

As Moody's Investor Service observes, colleges and universities are "consensus-driven organizations that are not accustomed to rapid implementation of expense reductions and budget changes" (Moody's, 2009). Bi-cameral and tri-cameral governance is an ideal model to maintain tradition and quality, but not to implement innovations or manage budgets in the face of increasing economic pressure. Most academic institutions take a collegial, equitable approach to budget cuts: across-the-board reductions in budget, evenly between academic departments and administrative support units. (Although since academic self-governance typically veers away from cutting faculty positions, administrative units usually suffer the steepest budget cuts.) Academic institutions are by their very nature conservative, tending to preserve the status quo and embracing change only in moderate, incremental ways. This conservative approach is perfectly designed to advance scientific knowledge over the decades, but ironically militates against decisive administrative change. This tendency to incremental management often looks like deference to the status quo, or procrastination: so far, the most common institutional responses to budget cuts have been deferred maintenance and construction, merging academic departments or research institutes, hiring freezes, salary freezes, and increased teaching loads. In the U.S., where private colleges have far less insulation from the economic downturn, sabbaticals are being cancelled, mandatory furloughs imposed, campuses are being merged or closed, and in an increasing number of cases, for-profit colleges are buying up ailing nonprofit colleges. Many U.S. colleges and universities have made more strategic, "vertical" cuts, eliminating programs, faculties, or schools, often in the humanities and specifically the modern languages. Hints of furloughs have reached Canada, and the 2010 O'Neill report encourages mergers among some Nova Scotia universities (*Top Ten*), but many of these more extreme fiscal realities are unlikely to impact Canadian institutions in the near future. Provincial governments build new campuses to win votes, and invest in bricks and mortar to demonstrate a commitment to post-secondary accessibility, but none have yet seen it as politically expedient to close a university or college campus. (When elementary and secondary school closures have been inevitable, provincial governments have typically downloaded the responsibility, and the political fallout, to district school boards.)

## TUITION INCREASES

In the past 20 years, PSE tuitions in Canada have risen significantly. In 1990, the average Canadian undergraduate paid $2,000 in annual tuition (in constant 2009 dollars); by 2009 that had more than doubled to $5,583 (CAUT, 2010). Tuition for professional programs, however, increased from similar starting points to vastly higher tuitions in 2009: Law to more than $8,500, Medicine to more than $10,200, and Dentistry to almost $14,000. Canadians are socially inclined toward public education, and a recent poll found that 60% of Canadians would support the elimination of PSE tuition altogether (CAUT, 2009).

Despite student protests to the contrary, university and college tuition fees in Canada are still remarkably affordable. Students in the U.S., Australia, Korea, and Japan pay vastly more of the cost of their education, although students in fifteen other OECD countries pay substantially less—particularly in Denmark, Finland, and Norway, where public sources account for more than 95% of PSE funding (CAUT, 2010). Nonetheless, compared to a student's opportunity cost of spending a year in higher education—anywhere from $20,000 to $70,000 depending upon student age and provincial employment rates—tuition of $1,500 to $7,000 is not the primary impediment to pursuing an education. In fact, recent studies have emphasized the importance of parental education and social barriers, above and beyond financial accessibility, as primary influencers of the PSE participation rate (Berger, 2007).

Tuition fees vary significantly across the country. Community college tuitions are highest in Prince Edward Island, Saskatchewan, and Alberta, and considerably lower than average in Ontario, Newfoundland & Labrador, and particularly in Manitoba (Berger, 2007). University tuitions, on the other hand, are highest in Nova Scotia, and considerably lower than average in Alberta, Manitoba, Newfoundland & Labrador, and of course Quebec, where they were frozen for 13 years prior to 2007. Artificially low tuitions in Quebec, which have not significantly raised comparatively low participation rates, have, however, had the effect of diminishing the resources of Quebec universities while raising trade barriers to prevent other institutions from recruiting many Quebec students. In Atlantic Canada, where provinces with very low and very high tuition are in close proximity, price-sensitive students have proven quite willing to relocate across provincial boundaries to pursue their education.

The most significant impact of rising tuition fees on prospective students, however, is that the higher perceived "price tag" fosters a consumer mentality and a focus on career return on investment (ROI). Institutions and government have gladly encouraged this ROI focus, by emphasizing the "million-dollar bonus" a university graduate apparently earns over his lifetime, to justify transferring more of the cost of PSE onto students and away from government. (AUCC has recently calculated the benefit as $1.3 million over high school graduates, and $1 million over college graduates.) The unintended result of this emphasis on ROI, however, as Jeff Rybak explains, is that students receive "the not-so-subtle message . . . that education for its own sake is rather frivolous" (Rybak, 2007). Students enrol in PSE not to learn, not to grow as individuals, but to obtain a credential that will ensure them greater career opportunities. Rybak observes that many students he counseled at the University of Toronto were making "safer" program choices, and choosing "safer" thesis topics or research areas, because higher tuition created a greater sense of financial risk for the student. The unintended consequence of tuition fee increases may ultimately be reduced interest in the liberal arts and sciences, and more focused demand for career-oriented and professional programs—which could be an impediment in what Richard Florida calls the dawning "creative economy" (Florida, 2002).

Nonetheless, tuition increases are continuing, and in some cases accelerating. Late 2009 and early 2010 saw proposals for some particularly aggressive tuition increases: in November 2009, the Northern Alberta Institute of Technology proposed a 40% tuition increase to bring its fees in line with those of SAIT Polytechnic, but the province denied the request; the same week the University of Alberta requested a 66% tuition hike for professional programs, and got approval from the same government. In April 2010, the University of Manitoba proposed tuition increases of 46% for Law, 54% for undergraduate business, and 78% for its MBA program. The same month in Quebec, McGill University proposed raising tuition for its MBA program from $1,672 to $29,500—a 1664% increase, although still a bargain compared to $70,000 at other institutions. The government of Quebec publicly opposed the move and promised to claw back funding equivalent to the MBA fees McGill charges, but at the time of writing, McGill administration was undeterred (*Top Ten*).

In a world of globalizing research and employment, international student recruitment, and competition, it seems inevitable that Canadian tuitions will eventually rise. At the very least, tuitions for institutions with global ambitions will need to rise significantly: with fixed government funding and immovable salary expenses, there are few other levers available to campus administrators, if they are to compete with better-funded U.S. institutions for faculty, research dollars, and top students. Rising tuitions will place increasing pressure on enrolment, pose new barriers to accessibility, increase demands for financial aid, and likely exacerbate student anxieties about ROI, focus on career outcomes, and expectations for campus services.

## PRIVATIZATION ON CAMPUS

Many North American institutions have recognized the potential for international student recruitment, and in the face of budget constraints have sought external partners to achieve faster results. Many have partnered with North American consultants to recruit more effectively overseas, or to join trade missions or postsecondary fairs. Many more have hired overseas agents to recruit students directly, sometimes on a thinly disguised commission basis. But in the past few years, several Canadian universities have made headlines for controversial decisions to partner with private-sector education companies, such as Navitas or Study Group International (both based in Australia), not only to recruit international students, but to educate them in "foundational" or "pathway" programs on or adjacent to the university campuses in Canada, until the students are prepared to transfer into the established academic stream (*Top Ten*).

In February 2006, Simon Fraser University contracted with Navitas to open "Fraser International College," and the SFU board of governors approved a ten-year renewal of the partnership in October 2010. Over the first four years of the agreement, they report a total of 1,260 students from 40 countries have passed through the FIC program, and that 900 graduates have transferred to SFU. In November 2007, the University of Manitoba administration signed a five-year contract with Navitas to manage the International College of Manitoba, without consulting the Senate or Board of Governors. In February 2008, McMaster was close to a deal to establish McMaster University College with Navitas, but campus outcry derailed the deal permanently. In January 2010, the University of Windsor senate voted against a SGI partnership for a business prep academy. As of February 2010, Navitas reported that it was negotiating with Dalhousie University, and in May 2010 that it was negotiation with Carleton University, to establish international foundation year programs on campus in Canada.

Critics of these partnerships, most notably and vocally faculty associations, are concerned about what they see as "the outsourcing of education" on public university campuses (CAUT, 2010a). Navitas instructors earn lower salaries, have no collective agreements, pensions, tenure, or academic freedom: in the U.K., such arrangements have been criticized as creating "a two-tier workforce in higher education" (UCU, 2010). Private-sector companies are trading on the reputation of the public university, charging the same international tuition fees, and paying royalties or fees to the institution for the use of resources such as classrooms, labs, computers, and health and career services. Some see Navitas paying for access to better facilities than the university's own faculty can afford. Others are concerned about the implicit guarantee of progression into second-year university programs after the completion of the foundational year (*Top Ten*). Spokespeople deny it, but the Dalhousie Faculty Association worries that Navitas would create a "back door" into Dalhousie that would put a "massive strain" on academic standards at the university (DFA, 2010). Brochures for the International College of Manitoba clearly state on the cover that they are "Your Direct Pathway to University of Manitoba," and feature the U of M coat of arms equal in size to the logo of ICM. Effectively, say critics, the institutions have outsourced the teaching of first year for international students. Of even greater concern than the current arrangements to deliver foundational programs, faculty associations claim that the Navitas business plan includes eventually delivering full degree programs in partnership with universities (UCU, 2010).

Perhaps the most extreme example of faculty outsourcing to date arose in Michigan in fall 2010: Washtenaw Community College announced that it was outsourcing 400 adjunct faculty positions to a temp agency, in order to save $800,000 annually in pension contributions (*Top Ten*). It is no coincidence that some of the most radical college strategies have been implemented in Michigan, a state at the epicenter of the economic recession. It currently seems unlikely that such desperate measures would appear on Canadian campuses, but that may depend entirely on circumstances.

## RISING LABOUR TENSIONS ON CAMPUS

Since 1970, what faculty associations would call the rising commercialization of the academic enterprise has led to political tensions on campus between administrators seeking to manage the institution efficiently as a market-driven business, and faculty who cherish centuries of traditional academic self-governance (Turk, 2008). Scholars and researchers are by their very nature intellectual individualists, following their own research interests and respecting academic freedom and autonomy as self-evident values. Few academics, however, are by nature intellectual entrepreneurs, alert to opportunities in their environment, and responding to unmet student enrolment demand or looming labour market shortages. While every self-respecting campus has a program review cycle, that review is often focused on academic quality, not relevance to student or societal demand. Canada's community colleges are much better at marrying educational function with marketplace needs, largely because their original mandates emphasize meeting local and regional industry and workforce needs. Colleges typically have program advisory committees comprised of representation from industry and community, and curriculum is reviewed regularly for currency and relevance.

As campus administrations have responded to budgetary and enrolment pressures by increasing class sizes, hiring part-time, adjunct, or teaching-stream faculty, freezing salaries and limiting benefits, formerly collegial relationships on campus have been growing more heated and adversarial. Just before Christmas 2007, the administration of St. Thomas University in Fredericton made history by preemptively locking out faculty, a first on a Canadian campus (*Top Ten*). The negotiation stalemate persisted until February 2008, when classes finally resumed. Labour tensions on Canadian campuses grew in 2008, with support staff strikes at Concordia University, New Brunswick Community College, and Seneca College, among others, and faculty strikes at Wilfrid Laurier University, McGill University, the University of Windsor, the University of Sudbury, Brandon University, Université Laval, and, of course, York University, where teaching assistants and contract faculty were on strike from November 7, 2008, until January 30, 2009. That bitter strike persisted throughout the undergraduate application season, resulting in a decrease of 3,897 applications direct from high school, a 13.7% decrease in "first-choice" applicants, and a 7.3% decrease in confirmed enrolments that September. Labour action continued to percolate on campuses across Canada in 2009 and 2010, when 27 CUPE locals (Canadian Union of Public Employees) across Ontario were renegotiating their contracts and multiple faculty associations won strike mandates (*Top Ten*).

It is difficult to predict with any accuracy the future of labour action on Canadian campuses, although it seems clear that a protracted strike can have a major negative impact on student enrolment in subsequent years. The long-term trends would seem to support a future with escalating labour tension, particularly at universities: since 1975, Canadian universities have seen a 30% increase in full-time faculty while experiencing a 100% increase in undergraduate enrolment (AUCC, 2007); over the same period, total university budgets have increased 150% but expenditures on academic rank salaries have fallen from 30% to 20% of institutional budgets (CAUT, 2010). These Canadian statistics are corroborated by a controversial Goldwater Institute report, Administrative Bloat at American Universities, which observed "diseconomies of scale" as instructional expenses increased 39% between 1993 and 2007, but administrative expenses increased 61% (Goldwater, 2010). With steadily increasing enrolments, capped government funding, rising course loads and class sizes, labour tension on Canadian campuses is unlikely to diminish in the foreseeable future.

## LOOMING DEMOGRAPHIC CHALLENGES

Canadian postsecondary institutions will face a full spectrum of demographic challenges in the coming decades. The natural birthrate in Canada has been declining since the popularization of oral contraception in the 1960s, and Human Resources and Skills Development

Canada projects the birthrate will slip into negative territory around 2027. AUCC believes that rising participation rates, international recruitment, and the recruitment of traditionally underrepresented groups will maintain fairly stable university enrolment over the next 15 years (AUCC, 2007), but the Canada Council on Learning projects overall PSE enrolment in Canada will drop by 120,000 students by 2025 (CCL, 2007). Canada's universities are in a privileged position when it comes to enrolment management, because most can simply lower entrance average requirements to maintain full enrolment. Combined with growing student interest in undergraduate and graduate degree programs, universities may skim off the highest-achieving college applicants and create new enrolment management challenges for Canada's community colleges.

Canada's population is distributed very unevenly across the country, and demographic trends look decidedly different depending upon region. In Toronto and the Greater Toronto Area, all projections point to massive increases in youth populations and heightened demand for university and college places well past 2030. Likewise, Calgary can anticipate positive demographic trends and enrolment growth—as well as plenty of recruitment activity in their backyard by institutions from across the country. While the population decline will be moderated in B.C. by plenty of in-migration, demographic projections call for an increasingly senior population attracted to B.C. for their retirement. (This may represent a boon for continuing education, but not for traditional full-time undergraduate programs.) At the opposite extreme, regions of Northern Ontario, Atlantic Canada, and the prairies face precipitous population declines over the coming 15 years, which will be felt most acutely in Newfoundland & Labrador, New Brunswick, PEI and Nova Scotia, and possibly Saskatchewan (although recent economic swings have benefited in-migration there).

As the birthrate has declined in Canada, most population growth has occurred through immigration. Between now and 2050, new Canadians and first-generation Canadians will be an increasingly dominant majority of Canadian youth. StatsCan projects that by 2017, the so-called "visible minority" will in fact be the majority for Canadians under age 50. Studies conducted by Academica Group for a number of government agencies have detected clear tendencies among new Canadian and first-generation Canadian applicants to Ontario universities: they are twice as interested in commuting to campus and living with their parents than living in residence, they are less interested in college and more influenced by their parents, and they are almost twice as interested in fields like science, commerce, engineering, and mathematics, and far less interested in the arts, humanities, social sciences, education, fine arts, or music (UCAS, 2005). Unless significant cultural change occurs, university humanities faculties may well face steadily intensifying enrolment challenges.

## SHIFTING FOCUS TO "NONTRADITIONAL" STUDENTS

From coast to coast, college and university administrations are aware that traditional demographics are in decline, but are committed to attract "non-traditional" students to more than make up the difference and maintain critical mass and institutional momentum. In some regions of the country, the focus is on Aboriginal students, who are underrepresented in higher education and on university campuses in particular. The recent financial scandals at First Nations University of Canada in Regina has not helped the cause of Aboriginal postsecondary participation (*Top Ten*). While economic hardship poses a real barrier to some urban Aboriginal students, the larger obstacles to Aboriginal participation in PSE are geographic, social, cultural, and educational. Aboriginal communities are often remote and inaccessible, and are sometimes unsupportive of a young person's aspirations to go away to university. Aboriginal youth face heightened identity anxiety over the decision to attend PSE, because it often simultaneously seems to them like a rejection of family traditions. Many Aboriginal youth struggle with math and science prerequisites in high school, and are academically unprepared for university. And sadly, some Aboriginal students arriving on campuses find the system too inflexible to accommodate their spiritual or family obligations, unwelcoming or alienating, and they fail to persist. All of these barriers should be addressed, and campus retention professionals should certainly make learning supports and cultural supports for Aboriginal students a priority, but in most regions of the country the actual number of Aboriginal students an institution can conceivable attract will not make up for demographic declines in the mainstream population.

On many campuses, the focus is therefore on the higher fee-paying international student, as a non-traditional market to sustain the academic enterprise. Canadian student recruitment efforts have been particularly successful in China, the U.S., France, and India (AUCC, 2007), but colleges and universities are establishing institutional partnerships with peer institutions in dozens of countries to attract students. On most campuses, international students comprise roughly 10% of the total student population, and while the market in some parts of the world is immense, there are practical limits on how many foreign students a campus can absorb before pressures on student support services become unmanageable. There is also a market-driven limitation: many international students come to Canadian campuses to study alongside Canadian students, and as the ratio shifts toward international students, an institution will eventually become less desirable as a Canadian destination. (Some campuses have also outsourced international "foundation year" programs, as noted above.)

Mature students are another non-traditional market for many Canadian institutions, although administrators may overestimate the market potential and underestimate the competition. Despite considerable institutional marketing and government policy efforts, and the doubling of university participation rates by youth aged 18–22, the participation rate of Canadians older than age 25 has not significantly budged in 35 years (CAUT, 2010). Plant closures and layoffs drive blue-collar workers back to college in particular, but generally only for short-term retraining programs that government will fund. More than half of applicants to Ontario universities over age 25 are actually considering community college instead (UCAS, 2009). Mid-career professionals are indeed a growing market for post-degree diploma programs and professional master's degrees, but their busy lives spent juggling employment, spouses, children, and elderly parents mean that online or distance education providers represent a more attractive option than the traditional campus experience. Many Canadian institutions still underestimate the competitive threat posed by the University of Phoenix, Kaplan University, Athabasca University, and Royal Roads University, and by the distance education offerings of American public universities: the fact is that non-traditional students may well prefer non-traditional forms of education, and established brands with economies of scale will pose a significant competitive threat.

## SHIFTING EXPECTATIONS OF TRADITIONAL STUDENTS

Although overall university participation rates have been rising in Canada, over the past 35 years almost all of that increase has occurred among the traditional university-bound cohort of 18- to 25-year-olds. There is no statistical evidence that tough economic times, degree inflation, accessibility initiatives, or other efforts at recruiting non-traditional students have had significant impact on the participation rates of students over the age of 25 (CAUT, 2010). So the "traditional student" will likely remain the focus for most institutions as they compete for enrolments in Canada. Traditional students are themselves a "moving target," as the annual "Mindset List" from Beloit College reminds us every September (Beloit, 2010), and a stack of sociology texts describing the "Millennial Generation" attempts to define (Howe & Strauss, 2000). While it is unfair and inaccurate to generalize across an entire generation, there are some clear trends that will almost certainly continue to affect enrolment management professionals across Canada for years to come.

## THE NEW CAREERISTS

Students have become increasingly focused on career outcomes of their postsecondary education (UCAS, 2000–2010), and recent surveys have found that Canadian students are focused on finding interesting work, work-life balance, interesting co-workers, and job security (Brainstorm, 2010). As a result, their dream employers are now governments, charities, and high-tech superstars Google, Apple, and Microsoft. Fully 57% of applicants indicate that careerist considerations drive their pursuit of higher education, compared to just 18% who cite a desire to pursue advanced study, and 14% who seek to develop themselves personally (UCAS, 2009). Application volumes to university programs in Ontario demonstrate that students respond within months to shifts in the labour market, losing interest in computer science or journalism as career opportunities are perceived to be in decline, and focusing on social work, nursing, and education when government employment appears most secure (OUAC, 2009).

There seems to be a movement among Canadian colleges, in particular, to meet the marketplace demand for career-oriented degree programs through applied degrees, joint and collaborative degrees, or even hybrid institutions like the University of Guelph-Humber or Seneca@York, which promise students the best of both worlds. Nine institutions in Ontario, Alberta, and B.C. have collectively established an organization called Polytechnics Canada to promote a middle path—degree-granting colleges and technical institutes that conduct applied research—even though their governments may not explicitly recognize them as "polytechnics" per se (*Top Ten*).

For decades, Canadian universities have been meeting student demand for more career-oriented, professional degree programs—but in recent years, some have been catering to student desires for career certainty by offering outcome "guarantees": the University of Calgary guarantees undergraduates will complete their program within four years; and the University of Regina guarantees employment in the student's chosen career within six months of graduation (provided that students uphold their end of a fairly comprehensive bargain). These guarantees serve to reinforce the rising tide of consumerism among PSE students, and reinforce the focus on completion and career returns, rather than quality of education or development of student character.

## BALANCING STUDY, EMPLOYMENT, AND CREATURE COMFORTS

Students are increasingly seeking work-life-school balance, not an immersive or fully engaged student experience. Although most undergraduate students continue to enroll full-time, the amount of paid employment they assume has risen steadily since 1976 (Motte, 2009). U.S. statistics have found in particular a rise in the percentage of college students working 20–24 hours per week at paid employment, and the U.S. National Center for Education Statistics has developed a special category for "part-time students who looked like full-time students" (NCES, 2004). As college and university students increasingly divide their time between studies and paid employment, hours spent studying declines (Babcock, 2010), time to degree completion rises (NCES, 2001), and, inevitably, student engagement and retention become more and more challenging.

Students' parents are increasingly well-educated, overprotective "helicopter parents," with apparently insatiable appetites for enhanced campus security, emergency notification systems, campus Webcams, and even tattle-tale vending machines (*Top Ten*). In the U.S., "College Parents of America" maintains a Web site, a blog called "Hoverings," and conducts an annual "Survey of College Parent Experiences." Some institutions have introduced parent-only tours and orientation programs, parent-specific Web sites, and formal "farewell" ceremonies to give parents the hint that they should cut the apron strings.

Student expectations for campus services are also rising, from pervasive Wi-Fi and luxurious computer commons to one-stop service centres, online registration, credit card tuition payments, and pet-friendly dorms. More and more institutions are constructing luxurious dorms with private bedrooms, much like students enjoy at home, or repurposing luxury hotels as residence space. Student admissions processes are becoming more flexible and responsive, from hand-held data collection during high school visits to personalized print-on-demand viewbooks, from customizable Web portals for applicants to online previewing of residence rooms and roommates (*Top Ten*).

## MORE AGGRESSIVE MARKETING

Canadian colleges and universities have traditionally been conservative recruitment marketers: continuing education departments and MBA programs have been the biggest advertisers, while foundation and capital campaign purposes have driven many national branding campaigns. In most cases there has been a collegial respect for institutional catchment areas, and a desire to avoid expending public dollars in an escalating marketing "arms race" with a zero-sum collective gain. Institutions have invested in detailed and insightful market research for well over a decade now, and increasingly have been attempting regional market share analysis and geotargeting, but to the casual observer, universities did not need to actively recruit students, and overt advertising would suggest a whiff of desperation.

In some ways, the marketing landscape started to change in 2004, when York University launched its "subway station domination" campaign—at the St. George TTC stop, immediately beneath the University of Toronto. Then in 2008, Lakehead University moved the bar for aggressive marketing still further, when it plastered downtown Toronto with its "Yale Shmale" teaser campaign, featuring a photo of then-president George Bush. (The campaign microsite explained that "graduating from an Ivy League university doesn't necessarily mean you're smart.")

Recent years have seen more examples of aggressive PSE marketing in Canada. In 2008, Colleges Ontario launched a mass media viral marketing campaign touting an imaginary pharmaceutical, "Obay," to emphasize to parents that their children should be permitted to consider college pathways to solid and lucrative careers. Later in 2008, Algoma University ran a Toronto-focused campaign for fictitious "Colossal University," denigrating its huge class sizes, impersonal attention to students, and "cookie-cutter" approach. (Algoma now uses a campaign focused on putting 681 km between you and your parents.) Memorial University of Newfoundland has blanketed transit routes to major university campuses across the country with advertisements for "graduate programs on the edge," and invites undergraduate applicants to "Rant Like Rick" in a video contest inspired by honorary graduate Rick Mercer. Brock University has clearly invested heavily in a national branding campaign featuring "Both Sides of the Brain." Lethbridge College has invited students to come to its "totally new'd" college (and assuring students "we'll explain to your parents").

Although the most obvious examples of aggressive advertising are originating in regions of Canada facing the steepest demographic declines, PSE advertising is also heating up in regions with intense competition among neighbouring institutions. Toronto's Centennial College has used grungy models in its advertising, explaining that "Einstein didn't own a hairbrush either," and that "The Freak shall inherit the Earth." Toronto's George Brown College tried to build a memorable brand on the slogan "Brown Gets You the Job," but was reportedly derailed by lawyers from United Parcel Service. Calgary's SAIT Polytechnic currently features senior citizens in its advertising, above the slogan "get a career you'll never want to leave," while Mount Royal University recently ran an airport-themed campaign encouraging prospective students to "get on board" because "your future is about to take off" (*Top Ten*).

In 2010, two American universities launched what some detractors might call an even more unseemly approach to advertising higher education: the music video. In the wake of the immense popularity of *High School Musical, Glee,* and *American Idol*, Yale University surprised the Ivy League by launching a 16-minute student recruitment music video in January 2010. Hundreds of talented Yale students, alumni, and "recent grads working in the admissions department" sang, danced, and played musical instruments through a remarkably detailed introduction to the residential college system, Yale's libraries, student services, history, and program offerings. (A disclaimer at the conclusion of the video apparently attempts to distance the institution from the production of the video, but the admissions department was pivotal.) Shortly thereafter, in April 2010, the University of Delaware launched an 8-minute music video on YouTube, featuring an introduction in which the university's president and registrar explicitly endorse the music video project.

Canadian universities, ever more conservative than their U.S. counterparts, have not yet embraced the student recruitment music video as a form of marketing, but they have encouraged their students and student associations to create amateurish "lipdub" videos based on popular songs. In Canada, these lipdubs originated with the Université de Quebec a Montreal and Université Laval in 2009, and were followed in 2010 by Campus St-Jean in Edmonton, Brock University, Dalhousie Student Union, the Mount Allison Student Association, the University of Waterloo, and the University of Victoria (*Top Ten*). The videos do little to promote academic values or program offerings, but emphasize student spirit and the friendliness of the student association.

## NEW COMPETITION FROM OLD INSTITUTIONS

The competitive landscape for student recruitment is changing. Canadian colleges and universities are quick to identify their peer institutions and "aspirational set" as key competitors for student recruitment. Sometimes quantitative market research confirms that these institutions are in fact true competitors in the marketplace, but in many cases institutions are surprised to discover that their real competitors are less direct. In regions experiencing economic growth, the labour market is the biggest competitor for postsecondary students, who face a significant opportunity cost if they forgo employment to attend school full-time. In many jurisdictions, the primary competitor for a community college is the local university, and likewise colleges are a serious consideration for about one-quarter of university applicants. In recent years, seven colleges in Alberta and B.C. have been redesignated as universities, transforming the competitive landscape and disrupting traditional transfer patterns (*Top Ten*). Nearly a dozen Ontario universities and colleges have announced plans to build new satellite campuses in the Greater Toronto Area to meet the projected enrolment demand, and a recent HEQCO report recommended that the province establish a new undergraduate teaching university in Toronto (HEQCO, 2009). The higher education landscape in Canada is not staying fixed, even for public institutions.

## MULTINATIONAL FOR-PROFIT COMPETITORS

Just as the Internet has proven to be a fundamentally disruptive technology for the music, newspaper, and magazine businesses, and may soon transform the book and movie industries, it has the potential to radically change any sector focused on the transfer of information that can be digitized. Higher education institutions will need to be alert to online competitors over the next decade, just as American institutions have been surprised to watch the sudden rise of the University of Phoenix and Kaplan University. In 2010, the University of Phoenix has more than 455,000 students (more than the entire enrolment of the "Big Ten" U.S. institutions), and 200 campuses across the U.S., Canada, Mexico, and internationally. The University of Phoenix generates almost $4 billion in tuition revenue annually, and commits 23.5% of net revenue to marketing. Despite tuitions as much as twice the rate of public universities, American for-profit providers have seen immense enrolment growth in the wake of the recession: 2009 enrolment at the University of Phoenix was up 22% from 2008, and Kaplan saw enrolment increases of 28% on enrolment of more than 100,000 students. (In the wake of controversy over government financial aid, the University of Phoenix reported a 10% drop in enrolments over the summer of 2010.) The University of Phoenix has established several Canadian campuses, primarily in western Canada, and a new brand, Meritus University, in Fredericton (*Top Ten*). So far, traditional institutions perceive little threat, but upstart competitors are often dismissed by established players in their early days, only to grow into strong competitors years later.

Thus far, the social biases of Canadians (and of course government-subsidized tuitions) have insulated public institutions from their more nimble but less trusted for-profit competitors. But as students focus more and more on career outcomes as the only metric that matters, employers—not academic accreditation boards—will hold the balance of power. If

Canadian employers respect a degree from an online or for-profit institution sufficiently, and students perceive more attractive program offerings or more convenient service or delivery options, significant enrolment could shift from traditional institutions to these new competitors, as they have in the U.S., despite tuition fee differentials. This is particularly true for the "non-traditional" students so many institutions hope to attract—mature students juggling busy lives, rural students far from a traditional campus, or even full-time undergraduates who simply want to juggle employment and work, and are fluent and comfortable in an online environment.

## DISRUPTIVE TECHNOLOGIES

The potentially disruptive power of the Internet on higher education should not be underestimated: online and for-profit institutions represent only the most conventional competitive threat as a result of the Web. For students seeking educational content, the Internet provides an incredible range of free options, from MIT's OpenCourseWare consortium to Webcast.Berkeley, and from iTunesU to TED.com. Lectures have been digitized, published, commoditized, and priced at free—all in the space of a few short years. Already, some traditional students on Canadian campuses report that they prefer to watch MIT lectures online, finding them more dynamic and comprehensible than their own professors. International studies are consistently proving that podcast lectures result in 15% better learning outcomes for students, are appreciated as an option by most students, and are in fact preferred by many students (*Top Ten*). Traditional lecture theatres may well become relics in the next few years; some campus planners are already reporting a focus on building smaller and more flexible learning spaces in new construction.

In 2010, experiments are just beginning with eTextbooks, iPads, and various tablet computers as part of the postsecondary curriculum. But as the traditional anchors of any campus—libraries and lecture halls—are distributed globally across the Web, these shifts will inevitably impact campus business models: institutions are no longer in the business of selling lectures to undergraduates, just as they have long since ceased to be in the business of preserving written books in libraries. The impact of eLearning will extend well beyond traditional humanities programs: instructors in SAIT Polytechnic's electrician apprenticeship program are already experimenting with delivering upper-year education electronically, and as surgeons increasingly direct surgical robots remotely via the Internet, someday even brain surgery could conceivably be taught in a virtual or simulated environment.

## THE DISINTERMEDIATION OF HIGHER EDUCATION

The biggest disruptive threat to any established knowledge industry is the "disintermediating" power of the Internet (Tapscott, 2006): people can get what they need directly from each other, without the need for intervening institutions (Li, 2008). Local booksellers experienced this power early on as Amazon and Indigo offered superior selection, price, and search capabilities. Kijiji and eBay have replaced the need for consignment shops (and perhaps soon, real estate agents). Even the mighty *Encyclopedia Britannica* appears to have lost the battle against Wikipedia, and the *Oxford English Dictionary* is relevant today only because it has an efficient online delivery mechanism (*Top Ten*).

Students can now obtain world-class lectures, textbooks, course outlines, and tests online without ever setting foot on a traditional campus. Open courseware makes course content available free online, anywhere in the world. The Internet already hosts eponymous institutions like the "Jack Welch MBA," "Trump University," and even Glenn Beck's "Beck University" (Top Ten). Dynamic and inspiring lecturers can easily reach an online audience as "free agents," without institutional support. "Wiki" Web sites are appearing to allow students to socially network among themselves, helping each other learn course content. (These include Cramster.com, UniversityJunction, Peer2Peer University, and even Stanford University's Engineering program.)

The next step in the disintermediation of higher education is the dawn of "Open Teaching," in which faculty are also available to students online, at no charge. Many faculty at traditional institutions are already allowing non-students to audit their online courses for free. An experimental Web site launched in the fall of 2009 is formalizing and expanding on the open teaching model: the University of the People (UoPeople. com) offers students open courseware, social networking among themselves, and access to volunteer faculty. In its first year, UoPeople has just two hundred students from 50 countries, in business and information technology programs, but it aims to revolutionize global higher education by offering university degrees to students in developing countries, virtually for free: it declares it will be "the world's first tuition-free, online academic institution dedicated to the global advancement and democratization of higher education." (In the pilot program, students enrol for $15 and pay $100 to take the final exam.) UoPeople is seeking full-blown degree-granting accreditation in the U.S., and aims for 10,000 students by 2014—about the size of the University of Phoenix back in 1990. UoPeople is no lightweight, either: it was founded by Israeli multi-millionaire Shai

Reshef, who sold previous online institutions to Kaplan and Laureate Education, and is currently chairman of Cramster.com.

## FACING A RAPIDLY-CHANGING ENVIRONMENT

The Internet's disruption of the music and newspaper industries took more than 15 years, and the full impact of disintermediation on higher education will likely take even longer, because traditional institutions still enjoy a virtual monopoly on degree credentials in Canada. But just because technological change has not yet transformed the business model of a campus, does not mean it will not do so in the years ahead. Bill Gates, founder of Microsoft, famously wrote:

We always overestimate the change that will occur in the next two years and underestimate the change that will occur in the next ten. Don't let yourself be lulled into inaction. (Gates, 1995)

In the face of evolving competition, steadily shifting student expectations, budget constraints, unpredictable political interference, transformations in the workforce, globalization, and technological change, Canadian college and university leaders need to be alert to emerging threats and opportunities—but they must also nurture a nimble, entrepreneurial, and innovative campus culture. Forward-looking institutions will need to challenge long-held assumptions about program offerings, delivery methods, physical plant, and student services. In the increasingly global landscape of higher education, future success will belong to those institutions that possess unique vision, are unafraid of change, and boldly find new ways to meet the sometimes contradictory demands of students, scholars, government, and the economy.

## REFERENCES

AUCC (2007). *Trends in higher education, Vols. 1–3.* Ottawa: Association of Universities and Colleges of Canada. Available at www.aucc.ca.

Babcock, Phillip and Mindy Marks (2010). *Leisure college USA: The decline in student study time.* American Enterprise Institute for Public Policy Research.

Beloit College (1998–2010). *Beloit college mindset list,* available annually at www.Beloit.edu/mindset

Berger, J. and Motte, Anne (2007). *Mind the access gap: Breaking down barriers to post-secondary education.* Canada Millennium Scholarship Foundation.

Brainstorm Consulting (2010). From *Learning to Work,* national survey of 16,000 Canadian college and university students.

CAUT (2009). *Poll: Canadians want tuition fees lowered or eliminated, CAUT Bulletin.* Based on a     Harris-Decima poll of 2,036 Canadians, November 2008.

CAUT (2010). *Almanac of post-secondary education in Canada, 2010–11.* Toronto: Canadian Association of University Teachers.

CAUT (2010a). *Outsourcing deals face stiff opposition at U of Windsor, Dalhousie.* Canadian Association of University Teachers Web site, 2010.

CCL (2007). *Report on learning in Canada 2007: PSE in Canada, strategies for success.* Canadian Council on Learning.

Cote, James E. & Anton L. Allahar (2007). *Ivory tower blues: A university system in crisis.* Toronto: University of Toronto Press.

DFA (2010). *An open letter to the Dalhousie University community,* on the Dalhousie Faculty Association Web site.

Florida, Richard (2002). *The rise of the creative class: And how it's transforming work, leisure, community and everyday life.* New York: Basic Books.

Gates, William H. III (1995). *The road ahead.* New York: Viking Penguin.

Goldwater Institute (2010). *Administrative bloat at American universities: The real reason for high costs in higher education.* Policy Report, August 2010.

HEQCO (2009). Glen A. Jones & Michael L. Skolnik, *Degrees of opportunity: Broadening student access by increasing institutional differentiation in Ontario higher education.*

Howe, Neil and William Strauss (2000). *Millennials rising: The next great generation.* New York: Vintage Books.

Kelly, Jim (2009). *Change key to solid future: LU leader.* The Chronicle-Journal, Thunder Bay Ontario, May 20, 2009.

Li, Charlene and Josh Bernoff (2008). *Groundswell: Winning in a world transformed by social technologies.* Boston: Harvard Business Press.

Moody's (2009). *2009 U.S. higher education outlook.* Moody's Investor Services.

Motte, Anne and Saul Schwartz (2009). *Are student employment and academic success linked?* Canada Millennium Scholarship Foundation Research Note 9, April 2009.

NCES (2001). *2000–01 Baccalaureate and beyond longitudinal study.* U.S. Department of Education, National Center for Education Statistics.

NCES (2004). *2003–04 National postsecondary student aid study,* U.S. Department of Education, National Center for Education Statistics.

OUAC (2009). Application and enrolment volume statistics published annually by the Ontario Universities Application Centre.

Rybak, Jeff (2007). *What's wrong with university: And how to make it work for you anyway.* Toronto: ECW Press.

Snowdon, Ken (2010). Percentage contributions to Ontario university operating budgets, data compiled for HEQCO and reproduced in the Globe & Mail.

Tapscott, Don and Anthony D. Williams (2006). *Wikinomics: How mass collaboration changes everything.* New York: Portfolio.

*Top Ten (2007–10).* This chapter references and consolidates news and information contained in thousands of news stories reported in Academica's *Top Ten,* a daily news brief edited by Ken Steele. The news items and links to original sources are available in a searchable database on the Academica Group Web site at www.academica.ca.

Turk, James L. (2008). *Universities at risk: How politics, special interests and corporatization threaten academic integrity.* Toronto: Canadian Association of University Teachers.

UCAS (1997–2010). *University college applicant study,* a national survey of 200,000 PSE applicants conducted annually by Academica Group.

UCU (2010). *Joint venture watch,* on the University and College Union Web site, U.K.

# CHAPTER THREE
## ACTIONABLE INTELLIGENCE: RESEARCH FOR SEM

**BY ROD SKINKLE**

In thinking about the content for this chapter we challenged ourselves to address several interrelated questions:

1) In our collective experience with SEM-related research, what learning (i.e., information, perspective, beliefs, etc.) would provide the greatest value to senior leaders in higher education?

2) Why does SEM-focused research appear to be so successful, and have such impact in some institutions, while much less so in others?

3) Are these variances most associated with institutional characteristics, or to the research (methodology, scope, budget, etc.) itself?

Reflecting on these important questions, we concluded that a discussion around the purposes, value, and framing of research for SEM would provide highest value discussion for institutional leaders. The following is structured not as a "how-to," but rather as "why," and "what to look for," discussion from a leadership perspective.

### RESEARCH: A SEM IMPERATIVE

As consultants who regularly work with institutions to provide SEM-related research programs, we have come to believe fervently that you should not conduct research unless you have clearly defined need and, equally importantly, a process to make use of the findings; therefore, a useful starting point is with the discussion of the institutional "needs" that are typically being addressed through research. This is the appropriate starting point for institutional leaders because the need leads directly to the "value" of research, or alternatively, the return on investment (ROI).

## THE PROOF IS IN THE PUDDING—NOT REALLY

We frequently turn to research when a problem surfaces. "Our applicant numbers to program X, a flagship program for us have dropped for two years in row—we need to know why." "We are seeing increasing attrition levels in second year on several key programs—we need to understand this." Many of you will be familiar with these types of scenarios, and they are certainly legitimate questions for which research is well suited to supply answers. Moreover, these are relatively specific needs that can help define specific research projects with clear ways to use the findings. These are examples of "problem focused" need for SEM research. Here the ROI seems relatively straightforward. A problem has been identified, there are costs associated with that problem, and research helps to solve that problem.

You will likely also be familiar with the flipside of this: "Our application numbers are up this year, so we have no need for recruitment focused research." And, "our retention levels are good in comparison to national averages, so we have no need for retention-focused research." After all, the proof is in the pudding, right? Here we have to say, "No—not really." There are multiple alternative explanations for enrolment and retention increases and more often than not they reflect external factors such as shifting demographics, urban growth, and/or downturns in the economy—to name a few. Thus, we should not conclude that you do not have problems with recruitment or other enrolment management processes from that information alone. In fact, problems have a way of not revealing themselves until the system is under increased stress, or in this instance, until the enrolment numbers are on the decline. Both the "problem" and "no problem" approaches to defining need provide a useful foundation on which to build a deeper consideration of the value of research in the SEM arena.

Returning full circle to the question of why research just seems to be more successful in some institutions than in others, we find three vital and systemic characteristics associated with institutions that get the most value from research. First, these institutions have built research programs systematically into their overall SEM planning processes. Second, they have learned to harness the potential of research to address the institution's highest and most strategic priorities. Third, institutional leadership have established a culture of evidence-based decision-making.

Our objective in the following pages is to demonstrate in concrete terms how to use and incorporate research to provide strategic advantage to the institution. This shift in perspective becomes clearer when SEM is viewed as the fully integrated process bridging the entire student experience, as argued throughout this text. From this perspective the real ROI potential of a strategic research program reveals itself. It is also, in our view, an area of genuine opportunity for institutional leaders providing (1) intelligence to help monitor and prioritize strategic opportunities and threats at the institutional level, and (2) access to the detailed data required to identify, prioritize, and justify the need(s) for action.

## DATA—WHAT DATA?

In essence, the above argument reflects a basic truism—leaders need data, and the higher up the leadership ladder you go, the higher the level of data required. The real challenge for leaders, however, is that data are everywhere and reasonably easy to gather, but data are not strategic intelligence. Data are really only the raw input to strategic intelligence. To bridge this gap from data to intelligence, leaders need to first define, or set in motion and guide a process to define, the institution's strategic information needs. These information needs will then help direct the type of data, and point to where and how best to gather it. Finally, this step is critical to ensure that research results provide maximum value to the institution. To address this challenge, the remainder of this is organized into three sections:

1) A Framework for SEM Research—All information is easier to internalize when it can be organized within a broader conceptual framework. In the case of SEM research, we find it particularly useful to organize the information within a model we term "The Student Relationship Continuum." This approach enables us to both categorize the types of research, and to visualize how and where each fits within the overall institutional data stream. This conceptual framework also is helpful in framing our discussion concerning the focus and level of research data that are appropriate to the different rungs on our institutional leadership ladder.

2) Case Studies—In the second section we review two different examples of institutional SEM-related research. Not only because a picture is worth a thousand words, but also because examples provide you with an effective paradigm for comparing and contrasting the research within your own institution.

3) Summary & Context—In the third and final section of this chapter, we distil the information and consider it within the context of key leadership roles and functions.

## FRAMEWORK FOR SEM RESEARCH

"The Student Relationship Continuum" model (figure 1) illustrates a number of core principles while also providing a useful framework to conceptualize and organize SEM-related research across the institution. The overarching principle, of course, is that the visual illustrates the continuity of the student's relationship with your institution and does so in terms of key SEM touch points. It is clear how different departments within your institution are accountable for the delivery of services that align with one or more components of the model. It is also immediately apparent how each component leads to the next and how each is contingent on success in all those preceding it.

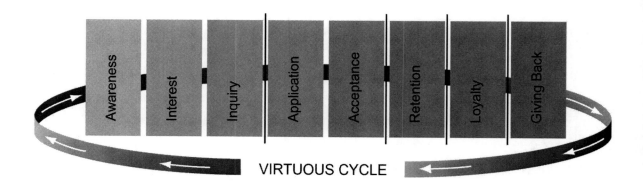

*Figure 1: Student Relationship Continuum*

The model suggests a number of critical points for institutional leaders that bear responsibility for one or more clusters of activities across the experience continuum.

- When viewed as a virtuous cycle, it is not particularly helpful to consider the relative importance of individual components in isolation, because each literally depends upon the preceding. From this perspective, dropping the ball at any one point in the relationship influences all the following interactions.

- As accountability for activities across the continuum increase, the opportunity and need for shared mission, coordination of activities, and communication across the student relationship continuum increases.

- The model also provides a useful way for leaders to frame the type and depth of information they have across the institution. This assists with the "big picture" perspective enabling leaders to spot the weaknesses in both understanding and accountability across the whole of the student relationship continuum (i.e., where are the gaps).

In Figure 2, below, we use the model to chart and audit the information available vertically and horizontally across the continuum. It is helpful to first plot the institutional departments along the continuum, recognizing that there will be both overlap across departments and considerable variability in the way that institutions assign responsibilities for these functions.

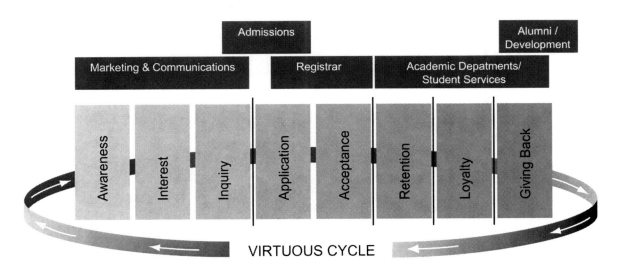

**Figure 2:** *Departmental Focus*

The Student Relationship Continuum reflects the continuity of components each of which represents key touch points for institution and student. However, the interstitials are also transition points from one state to the next, and institutions usually monitor the volume of flows across these transition points. However, it is typically research that enables us to monitor the effectiveness of the flows in terms of barriers and impediments, or aids and supports. Each is a decision/action point for students and each is a real or potential intervention point for institutional services.There exist long traditions of process and deep bodies of knowledge concerning theory and best practices relevant to each of the above clusters of service. Not surprisingly, there is also a significant number of research tools to provide measurement and insight across the continuum. In Figure 3 below, we can overlay examples of such tools along the continuum.

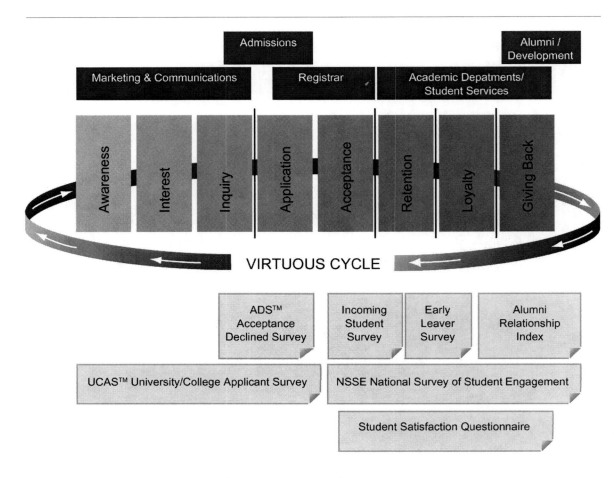

**Figure 3:** *Research Resources*

Figure 3 illustrates how a variety of student experience research resources can be placed along the Student Relationship Continuum, facilitating a "big picture" view of research. Leaders can readily determine where the gaps in information are. Ultimately, the framework illustrates how leaders can utilize research to provide a continuum of intelligence that aligns with the institution's most important (strategic) information needs.

Consider the following stream of integrated strategic intelligence objectives.

- Market Intelligence—aligns with "Awareness" and "Institutional Marketing" on the continuum—and represents strategic information about an institution's reputational advantage, market share and positioning relative to competitors, prospective student markets, and market forces that may impact an institution's ability to realize its enrolment and financial goals.

Research in these areas provides strategic insights for developing a marketing strategy and can be used to gauge return on investment of marketing efforts (Steele, 2009).

- Admissions Intelligence—aligns with "Inquiry through to Enrolment" and "Recruitment Communications and Admissions" on the continuum—and represents strategic information about the effectiveness of the institution's recruitment and admissions processes in influencing prospective student decision-making processes.

- Student Success Intelligence—aligns with "Retention" and "Academic Departments, Student Services and some Registrar functions" on the continuum.

   Research in these areas provides strategic information about student satisfaction and engagement and the effectiveness of co-curricular and student life services in meeting the needs of current students.

- Institutional Advancement Intelligence—aligns with "Loyalty and Giving" and "Alumni Development" on the continuum.

These areas are highly underdeveloped in Canadian PSE and represent strategic information about the effectiveness of the institution in building student affinity throughout the student life cycle (Skinkle, 2005).

   The next step is to illustrate how this research can support SEM objectives. To achieve this we present two examples that illustrate how institutions have come up with innovative approaches to the use of research in support of top level SEM objectives.

## SELECTIVE CASE STUDIES

Recall how in Chapter One we acknowledged that even while there is a growing appetite among Canadian institutions for SEM, many still struggle with a number of the highest management imperatives. The examples provided were: 1) proactively exploit external opportunities and mitigate threats, 2) convert raw data into actionable intelligence, 3) utilize technology to enable enrolment strategies and practices, 4) position the institution effectively among competitors, 5) significantly impact student success and retention, 6) align enrolment efforts with the goals and capacity of the academic enterprise, and 7) build organizational capacity to sustain competitive advantage. We will refer to these periodically in relation to the following case studies.

**CASE STUDY 1:** The University of Waterloo—We start with a large research-intensive university known to virtually everyone in Canada, not to mention a strong international presence. The University of Waterloo has worked with Academica Group to conduct applicant research for more than 10 consecutive years. No—that's not why we're featuring them here. It is because it is hard to find a school that better exemplifies the use of proactive consumer research to continuously refine their market positioning. With their consent, we share one example of this work with their peer community.

We developed the University/College Applicant Survey (UCAS™) with the goal of providing schools with strategic intelligence focused on the marketing and communications through to the acceptance components of the (first five bars) student relationship continuum. The instrument examines everything from the most tactical (how much time did you spend on our competitor's Web site) to most strategic (e.g., perceived reputation on the most critical brand attributes). Figure 4 below illustrates one way the information can be presented.

*Figure 4: Reputation Septograph*

In addition to these quantitative measures, we collect word association data that provide another view of the institution—words that come to mind among applicants when thinking about your school. There are literally hundreds of data points that client schools use from this type of research, so it's risky to home in on a particular aspect; however, there is one particularly striking example that warrants the risk.

A number of years ago the Director of Marketing and Undergraduate Recruitment at the University of Waterloo began to notice the frequency with which the school was associated with the term "innovation." This made a lot of sense because the school literally pioneered cooperative education in Canada and is also well known for its incubation role in early days of the birth of Research in Motion (think BlackBerry). The university is also widely recognized for its preeminance in Technology and Science, made enormously more preeminant as a widely publicized feeder of graduate talent to Bill Gates' Microsoft corporation. No surprise then that this was a strong association in the minds of the public (and prospective students live in the public). However, the data reinforced the strategic value of this association. But the thinking did not stop there. The University of Waterloo, an institution that was born just over 50 years ago, couldn't hope to win on reputation attributes that tend to go with a long "tradition," such as the Harvards and Yales or the Queens and McGills of the planet. Interestingly though, the attribute "tradition" is a notion that, along with all its strengths, has trouble cohabitating in peoples' minds with innovation. And, in fact, the data reinforced that too. Now a potentially valuable identity pairing becomes decisively more strategic. Why? Because it achieves four of seven vital high-level management imperatives that we noted previously:

1) proactively exploit external opportunities and mitigate threats,

2) position the institution effectively among competitors,

3) align enrolment efforts with the goals and capacity of the academic enterprise,

4) convert raw data into actionable intelligence.

The recruitment and marketing professionals at the school recognized this and gradually orchestrated increasing pairings between the school and the term. Indeed, at this point, everything concerned with marketing undergraduate programs goes through the innovation filter. Through further testing, the school adopted the tag line "ideas start here"—a simple and effective way to convey the essence of "innovation" in everyday language.

This is not a book about branding; however, it is worth noting that it is not advisable to attempt to own an "attribute," however desirable, that is not consistent with your brand (Tybout & Calkins, 2005). In this instance, the research provided evidence that the school's brand footprint was such that it could realistically claim this adjective and importantly, deliver on it.

**CASE STUDY 2:** A study involving a midsize institution on Canada's west coast provides an excellent example of research to support institution-wide SEM objectives. As this project is ongoing we will keep the school anonymous; however, we bring this example forward at this point because it is not only the results but also the bold and innovative use of research and the manner in which it has been developed and integrated by the institution that provide the highest value learning for institutional leaders.

The research leadership within this institution presented us with a genuine opportunity: to assist in the design and execution of a truly integrated and actionable research program. A program customized to their circumstances that was flexible and sustainable, while providing ongoing timely intelligence to their SEM committee. A tall order—sure, but it is instructive to recognize the real leadership golden nugget here. Recall in her study of SEM practice leaders (see Chapter Eight), Lynda Wallace-Hulecki isolated a sequence of strategies and practical tips exemplified by these leaders: Tip number 2: adopting the use of research and data: the language of academics.

There are a couple of dots to connect here. The first inspirational move, of course, was the establishment of a multidisciplinary SEM committee, but the second, from the Institutional Research leadership, is the realization that if such a committee had both input and access to a source of ongoing reliable research intelligence, their potential to impact change would be immeasurably greater.

The SEM committee had been mainly concentrating on recruitment and other front-end processes, and was looking to move "along the continuum" into retention initiatives. The group had articulated their next priority would be a deeper understanding of retention within their institution. While there are several retention and student engagement focused instruments available, the IR leadership wanted to develop a customized longer view approach with enhanced flexibility to pursue local SEM-directed information needs and priorities.

To address this need we deployed our Student Consumer Panel design, which utilizes a combination cross-sectional and longitudinal design. The project should be considered a four-year longitudinal study.

## SAMPLE/DESIGN

This school had worked with us previously and knew the hands-on value of the University/ College Applicant Survey UCAS™, in which dozens of schools in Canada and the U.S. participate. Starting with this applicant survey, we added our newly developed Retention Module that assesses applicant expectations on an array of interaction and engagment behaviours.

With our applicant research, we routinely invite respondents to participate in our ongoing Consumer Panel studies. For this school, we built on the sample by inviting both incoming and first- and upper-year students distributed by year, as in Figure 5 below, for a total of approximately 1000–1200 students.

| Target Group | Applicants | First-Year Student | Second–Fourth Year |
|---|---|---|---|
| Research Focus | Applicant Perceptions | Entering Student Engagement | Engagement/Retention |
| Sample Size | N = 2000 | N = 750 | N = 350 |

*Figure 5:* Sample Size by Year of Study

This design is powerful and efficient because we recruit a cross-section of students from first-year, right to fourth-year programs while it is simultaneously longitudinal, because we track the entire sample as students move through their college experience. It has the benefits of immediacy (i.e., can gather information from across all years) and the strengths of longitudinal research designs (Cook & Campbell, 1979).

## STRATEGIC INFORMATION OBJECTIVES

The overarching purpose of the research is to better understand the college experience through the eyes of its students in order to develop actionable improvements. There are two categories of information that will help us identify actionable information. The first category we describe as theoretical or pedagogical. This refers to the study of the broad constructs such as student engagement, progression/retention, etc. This type of data becomes actionable intelligence in the hands of the appropriate academic and student support services professionals. The second category refers to the less theory driven but equally valuable opportunities available through the collection of ongoing feedback on a wide range of student experience and perceptions. Also noteworthy, the Student Consumer Panel presents the opportunity to "road test" student development concepts and service ideas on an as needed basis. The following list shows the major strategic research themes: 1) Recruitment & Marketing Best Practices, 2) Entering Student Engagement, 3) Progression/Retention Factors, 4) Ongoing Student Experience Feedback.

## LEADERS & SEM RESEARCH

Through previous sections we have considered research as a SEM imperative, presented the Student Relationship Continuum as a framework to provide context and structure for institutional research, and reviewed two examples to demonstrate the application of SEM research. In this third and final section, our goal is to distil the information and consider it within the context of key leadership roles and functions. Throughout this book, much has been said about the vital role of leadership in setting the example, establishing the culture, and enabling the processes to achieve a well-integrated and high functioning SEM organization. Here our objective is to home in on these leadership roles specifically as they apply to research for SEM.

## INSPIRING RESEARCH

Certainly much has been written about the subject of leadership. Most would agree that a key function of leaders is to "inspire." In their best-selling book on this subject, published in 2005, Kouzes and Posner summarize years of research with the identification of the top five leadership traits:

1. **Honest**

2. **Forward-Looking**

3. **Competent**

4. **Inspiring**

5. **Intelligent**

   While the above are all clearly important with respect to leadership in general, number four, "inspiring," can be particularly crucial with respect to leading SEM research on campus. This is because research is a revered, sacred activity in our institutions of higher education, and an almost black-box-like activity full of complex methods and statistical jargon. Like higher education itself, participation in research can be a rewarding and transformative experience, both for the sheer joy of discovery and for the improved effectiveness it can bring to employees in their day-to-day work. It is inherently rewarding on many levels.

Many years ago a senior VP charged this investigator (then a Coordinator of Research for Student Services) with an extraordinarily broad research challenge: Go and conduct research to improve the quality of undergraduate student life. This seemed at the time a pretty broad and vague mandate. Nevertheless, we began by recruiting what was quite possibly the first-ever student consumer panel in Canada. Throughout the academic year we explored this broad research mandate through a succession of quantitative and qualitative studies with students. Once the students got over the shock of someone actually asking their opinions on this subject, it was truly remarkable how much we learned. We accumulated a wealth of ideas and perceptions ranging from relatively discrete service improvements to enterprise-wide intelligence with potentially game-changing perceptions concerning academic advising and related student experience.

The point of this anecdote is that this opportunity, which seemed quite vague then, now twenty plus years later seems inspired. It was inspired by a senior administrative leader who recognized the potential. This was precisely the type of "listening to the users" Peters and Waterman (2004) described, in their now classic book *In Search of Excellence*, which provides organizations with competitive advantage because it leads to creative breakthroughs in service, and helps to keep the organization "quality obsessed." This example reinforces something that you will not find in a text about research methods—that leaders can inspire respect and demonstrate the value of research through example.

## RESEARCH SCOPE & FOCUS

As one moves down the leadership ladder the scope of interests naturally narrow to reflect the scope of responsibility and the focus also narrows toward more immediate management needs. This is where you will find more problem-focused research questions. As we stated previously, there is nothing wrong with this in the sense that research is about providing intelligence to help solve problems that arise, and there will always be unanticipated problems, and opportunities, that arise seemingly from nowhere. In fact, it is not uncommon during the course of these discreet investigations, to discover information of much broader strategic value. Thus, it is an important function of leadership to encourage and enable this type of focused and more opportunistic research.

Still there is no sidestepping the reality that these are reactive uses for research and, moreover, that the institution will typically derive less strategic value (ROI) from this approach. As you move up the leadership ladder, the scope broadens and you move increasingly toward the institution's highest and most vital challenges. This is where the senior leadership can exercise their broader perspective to ensure that research aligns with the most important strategic objectives of the organization. As noted at the outset of this chapter, this is also an area of genuine opportunity for leaders to identify top-level strategic opportunities and threats for the institution.

## ORGANIZATIONAL CAPACITY

To realize this opportunity, leaders also need to attend to the more fundamental challenges associated with the development of organizational capacity. These are addressed in detail with respect to overall SEM capacity in Chapter Eight. Here we are referring specifically to the organization's capacity to both execute research and to ensure the institution has the capacity to maximize the benefit from research.

Several organizational capacity issues are foundational:

1. A culture of evidence-based decision-making—this is truly the purview of leadership. Only they establish, via direction and reward, the appetite for evidence and the climate wherein it is valued. Many institutions have existing data that they are not benefiting from; however, as this culture develops, administrators are encouraged and empowered to use existing data more often and more strategically. Likewise, they will be more likely to recognize and develop further information needs (i.e., strategic research objectives).

2. Clarifying and communicating the organization's top-level information needs are also strictly the role of institutional leadership. As noted above, leaders have the opportunity to use their broader scope to focus on the organization's highest strategic objectives. Once those objectives are established, however, leaders need to ensure the articulation of the information required to reach these strategic objectives. What information do we have internally? What information do we need to gather?

3. Prioritizing information needs in relation to the competing demands—as we have dis-

cussed previously, given the organizational realities of budget and competing demands for resources, this is one of the most important organizational capacity challenges. This type of top-level organizational research is an investment, plain and simple, and institutions have to make the investment before they can realize the return.

4. Ensuring the capacity to act on intelligence—even when information needs and priorities have been identified and resources allocated (discussed below) it will have limited impact unless leadership has established the mandate and processes to act on findings. As many leaders will attest, this is much easier said than done. These top-level objectives tend to cross over institutional silos and ultimate accountability tends to be difficult to establish. Thus, interdepartmental collaboration is a prerequisite condition of effective SEM research. This capacity requirement goes beyond simple bidirectional communications to a point that demands an integrated, cross silo perspective.

The above capacity matters are, in our view, the most fundamental. These are the cultural hallmarks that tend to define organizations that regularly make use of strategic intelligence.

## EXECUTION AND RESOURCES

In addition to these organizational capacity challenges, it is also important to consider the leadership roles with respect to two vital, if more pragmatic, challenges: 1) What is the best approach to initiate and oversee the execution of SEM research, and 2) How do institutions resource this research.

To the first question, we recommend strongly the establishment of a multidisciplinary SEM committee as a best practice approach to initiate and help define SEM research. Once leadership has established the broad organizational capacity requirements noted above, the SEM committee is empowered to contribute directly to the establishment of research objectives, and interpretation of findings and implications. This is also an effective strategy that simultaneously improves the relevance of research while enhancing the use and dissemination of findings.

With respect to the second question, resourcing of the research, institutions vary widely in terms of internal expertise and resources. Furthermore, leaders should expect that this topic often elicits mixed, and even somewhat controversial, reactions across university and college campuses. After all, are not our institutions of higher learning brimming over with relevant subject matter knowledge (e.g., business and market research) and skills? Our experience with this matter has been pretty consistent. It is not a matter of expertise but rather of focus and capacity. The professoriate is correctly focused on their areas of research specialization and this is their highest best use for the institution.

Concerning nonacademic institutional research resources (IR), capacity tends to vary a great deal across institutions. Certainly the appropriate leaders, including IR leadership, should be involved in the design and coordination of SEM research. Whether the institutional research offices have the resources and expertise to execute institution-wide SEM research is also highly variable. This capacity variance is not only a function of size but also of focus. Larger institutions with more resources tend to have correspondingly larger demands for the more expedient budget and resource management focused information. For leaders determined to champion this type of SEM-related research, this is a question that concerns both the "resources" and "efficiency." It is often most efficient to deploy the top internal talent to work with external consultants with the goal of developing the most efficient and sustainable internal research capacity. Since this author provides SEM and other PSE research consulting, it is difficult to discuss the subject without seeming to "sell" consulting services. Still, it is a very important topic that most PSE leaders have and/or will continue to confront.

With respect to the above matter, leaders will need to weigh several interrelated factors. The first consideration is the SEM expertise. Whether using internal or external SEM champions, these champions are deploying research for the express purpose of identifying strengths, weaknesses, opportunities, and threats (SWOT) across the student continuum. Their ultimate objective is to support the development of optimal SEM processes, specific to an institution's particular circumstances. Therefore, the SEM expert needs to be directly engaged in the research design and interpretation of findings. The second and related consideration is the research expertise. The researchers need to understand the PSE environment and, most importantly, the SEM processes and goals that the research seeks to inform. The third consideration is the need for objective and reliable information. In an academic environment, it does not pay to underestimate this consideration. Finally, there is the practical matter of the resources to execute in a timely manner to support the ultimate purpose—the development of optimal SEM processes.

Whatever your current situation, we recommend dedication to the goal of "developing the most efficient and sustainable internal research capacity." As Dr. Black argued in the introductory chapter, your only truly sustainable competitive advantage is your "organizational capacity." If this organizational truism was not well understood in the past it should be abundantly clear now. We have seen relatively new colleges and universities move from start-up, with no reputation, to overtake long established institutions with venerable status, in a space of 20 years or less. This author has spoken to university presidents who do not share this fundamental perspective; neither on the threat nor opportunity side. There is an underlying complacency here, born of a different era when age and geography tended to define status and market potential. It's easy to be lulled in this environment because institutions do not tumble overnight. They lose ground in small, ever so subtle increments. Overreliance on throughput data can tend to reinforce this problem. By the time you observe change with this level of data, the antecedent variables are way out in front. Ken Steele's chapter provides a glaring reminder of the variety of environmental conditions driving changes in the landscape of higher education—with unprecedented speed. As in nature, the organism that anticipates threats and exploits opportunities thrives.

## SUMMARY

We've argued that your starting point, as leaders, is with a deeper view of the "need" for research. Think of research as the eyes and ears, gathering data, which is the input to the brain. The brain, of course, is your senior leadership who collectively possess the experience and context to make the best use of the data. It is not really possible for professionals farther down the leadership ladder to structure and resource broad-based mission critical research programs in isolation.

We have presented the Student Relationship Continuum as a useful framework to conceptualize and organize research. The continuum model mirrors the student experience, which is itself a contiguous and personal journey. For leaders this framework reinforces two essential principles: 1) the view of the student experience as a "relationship" that is holistic and a virtuous cycle beginning with the first time a student becomes aware of your school (I wonder what the context and first impression was); and 2) the framework helps to reinforce the cross-silo interdependencies and suggests how research can play a crucial role in enterprise-wide communications.

When it comes to resourcing research and ensuring the highest ROI, there are a number of pivotal organizational capacity issues that are the purview of institutional leadership. Our example on Canada's west coast illustrates there are innovative and cost-effective ways to build in exciting research and to ensure that the information is fed directly to key decision-makers within the context of a broad multidisciplinary SEM group. Experienced IR leaders know full well how to get the most value out of research. The most seasoned have led many studies, large and small, and the most common refrain we hear from them is that the results were never really used, sometimes not even shared. This author and my colleagues in various institutions are often befuddled by a commonly heard question from the most senior leadership: *"How can I even contemplate spending on research when we are cutting teaching faculty and other administration, due to shrinking resources?"* The more logical question would be the other way around: *"How can I justify adding more faculty or other administrative resources in the absence of good intelligence to direct that spending toward our most mission critical objectives?"*

## FOOTNOTE

[1] However, because of their closer proximity to the front lines, they can provide valuable guidance toward both design and interpretation of research.

## REFERENCES

Black, J. (2008a). *New directions in strategic enrollment management.* VA: Strategic Initiatives.

Cook T.D. & Campbell, D.T. (1979). *Quasi-experimentation: Design & analysis issues for field settings.* Boston, MA: Houghton-Mifflin.

Kouzes, J. & Posner, B. (2007). *The leadership challenge.* 4th Ed. John Wiley & Sons.

Peters, T. & Waterman, R. H. (2004, 1982) *In search of excellence.* HarperCollins Publishers, New York, NY.

Steele, K. (2009). *Selling the academy without selling out.* Academic Matters, February-March.

Skinkle, R. & McKinley, P. (2005). *Strategic engagement of alumni: Integrating research and alumni relations.* Presentation: International Conference Annual Proceedings of Association of Professional Researchers for Advancement. San Diego, CA.

Tybout, A. & Calkins, T. (2005). *Kellogg on branding.* John Wiley & Sons, Hoboken, New Jersey.

## ACKNOWLEDGEMENTS

*For 25 plus years, it has been my good fortune to collaborate on research projects with many dedicated and passionate higher education professionals across this country. This chapter is really my attempt to bring together the learning and enthusiasm from those collaborations. I want to sincerely thank those many clients who have, and continue to provide us the privilege of working with them.*

*I particularly want to acknowledge an early mentor and dear friend, Dr. Tom Siess, former Director of Students Services at The University of Western Ontario. Tom was a pioneer who envisioned and realized the potential of applied research as an ongoing practice to advance student affairs.*

*Finally, for their generosity and valuable advice in reviewing early versions of this chapter I wish to thank Tina Roberts, Director, Marketing and Undergraduate Recruitment, University of Waterloo and Paul Merner, Associate Vice President, for SEM, Camosun College.*

# PART TWO

# INTRODUCTION
## ENROLMENT ENABLERS AND CORE STRATEGIES

With the Canadian enrolment context in mind, now we turn to the enablers of enrolment strategy as well as the strategies themselves. Through our visits to hundreds of campuses, we have observed a seemingly infinite number of enrolment and branding strategies considered to be best practices that have yielded minimal results, cost thousands of dollars and staff hours, and left the organization deflated and searching for alternative solutions. The problems we uncovered were usually not in the strategies per se, but in the execution.

Failure to understand and work within an academic culture or view SEM through an academic lens can be contributing factors to unsuccessful strategies. Chapter Four reveals the importance of creating a culture of shared responsibility for enrolment outcomes with the academic community. The author also presents six strategies and nine practical tips that provide insights on how to foster campus-wide engagement in SEM planning.

In Part Two, Chapters Five and Six focus on reputational and student success strategies. Chapter Five explains the two sides of institutional branding: 1) promotion and positioning, and 2) brand promise delivery. Both are essential to possessing a brand that is compelling and real. Chapter Six conveys the importance of a student success culture along with insights on how to create and sustain such a culture. Most importantly, this chapter focuses on ensuring the conditions for student success are in place.

Poor execution of strategies can also be attributed to the lack of organizational capacity or other enabling factors such as technology—the focus of Chapters Seven and Eight. Now, more than ever, enrolment enterprises are dependent upon technology to deliver information, transact business, serve students, and market the institution. Chapter Seven discusses emerging technology trends and related institutional opportunities to leverage technology. While technology represents a vital element of organizational capacity, Chapter Eight explores other defining features and characteristics associated with a high performing "enrolment" organization. In addition, Chapter Eight provides a brief overview of the common barriers to achieving optimal organizational performance, followed by a model and guidelines for building organizational capacity to create the conditions for optimal SEM performance.

# CHAPTER FOUR
## REFRAMING SEM FROM THE ACADEMIC LENS: THEORY IN PRACTICE

**BY LYNDA WALLACE-HULECKI**

Both the literature and research conducted by this author substantiate a brutal fact: while many institutions operate with the goal of increasing enrolment and net revenues, few have the ability to define optimum enrolment capacity within the academic program context and manage the nexus between enrolment, academic quality, and revenues. This chapter discusses the symbiotic relationship between enrolment management and academic program planning and innovation, the power of SEM in focusing strategic planning efforts on a student-centred purpose, and the importance of leadership in managing change. The chapter is structured in two parts. Part I discusses SEM as an academic imperative and the importance of creating a culture of shared responsibility for enrolment outcomes with the academic community. Part II draws from a study conducted by this author on exemplary practices in fostering a SEM ethos within an academic context, and presents six strategies and nine practical tips that may provide insights and value to you in fostering campus-wide engagement in SEM planning at your institution.

## PART I: SEM AS AN ACADEMIC IMPERATIVE:
### THE THEORY IN PRACTICE: LEVERAGING THE POWER OF SEM IN STRATEGIC PLANNING AND CHANGE

In today's Canadian higher education context, postsecondary institutions face unprecedented challenges in managing the nexus between student enrolment, financial imperatives, and academic mission. Since the early 1970s, SEM has evolved in concept and process. What was initially conceived as an operations management function within admissions and marketing has become an organizing construct applied by a growing number of institutions to strategically influence the alignment of these three imperatives. Throughout its evolution to date, the literature is replete with references to the codependencies between the concepts and processes associated with the strategic management of enrolment, and the broader institutional processes of strategic planning and resource management linked to accountability (Black, 2008; Bontrager (Ed.), 2008; Hossler, 2008; Norris, Baer, Leonard, Pugliese, & Lefrere, 2008; Massa, 2001; Dolence, 1993, 1997 ).

Within an ever-expanding and diverse system of higher education providers (private, for-profits, public, virtual), many institutions have been challenged by a more competitive environment. To survive, colleges and universities have mimicked the private sector in their approaches to student recruitment and marketing in order to increase market share of students and to secure greater portions of revenue from student enrolment (Hossler & Hoezee, 2001). Opportunities to diversify the enrolment mix have been pursued largely by increasing access for the traditionally underserved, which represent the largest growing segment of the population in many jurisdictions. As a result, institutional leaders are increasingly recognizing the need to infuse a more strategic and systems approach to enrolment planning, with particular attention on the relationships between enrolment goals, academic development directions, and resource management decisions (Hossler & Hoezee, 2001; Hossler, 2008).

In reality, enrolment planning is not a "quick fix" to an enrolment problem that can simply be achieved by pressuring admissions and enrolment professionals for improved results, or by throwing marketing dollars at an enrolment problem. Rather, it is a tool for achieving sustainable competitive advantage through changing environmental conditions (Black, 2008a, 2008b). Enrolment planning becomes strategic when it is an integral component of institution-wide planning and resource management processes, fused with the academic enterprise, and when it advances transformative change.

## DEFINING THE ACADEMIC IMPERATIVE

The fusion of enrolment management with the academic enterprise is a necessary condition to optimize enrolment. The combination of the "quality" and "relevance" of what is offered, how it is delivered, and the student support systems both within and outside the classroom create the conditions for a positive student learning experience, which in turn translates into an institution's reputational advantage for distinctive excellence. If managed well, an institution's reputation can protect it from adverse environmental forces, and serve as institutional currency in attracting and retaining high-value students as well as faculty and other employees.

In a rapidly changing and highly competitive marketplace, high performing organizations must be flexible, nimble, and responsive (Blanchard, 2010), while remaining focused, steadfast, and "relentlessly disciplined" in the pursuit of a sustained level of high performance and competitiveness (Collins, 2005). Having the "right" programs, in the "right" markets, delivered in a manner that is conducive to the learning preferences of potential students you serve is mission critical (Black, 2008c). For these reasons, academic program innovation and development is the cornerstone of the enrolment enterprise, and the academic program mix is central to enrolment success.

Developing and maintaining a strategic fit between an institution's goals and capabilities and its changing environment is a function of strategic planning (Bryson, 2004). There is a symbiotic relationship between enrolment management, institutional strategic planning, and academic program planning processes (Dolence, 1993, 1997). At the core of an institution's strategic plan is the academic mission and program plan. Enrolment planning and the resultant SEM plan are integral components of the academic plan and planning process. Enrolment planning brings a systems perspective to strategically focus the institution on its program areas of distinctive competence and competitive advantage. An outcome of the academic planning process is the articulation of broad institutional enrolment planning parameters that may include, but are not limited to:

- Optimal enrolment size

- Desired program and credential mix

- Desired instructional delivery mix (traditional, online, blended)

- Desired student profile

- Desired levels of student intake, persistence, and completion

- Desired reputation and image

- Relationship of enrolment to net revenues

From these, enrolment priorities and strategies are formulated with a view to:

(a) Uncovering the institution's existing competencies;

(b) Leveraging the use of strategic intelligence (research and data) to improve competitiveness;

(c) Fostering collaborative leadership in strategy development;

(d) Engaging institutional constituents and cultivating buy-in to the process;

(e) Identifying strategic opportunities to advance the institution's market position and enrolment goals; and

(f) Clarifying organizational capacity conditions for sustained high performance (e.g., people, budget, structures, information, systems, etc.).

The articulated enrolment objectives and targets are defined in measurable terms in alignment with the academic mission, faculty interests and expertise, organizational capacity constraints, market demand, competitive context, student selectivity, student diversity and quality objectives, institutional incentives and support systems, as well as financial exigencies. The process of establishing enrolment goals and targets is not atypical of most strategic planning processes, which normally involve five primary stages:

1. Organize—Establish a SEM planning process (e.g., sponsor, leadership team, mandate)

2. Research—Conduct market research, an environmental scan, and a review of institutional business intelligence information

3. Plan—Facilitate stakeholder dialogue to identify and prioritize high impact strategic opportunities

4. Implement—Formulate cross-functional strategy teams to develop strategies, tactics, and associated key performance indicators and metrics

5. Assess/Adjust—Evaluate the outcomes and return on investment of strategies implemented, and adjust the plan accordingly

When effectively aligned with budget plans and priorities, the resultant SEM plan becomes the lever by which the academic plan is realized, and a touchstone for measuring the effectiveness of institutional enrolment performance. In this way, the enrolment management plan becomes an integral component of the institution's strategic plan, rooted within the academic context, and linked to resource management decisions. Thus, academic program development and innovation becomes the cornerstone of the enrolment enterprise, enrolment becomes the lifeline to institutional vitality, and the enrolment planning process becomes the vehicle by which to realize continued success in achieving enrolment and financial performance goals.

## CRITICAL ROLE AND FUNCTION OF INSTITUTIONAL LEADERSHIP

If enrolment management is the vehicle for change, leadership is the engine. In high performing organizations, leadership is what moves the entire organization in a common direction (Blanchard, 2010; Collins, 2001). In the Jim Collins book, *Good to Great,* the author describes a common phenomenon among companies that is equally as prevalent among colleges and universities. Collins calls it "the flywheel"—the belief that one dramatic strategy or effort transforms an organization from good to great. The flywheel will turn if everyone is pushing in the same direction with equal vigor. Mobilizing a campus community around a common enrolment purpose is the secret to producing dramatic, sustainable results (Black, 2010). Leadership is the engine by which the flywheel turns.

By design, enrolment management involves solving complex problems, taking calculated risks, and reaching across departmental and divisional boundaries (Black, 2003b). Enrolment management requires negotiating campus-wide investment in strategies that serve the organization as a whole. Therefore, SEM requires strength of institutional leadership.

Historically, colleges and universities are known to be adverse to change (Goff and Lane, 2007). In fact, few higher education institutions operate as "flexible, nimble, and responsive" organizations, and the existence of a comprehensive, integrated, and actionable strategic enrolment plan is rare (Black, 2008a). While many institutions have adopted strategies related to the administrative aspects of enrolment operations associated with student recruitment and admissions, marketing, retention, and customer service, few have effectively aligned enrolment strategies with the academic priorities of individual faculties/schools, and fostered a culture of shared responsibility for enrolment outcomes with the academic community. Moreover, when queried about enrolment, more often than not faculty will respond that enrolment is an administrative responsibility of the administration. Therefore, institutional leaders face two primary challenges in creating a high performance enrolment organization:

1.  To foster a campus-wide SEM ethos that is rooted within the academic context, and

2.  To build a high performance enrolment organization at the operational level.

The remainder of this chapter focuses on the organizational conditions necessary to address the first challenge, as well as strategies and practical tips for institutional leaders in implementing these conditions. The second challenge is the subject of another chapter in this book on building organizational capacity for SEM.

# PART II: SEM AS A CAMPUS-WIDE SHARED RESPONSIBILITY

Fostering a campus-wide SEM ethos that is rooted within the academic context requires more than the formulation of a SEM committee. Research conducted by this author with exemplary leaders in the field of SEM explored the strategies and practices they used in cultivating shared responsibility for enrolment outcomes with the academic community. The research approach involved a survey of, and interviews with, five internationally renown enrolment leaders who were reputed for their effective leadership in realizing positive enrolment change. Results stemming from the research substantiated the relevance of the theoretical underpinnings to effective SEM practice described earlier in this chapter, provided insights on the antecedents for the successful execution of SEM as a change process, as well as practical strategies for leading the charge in cultivating a SEM ethos within the academic context. These strategies included:

1. Cultivating a change in culture

2. Adopting the use of research and data: the language of academics

3. Inspiring a campus-wide focus on the student experience

4. Actively engaging academic deans and faculty in SEM planning, decision-making, and change

5. Incentivizing change tied to accountability with consequences

6. Visibly leading the charge

The antecedents for cultivating a SEM ethos within the academic context are presented below, followed by a brief discussion of each of the six strategies, including practical tips from the field.

## ANTECEDENTS FOR CULTIVATING A SEM ETHOS WITHIN THE ACADEMIC CONTEXT

Five planning principles and six critical success factors emerged in the research as fundamental antecedents for garnering shared responsibility for enrolment outcomes with the academic community (refer to Chart 1, below). Taken at face value, these statements are like platitudes, where few would disagree. However, living these principles through action is hard work for even the most adept leader. In reality, any of these conditions can meet with resistance. As one study participant advised:

[T]he academic community operate as independent contractors who you have to convince to work together in the spirit of the collective whole. This takes negotiation and leadership, which starts with an understanding of campus culture. Be a student of the institution by walking around and talking to people. Keep asking, who do I need to talk with to understand how things work? Get a good sense of what the president, provost, vice-presidents value, among other influential members of the campus community. Seek to understand where the rubber hits the road in each of these areas before you take action. Then be consistent. (Wallace-Hulecki, 2007)

***Chart 1:*** *Planning Principles and Critical Success Factors*

| CORE PLANNING PRINCIPLES | CRITICAL SUCCESS FACTORS |
|---|---|
| • Right people at the table | • Compelling case for change |
| • Involvement of faculty, staff, and students from across divisions | • Visible support of "executive" leaders |
| • Interactive and participatory process | • Enrolment champion in a position of influence |
| • Respect for leadership style of the academic dean and unit heads | • Investment in quality research and analysis |
| • Evidence-based decision-making | • Readiness for change and for challenging the status quo |
| | • Accountability tied to resources |

Equally as important to creating the conditions for success is an understanding of the barriers that inhibit progress. Two barriers were repeatedly referenced in the research as leadership challenges, and include:

1. **Complacency**—Once an initial enrolment urgency is addressed, the tendency is to fall back to a state of complacency. One strategy suggested by a study participant to counteract

the forces that drive complacency is to place "enrolment" in its broadest sense as a standing agenda item at meetings of the board of governors, executive council, faculty senate, deans' and chairs' advisory meetings, and the like. This signals the ongoing strategic significance of enrolment, and holds those in leadership roles accountable and purpose-centred over the long haul.

2. **Challenging the status quo**—The great irony is that colleges and universities are by definition institutions that generate new knowledge; yet in reality, they are incredibly tradition-bound places (Goff and Lane, 2007). In order to foster an environment in which challenging the status quo is tenable, an internal education process is needed. As one study participant noted:

> The first call to order was to get people to understand all the [enrolment] dynamics at play, and what their involvement could be to help reshape that scenario. During that nine month period, we . . . were on parallel tracks with raising awareness, raising commitment, and raising understanding; and creating an enrolment management plan that was to have a price tag associated with it—a level of commitment the institution had never before made. (Wallace-Hulecki, 2007)

## STRATEGIES AND PRACTICAL TIPS FROM THE FIELD

As mentioned previously, six strategies emerged in the research for cultivating a SEM ethos anchored within the academic context. Each of these strategies will be discussed here. Practical examples of the application of these strategies are presented that emanate from the sage advice of the study participants, who collectively possessed over 200 years of higher education leadership experience, as well as this author's own experiences as a strategic planner/researcher and SEM leader for more than thirty years. These perspectives are intended solely to stimulate your thinking in the hope that you may glean value from the lessons learned from others who have successfully forged this road.

## 1. CULTIVATING A CHANGE IN CULTURE

In simple terms, organizational culture refers to "how things get done around here" (Blanchard, 2010, p. 241). While there are different meanings and interpretations of culture, from a functional perspective (versus semiotic), culture refers to the core enduring values and beliefs that manifest in organizational behaviour. An organization's culture is reflected by what is valued, the dominant managerial and leadership styles, the language and symbols, the procedures and routines, and the definitions of success that make an organization unique (Cameron and Quinn, 2006). There is substantial literature on the powerful effect that organizational culture has on the performance and enduring success of organizations (Blanchard, 2010). Empirical studies have demonstrated that when values, orientations, definitions, and goals stay constant—even when procedures and strategies are altered—organizations quickly return to the "status quo" and transformational change efforts fail (Cameron and Quinn, 1999, 2006).

Many believe that planning and control processes in organizations are strongly influenced by culture. For example, an organization's approach to planning is related to cultural factors associated with: 1) the degree of structure versus autonomy in strategic decision-making, 2) tolerance for a long-term orientation versus short-term quick results, 3) emphasis on the interests of "groups" versus the "individual", and 4) the mechanisms for negotiating agreement and handling conflicts. In relation to an organization's approach to control, cultural factors such as who and where are the sources and locus of power emerge (Hofstede and Hofstede, 2005).

SEM is largely about culture change (Kemer, Baldrige, and Green, 1982; Hossler and Bean, 1990; Henderson, 2001). The fundamental tenet underlying a SEM ethos is that it fosters campus-wide buy-in and engagement in a highly collaborative and participatory approach to enrolment planning, where improving the student experience and student success are focal points of attention (Black, 2008b). However, academic institutions traditionally are highly decentralized and autonomous organizations (Hossler and Hoezee, 2001). Academic planning typically occurs at the faculty/school or department level, and individual faculties/schools often operate with considerable autonomy. This norm engenders independence and autonomy, as compared to a highly collaborative integrated model of academic and enrolment planning that underlies SEM.

Therefore, when viewed from an academic lens, it can be expected that natural tensions will arise given the inherent differences between the traditional value-orientations of an "academic-driven" culture and a "student-centred" SEM ethos. Effective leadership within a cultural context brings balance between achieving the objectives of an organization and building political loyalty from within the organization (Cameron and Quinn, 2006). It requires building constructive relationships to influence others in achieving a common vision for change. In doing so, institutional leaders must align the vision for change with the intrinsic values and beliefs that instill passion and a sense of pride among campus constituents. Within an institutional context in which a traditional academic culture prevails, bold leadership is required to shift the cultural values to one that has concern for the collective "we," rewards performance on the strength of "group," develops a "collaborative" approach to governance, and fosters a spirit of the "strength of oneness."

The process of culture change requires persistence and sustained attention over time (Hofstede and Hofstede, 2005). The literature is replete with references to methods for motivating and influencing culture change. Among the most notable is the communication of a sense of urgency as an impetus and catalyst for a change effort (Kotter, 1995).

## PRACTICAL TIP #1: Create a Compelling Case for Change

All five study participants confirmed that it was the connection between enrolment and institutional budget, and the relationship between enrolment and the institution's market positioning that created a sense of urgency that leveraged their respective SEM initiative. Effectively managed, communication of a sense of urgency can catapult the transformative change process; poorly managed, it can be detrimental. The most effective source of communication regarding a sense of urgency comes from members of the institution's executive—the president and provost. The message must articulate the relationship between enrolment and the institution's aspirational directions, the importance to academic quality and the institution's financial well-being, and must be accompanied by a call to action for the institution to adopt a more strategic approach to enrolment management. Study participants agreed that when communicating the message, care must be taken not to lay blame for the urgency at hand. Rather, the call to action should be associated with the changing environmental context, the need for agility in planning, and the necessity of uncovering the root cause(s) of the challenge. In doing so, a sense of urgency can foster buy-in to the need for collective action among campus constituents. For purposes of illustration, the following is an account by one study participant of how a sense of urgency was used in a positive manner to launch a SEM planning process at one institution.

A town hall meeting was called by the president for purposes of communicating the changing institutional competitive context and enrolment challenges facing the institution. The president's message was reinforced by a credible external expert, who presented on environmental trends and issues impacting enrolment in comparable institutions across the region and country. Following the presentations, the president announced a "call to action" in the form of the establishment of a SEM planning council. The president highlighted the strategic importance of the SEM planning council by announcing the cross-divisional appointment of two co-chairs—the provost and division leader responsible for enrolment/student services. The announcement also included: (a) the designation of a respected and skilled senior officer as the enrolment champion who would assume responsibility for facilitating the SEM planning process; (b) appointments to the SEM planning council of other respected institutional leaders from across divisional boundaries (not necessarily holding administrative positions); and (c) the establishment of a renewable budget allocation to seed priority initiatives over the coming years. The president recognized the symbolic nature of the announcement, and knew that announcements regarding resource allocations, internal appointments, and the like, often impact faculty and staff morale, and can engender trust or distrust in a change effort. Therefore, the expertise of the public relations office was secured to develop a well-defined internal communications plan associated with the work of the SEM planning council. (Wallace-Hulecki, 2007).

## 2. ADOPTING THE USE OF RESEARCH AND DATA: THE LANGUAGE OF ACADEMICS

Continuing with the analogy of SEM as a vehicle for change and leadership as the engine, then data become the fuel. For a SEM plan to be strategic, it must be guided by research and data that are the sources of strategic intelligence in decision-making, in educating others, in targeting efforts, in planning, and in evaluating the effectiveness and return on investment of strategies introduced. Research and data also provide actionable intelligence at the operational level, where the right information is available to the right people at the right time to effect real-time change in enrolment operations. For example, research and data are critical to monitoring the impact of such tactics as marketing strategies in generating prospective student inquiries and applications, financial aid leveraging strategies in yielding admission acceptances, student communications strategies in realizing enrolment yields, among others. Moreover, as the "language of the academics" (Henderson, 2004), research and data serve to build institutional understanding of the drivers underlying change, help to shape institutional directions and aspirations, and reinforce the need for shared responsibility of enrolment outcomes.

### PRACTICAL TIP #2: Foster a Culture of Evidence

There was resounding agreement among the study participants that there is no alternative to making investments in the quality of the information you have at your fingertips. Too often organizations function by people making on-the-ground decisions with no data. Oftentimes the data required are available to management, but the staff are unaware of its existence. In other cases, the basic data exist within the institution's database management systems, but the data are not easily accessible to or retrievable by staff; therefore, this is an area often requiring strategic investment of resources and a commitment of leadership to evidence-based decision-making. The dedicated services of a skilled enrolment analyst either aligned with the enrolment leader or within the Institutional Research office is vital. However, to foster the effective use of research and data to inform operational and strategic decisions, commonly referred to as a "culture of evidence," requires more than generating the information. Institutional leaders must promote the routine sharing of information at all levels within the organization and its systematic application in decision-making processes. Drawing from this author's own experience, an example of a commitment to the systematic application of data in the decision-making process stems from her experience as the director of research and planning at one institution, as follows:

A new president began his tenure with a mission to ready the institution, a two-year public college, for a transformative change in mandate. At the time, the institutional research (IR) office served primarily as an administrative function in responding to government accountability requirements and in support of the president's planning needs. The new president recognized that in order to advance a transformative change agenda, faculty would need to be engaged in discussions that would challenge prevailing assumptions and values that went to the heart of the academic enterprise—the institution's mission, program and credential mix, and the role of faculty. Among the many strategies introduced by the president, was an infusion of resources into the IR office to create an enrolment management reporting system to support academic program planning and innovation linked to resource management. The system was targeted to the needs of the academic community in understanding the profile, interests, and education goals of their students; the dynamics associated with the admission and persistence of students through to program completion; and the associated implications for program costs, faculty workload, space allocations, and budget. As new information and reporting tools came available, the information became the baseline intelligence that launched each cycle of academic program planning and budgeting, as well as program review and development. Through this process, the president used a consistent base of research and data to build understanding of the drivers underlying change, to shape institutional directions and aspirations, and to reinforce the importance of enrolment to the ongoing health and well-being of the academic enterprise.

## 3. INSPIRING A CAMPUS-WIDE FOCUS ON THE STUDENT EXPERIENCE

Students are at the heart of enrolment management. The success of students in achieving their educational goals—and of the institution in achieving its mission—relies in large measure on an institution's ability to optimally allocate its resources to support all students in achieving their educational goals. There is abundant literature that reveals the power of proactively connecting students with faculty, staff, and their peers. To some degree, relationships influence a student's desire to select, persist, engage in learning, participate in extracurricular activities, and become loyal to the institution (Black, 2008a).

A high-performing enrolment organization cultivates student relationships from the initial point of inquiry throughout the student life cycle—commonly conceptualized in SEM literature as the "cradle to endowment" model (Henderson, 2001). The underlying tenet of this model is that enrolment management focuses largely on managing the relationship between the student and institution through a process of seamless service delivery (within and outside the classroom), where the resources of the institution are brought to bear on meeting the needs of each individual student. To achieve a seamless service experience for students, planning and decision-making structures must be in place that promote collaboration and coordination across functions and divisional boundaries in the delivery of programs and services relative to the needs of target student segments. Through such planning and decision-making processes, a campus-wide commitment to a student-centred purpose shapes institutional strategic directions, priorities, and decision processes; redefines operational processes, systems, policies, and practices; and ultimately permeates the organization's culture.

When enrolment is viewed as a lifeline to institutional vitality, and becomes a lever for improving the student experience, enrolment professionals become central to the academic enterprise and work as partners with the academic community. This model of education focuses all institutional resources on the student learning process, where the term "learning" is conceptualized to reflect the broader aspects of student development. Within the student affairs literature, and most notably in the seminal publication, *Learning Reconsidered: A Campus-Wide Focus on the Student Experience,* published jointly by the National Association of Student Personnel Administrators (NASPA) and the American College Personnel Association (ACPA), this reimaging of the learning process to bring a campus-wide focus on the student experience is referred to as "transformative education" (Keeling, 2004). The following examples demonstrate strategies applied at several institutions for raising awareness of the importance of enrolment as an academic imperative, and inspiring a campus-wide focus on the student experience.

## PRACTICAL TIP #3: Communicate the Academic Imperative

The importance of enrolment as an academic imperative is signaled when it is embedded in the institution's strategic plan and annual budget planning process; and when the campus community is engaged in meaningful dialogue to foster buy-in and invigorate idea generation. Successful strategies applied at several institutions include:

- Invite third party experts to present seminars to the campus community on the changing higher education landscape and innovative strategies that comparator and competitor institutions have introduced in response to changing enrolment conditions (e.g., Web site developments, innovative marketing strategies, first-year experience programs, academic program innovations, policy renewal, application of technology in the delivery of programs and services).

- Host regular "joint retreats" between the board of governors and faculty senate, and between academic and student affairs leaders, to foster understanding of the importance of collective action in addressing enrolment challenges. These retreats may be facilitated by the internal SEM leader and/or by an external SEM expert, and actively involve members of the institution's SEM planning council. Of utmost importance is that institutional leaders use these forums effectively in demonstrating a willingness to listen to the views of others, to take decisive action in keeping with predefined SEM planning principles endorsed by the SEM planning council, and to openly recognize and celebrate successes that have been achieved along the way.

- Host seminars with distinguished scholars who are recognized for advancing innovations in their fields of practice, such as in the use of technology in teaching and learning, fostering developmental advising practices, developing a service culture, leveraging knowledge management, applying a transformative education model of service delivery, to name a few.

- Undertake a third party review of existing SEM practices (e.g., student recruitment, marketing, retention, enrolment planning) in order to identify high impact strategies for improving the student experience. Use the review process as an opportunity to educate the campus community on SEM as a concept and process, as well as to break down silos of practice through the active participation of faculty, staff, administrators, and students from across divisional boundaries.

- Facilitate campus-wide roundtable discussions, brown-bag lunches, and the like, to engage faculty and staff in discussions on matters of common concern. For example, at one institution, a "Conversation Café" discussion forum (refer to www.conversationcafe. org/) was used to seek input from campus constituents on how to promote institutional quality through the recruitment and retention of outstanding faculty, staff, administrators, and students (which are codependent); as well as to define the critical success factors to achieve these ends. This was a fun-filled event where administrators functioned as "servers" and "note-takers," rather than as presenters or facilitators.

These types of initiatives are time-intensive, and require careful planning and execution; therefore, it is important that you set boundaries regarding how much time you spend on gaining institutional buy-in versus getting things done. Oftentimes, you will need to work on dual fronts of building awareness while moving forward on tactical decisions in tandem. If properly orchestrated, these initiatives can serve to build organizational capacity for SEM—a topic discussed in another chapter.

## PRACTICAL TIP #4: Demonstrate Support of Executive Leadership

The most visible forms of leadership involve the president and provost in communicating the importance of each unit and individual to contributing to the change agenda. For example, the president at one institution made an annual event of speaking to recruitment and admissions officers from both administrative and academic units at the annual kick-off of the recruitment and admissions cycle. The president's message conveyed how important a role these individuals served as ambassadors of the institution and as influencers in life decisions of students. Similarly, the president and provost attended new faculty orientation to encourage their engagement in student recruitment and orientation activities. At another institution, emeritus faculty who were highly acclaimed for teaching excellence were personally invited by the provost to serve as mentors to new faculty in creating the conditions for student engagement and success in their approach to classroom instruction. In these ways, executive leaders demonstrated their support of SEM as a campus-wide shared responsibility.

## 4. ACTIVELY ENGAGING ACADEMIC LEADERS IN SEM PLANNING, DECISION-MAKING, AND CHANGE

A common focus on student learning (broadly defined) helps to anchor an enrolment management effort on improving all aspects of the student experience within and outside the classroom. The active engagement of faculty in SEM planning is imperative. Faculty need to understand the importance of enrolment to the quality and financial vitality of the academic enterprise. They need to recognize the value their participation adds to the institution's efforts, as well as to their own lives and roles as faculty. While building awareness and understanding of the need for change is a necessary first step, it is insufficient to motivate and effect culture change. Fundamental to a transformative change process is an organization's readiness for change, and the ability and willingness of individuals to consider and embrace change. While there is no shortage of change management models, many are based upon the leadership and research of John Kotter, a Harvard professor and world-renowned change expert. In his 1995 book, *Leading Change*, Kotter introduced the following eight-step change management process:

1. Establish a sense of urgency

2. Form a powerful coalition

3. Create a vision for change

4. Communicate the vision

5. Remove obstacles

6. Create short-term wins

7. Build on change

8. Anchor the changes in corporate culture

SEM planning requires the fusion of strategic planning and change management. While the theories and models presented in the literature offer useful conceptual frameworks, in practice the approaches taken are generally less methodical (L. Wallace-Hulecki, 2007). Based upon the author's more than thirty years of experience in leading strategic change, it has been observed that "student success is everyone's business" is rhetoric that is oft espoused in strategic plans and annual reports, rather than demonstrated in the behaviours and practices associated with how services are delivered to students every day. Culture change within mature organizations, such as higher education institutions, must be intentional and carefully managed. Advancing a shift in culture requires the collective will of institutional leaders at all levels, involving both those in formal leadership roles as well as others who are key influencers. However, formal structures both enhance and constrain what organizations can accomplish (Bohlman and Deal, 1997); therefore, the introduction of structural change in association with SEM must be carefully considered. Designing a workable structure that leads to optimal organizational performance must take into account the capacity needs of the organization as it looks to the future—that is, its size, age, core processes, environment, culture, strategy and goals, technology, resources, and workforce characteristics. The conceptual framework of SEM as a "cradle to endowment" model of student relationship management suggests the use of structures that foster cross-functional and cross-divisional collaboration and coordination. Determining the nature of the structures and who among the campus constituents should assume lead roles in guiding the change process are crucial to successfully mobilizing positive change. Insights and suggestions from study participants for forming a powerful coalition that fosters collaboration and coordination, and for selecting the right people to sit at the table, are offered below under practical tips #5 and #6.

## PRACTICAL TIP #5: Forming a Powerful Coalition that Fosters Collaboration and Coordination

In launching a SEM change agenda, research conducted by this author suggested that a coordinating council or leadership team was often used as a forum for enrolment planning and decision-making, and task teams that involved individuals from across divisional boundaries and functions were often used to facilitate the execution of enrolment strategies (Wallace-Hulecki, 2007). For example, the use of an existing standing committee such as the deans' council—augmented by additional decision leaders from across divisions—can demonstrate the importance of enrolment within the academic context. Suggested strategies to foster active engagement and collaboration among participants included:

(a) appoint a co-chair to facilitate enrolment planning discussions along with the provost;

(b)  set aside adequate time (1–2 hours) at least monthly to address SEM matters;

(c)  prepare white papers or decision documents to inform and focus discussions;

(d)  assign different members of the SEM planning group to work in collaboration with the SEM leader in preparing the discussion documents and to lead discussion on those topics; and

(e)  ensure that at the end of each meeting there is agreement on the action(s) to be taken, and that responsibilities have been appropriately assigned with accountability for reporting back to the committee on progress made.

## PRACTICAL TIP #6: Selecting the Right People to Sit at the Table

The decision regarding who to involve on a SEM leadership team and sub-teams is often a political one. Having the right voices at the table provides politically savvy leaders of change with opportunities to position enrolment-related requests and concerns among key power brokers. Guidelines that may be useful in the decision process include:

- Formulate a "powerful coalition" that includes decision leaders and key influencers from across organizational boundaries, such as academic deans, vice-presidents/associate vice-presidents responsible for student services, registrar, institutional research, chief financial officer, IT director/CIO, directors of the academic development centre, continuing education, among others.

- Include faculty members who are primary influencers within academic units. Consult the academic deans in identifying who these individuals are. Extend a personal invitation from the provost to the designated individuals. Invite each individual to a meeting with the provost in order to explore their perspectives and interests in relation to the work of the SEM planning council.

- Seek to establish an appropriate balance of innovative thinkers, problem solvers, and influencers.  While some degree of dissonance can be healthy, and can foster understanding of differing perspectives, as well as stimulate "out-of-the-box" thinking, too much single-minded thinking or alternatively, negativism, can be counterproductive.

Beyond selecting the right individuals to sit at the table, it is important to nurture trusting relationships with each member both within and outside the work of the SEM leadership team and sub-teams. Fostering trusting relationships occurs primarily through one-on-one communication; therefore, it is important to make time to take individual members to lunch or for coffee in order to seek their insights on potential barriers to the success of the change agenda and their perspectives on how to manage the change process, while exerting political skills to push the SEM agenda forward.

## 5. INCENTIVIZING CHANGE TIED TO ACCOUNTABILITY WITH CONSEQUENCES

More than planning is required to realize transformative change in the pursuit of a student-centred vision. Campus leaders at all levels and across divisional boundaries must perpetuate the vision through their words and actions (Black, 2003b). In a strategic change process, your treatment of people is "leadership in action" (Blanchard, 2010). Modeling commitment to change is demonstrated by how you engage campus constituents in planning, by linking the planning process to resource allocation and budget decisions, by removing barriers that inhibit the successful execution of strategies in the workplace, by the use of incentives and reward systems that align with faculty and staff values and passions, and by holding individuals accountable for results with tangible consequences (both positive and negative). It is important to consider whether or not your business model, and principles associated with funding and resource allocation decisions are aligned with your values underlying the change agenda. In the context of SEM, at issue is whether the existing business model aligns with the strategic enrolment goals of the institution and incents an appropriate balance between collaboration and entrepreneurism for achieving enrolment outcomes. Perspectives and strategies on linking SEM to resource management decisions, and on fostering shared responsibility for enrolment outcomes tied to accountability are presented as practical tips #7 and #8 below.

### PRACTICAL TIP #7: Linking SEM to Resource Management Decisions

Both the SEM research conducted by this author and personal experience suggest that the business models in place at many institutions tend to promote internal competition for enrolment and tuition-based revenue, rather than collaboration in realizing new students and new sources of revenue. While a certain amount of internal competition across schools/faculties can be healthy, oftentimes it can be counterproductive. Inefficiencies can be created when limited resources across organizational units are working in competition to attract and recruit essentially the same targeted students, or to even mine each others' students. The end result may yield high financial cost and low enrolment gain, not to mention erosion to an institution's image and reputation in the community resulting from uncoordinated activities. Wholesale change in an institution's business model is not often practical or desirable; however, strategies can be introduced to bring the values and principles underlying SEM into balance with the institution's financial imperatives. For example, a predictable level of resources may be established within the budget planning process to fund incremental costs associated with high priority SEM initiatives. This may take the form of a renewable fund that is used as an incentive to "cost-share" cross-departmental or cross-divisional initiatives that are intended to yield new enrolment, increase conversion, improve retention rates, etc. This fund would need to be substantial enough to serve as an incentive for collaboration, while being tied to accountability with consequences.

## PRACTICAL TIP #8: Fostering Shared Responsibility for Enrolment Outcomes Tied to Accountability

The use of financial incentives tied to accountability and performance management can best be illustrated by drawing from an example presented by one study participant in addressing an enrolment challenge within a single school/faculty. The school/faculty was experiencing an increasingly serious decline in enrolment. After infusing resources into the marketing of the school-based programs, no appreciable gain in enrolment was realized. As the study participant remarked, "Interestingly enough, it was the recognition that the problems of building enrolment are the problems of the strength of the academic product, its resonance with the marketplace, its competitive context. You could not just price it more or market it more" (Wallace-Hulecki, 2007). In considering the issues at hand, a program of action was introduced that fostered shared responsibility for enrolment outcomes as reported by the study participant below.

The issues at hand required a focused program innovation and development plan at the school/faculty level. To support this effort, the provost, dean, and enrolment manager (the study participant) developed a plan of action tied to accountabilities, timelines, and support resources. A cost-sharing model was agreed upon to support the initial planning, research, and strategy development stages of the process. Appropriate reward systems linked to performance metrics were negotiated to incent collaboration across units (e.g., incremental/decremental allocations of professional development funds to departments, release time for faculty/staff to introduce required curricular innovations). To support the dean and faculty in this process, the enrolment leader facilitated the engagement of appropriate service units to provide expertise in:

- market research and analysis of enrolment trends,
- facilitating an integrated enrolment and program planning process with faculty and key enrolment services personnel (e.g., admissions, recruitment, student transitions, academic advisors)
- developing program-specific marketing and recruitment campaigns appropriate to target student audiences (e.g., high school direct students, mature students, etc.), and
- developing student success strategies (both curricular and co-curricular) appropriate to the needs and preferences of target student segments.

In this manner, the resources of the institution were brought to bear on an enrolment challenge within a specific school/faculty, the leadership role of the academic dean was respected in leading the process, and accountability for addressing the challenge rested with a collective team, who worked in collaboration with the dean, faculty, and enrolment leader. The outcomes of this initiative were tied to performance management of individuals as well as to budgetary decisions with consequences.

## 6. VISIBLY LEADING THE CHARGE

One fundamental requirement in leading change is the designation of a "champion" of the change effort—a senior leader who has overall responsibility for the day-to-day leadership of the SEM planning and change management process. The development, implementation, and ongoing renewal of the SEM plan requires the focused attention of a single individual—rather than as an add-on to be administered off the side of someone's desk (Wallace-Hulecki, 2007). As SEM has evolved as a professional field of practice, so has the role and function of the professional SEM leader (Black, Ed., 2001; Black, 2003a, 2003b, 2003c, 2003d; Huddleston in Black, Ed., 2001; Goff and Lane, 2007). The literature suggests that the pursuit of a high-performing enrolment organization requires a SEM leader who is adept at leading change and in bringing alignment between the organization and the changing environmental context. Operationally, the SEM leader must work in harmony with the provost/chief academic officer and have a seat at SEM planning and resource management decision-making tables. In some cases, the position has oversight of enrolment operations (e.g., admissions, recruitment, registrar, financial aid, student services); in other cases, the position is akin to an internal consultant (Goff and Lane, 2007). Regardless of whether or not the position has oversight of enrolment operations, the SEM leader must occupy a position of influence in strategic decision-making (that extends beyond their own portfolios) with responsibility and accountability for engaging the campus community in a process of enrolment planning, idea generation, strategy formulation, and implementation.

A review of position postings in Canada over the past two years conducted by this author suggested that the role of the enrolment leader increasingly reports directly to the provost or president. This review confirmed the multi-faceted attributes of the sought-after incumbent to these positions, such as demonstrated ability as a "systems thinker" and "influencer of change." Other attributes included "political acumen," "data literacy," "innovator," among others. In terms of education and experience, position postings called for an educational background related to the field of enrolment management, such as in student development, higher education leadership, and/or in organizational assessment and performance measurement; as well as a proven track record in facilitating change management and in realizing enrolment performance improvement. Admittedly, this is a tall order to find in any one individual; however, an investment in finding the very best individual is critically important and represents a critical success factor to achieving transformative change. SEM is a maturing profession, and highly skilled professionals in this field are in limited supply. Practical strategies for filling the void if such an individual is not readily available are offered below.

### PRACTICAL TIP #9: Designate an Enrolment Leader to a Position of Influence

The SEM research conducted by this author confirmed the critical importance of selecting the "right" individual to fill the role of the SEM leader. As succinctly stated by one study participant, "[S]eek an individual who can maintain a balanced leadership style—not overly autocratic or overly collaborative; is student focused, knowledgeable in the business aspect of enrolment (e.g., admissions, recruitment), politically astute, data literate, as well as who has a good sense of humor" (Wallace-Hulecki, 2007). Several practical strategies to fill the void if such an individual is not readily available include:

(a) Secure temporary support of a skilled academic or administrative professional within the institution to work in tandem with a highly regarded and capable enrolment/student affairs leader;

(b) Secure the expertise of a professional SEM consultant to mentor a newly appointed individual, or a less experienced SEM professional; and/or

(c) Secure the expertise of a professional SEM consultant to facilitate the initial SEM planning and implementation processes through which a potential candidate(s) for the role may be identified.

## SUMMARY

The process of SEM planning can be revolutionary in terms of positioning an institution for enrolment success. SEM planning has the potential to change the institution's culture—creating a source of sustained competitive advantage; however, relatively few colleges or universities have successfully fused SEM within the academic context. If you subscribe to the notion that academic program innovation and development is the cornerstone of the enrolment enterprise, then the success of your efforts in creating a high performance enrolment organization hinges on your ability to create the conditions for shared responsibility of enrolment outcomes with the academic community. This requires bold and "relentlessly disciplined" leadership in cultivating a change in culture, adopting the systematic use of research and data, inspiring a campus-wide focus on the student experience, actively engaging academic deans and faculty in SEM planning and change processes, incentivizing change tied to accountability with consequences, and in visibly leading the charge. Are you up for the challenge?

## REFERENCES

Black, J. (Ed.). (2001). *The strategic enrollment management revolution.* Washington, DC: American Association of Collegiate Registrars and Admissions Officers.

Black, J. (2003a, October). *Defining enrollment management: The structural frame.* [White paper]. Retrieved from http://www.semworks.net/about-us/resources/jim-black-publications.php

Black, J. (2003b, October). *Defining enrollment management: The human resource frame.* [White paper]. Retrieved from http://www.semworks.net/about-us/resources/jim-black-publications.php

Black, J. (2003c, October). *Defining enrollment management: The political frame.* [White paper]. Retrieved from http://www.semworks.net/about-us/resources/jim-black-publications.php

Black, J. (2003d, October). *Defining enrollment management: The symbolic frame.* [White paper]. Retrieved from http://www.semworks.net/about-us/resources/jim-black-publications.php

Black, J. (2008a, January). *The art and science of enrollment planning.* [White paper]. Retrieved from http://www.semworks.net/white-papers.php

Black, J. (2008b, May). *Enrollment management: A systems approach.* [White paper]. Retrieved from http://www.semworks.net/white-papers.php

Black, J. (2008c, May). *Perfecting enrollment strategy.* [White paper]. Retrieved from http://www.semworks.net/white-papers.php

Black, J. (2010, May). *Creating a retention culture.* [Whitepaper]. Retrieved from http://www.semworks.net/white-papers.

php

Blanchard, K. (2010). *Leading at a higher level*. New Jersey: Blanchard Management Corporation Publishing.

Bolman, L. & Deal, T. (1997). *Reframing organizations: Artistry, choice and leadership* (2nd ed.). San Francisco: Jossey-Bass.

Bontrager, B. (Ed.). (2008). *SEM and institutional success: integrating enrollment, finance and student success*. Washington, DC: American Association of Collegiate Registrars and Admissions Officers.

Bryson, J. (2004). *Strategic planning for public and nonprofit organizations: A guide to strengthening and sustaining organizational achievement* (3rd ed.). San Francisco: Jossey-Bass.

Cameron, K. S., & Quinn, R. E. (2006). *Diagnosing and changing organizational culture: Based on the competing values framework*. Revised Edition. San Francisco: Jossey-Bass.

Collins, J. (2001). *Good to great*. New York, NY: HarperCollins Publishing Inc..

Collins, J. (2005). *Good to great and the social sectors*. New York, NY: HarperCollins Publishing Inc.

Copeland, T. (2009). *The recruitment and outreach scorecard: moving from a tactically driven to a strategy driven enrollment office*. College and University Journal, 84 (3), 35-39. Available from http://www.enrollmentmarketing.org/research/College-University-Recruitment-Outreach-Scorecard-Tim-Copeland.pdf

Dolence, M. G. (1993, 1997). *Strategic enrollment management: A primer for campus administrators*. (2nd ed.). Washington, D.C.: American Association of Collegiate Registrars and Admissions Officers.

Goff, J. W., & Lane, J. E. (2007). *Building a SEM organization: the internal consultant approach*. [White paper]. Pre-conference article for the 2007 AACRAO Strategic Enrollment Management Conference. Retrieved from http://consulting.aacrao.org/publications-events/publications/ building-a-sem-organization-the-internal-consultant-approach/

Henderson, S. E. (2001, November). *On the brink of a profession: A history of enrollment management in higher education*. In Black, J. (Ed.). (2001). The strategic enrollment management revolution, 3–36. Washington, DC: American Association of Collegiate Registrars and Admissions Officers.

Henderson, S. E. (2004, November). *Refocusing enrollment management: Losing structure and finding the academic context*. Fourteenth Annual Enrollment Management Conference, Orlando, Florida.

Hofstede, G. & Hofstede, G. J. (2005). *Cultures and organizations: Software of the mind*. New York: McGraw Hill.

Hossler, D. (2008). *The public landscape: Financing higher education in America*. In Bontrager, B. (Ed.). SEM and institutional success: integrating enrollment, finance and student success, 2–13. Washington, DC: American Association of Collegiate Registrars and Admissions Officers.

Hossler, D. & Hoezee L. (2001). *Conceptual and theoretical thinking about enrollment management*. In Black, J. (Ed.). (2001). The strategic enrollment management revolution, 57–76. Washington, DC: American Association of Collegiate Registrars and Admissions Officers.

Hossler, D., Bean, J. P., & Associates. (1990). *The strategic planning of college enrollments*. San Francisco: Jossey-Bass.

Huddleston, T. (2001). *Building the enrolment organizational model*. In Black, J. (Ed.). (2001). The strategic enrollment management revolution, 125–148. Washington, DC: American Association of Collegiate Registrars and Admissions Officers.

Keeling, R. (Ed.). (2004). *Learning reconsidered: A campus-wide focus on the student experience*. The National Association of Student Personnel Administrators, and The American College Personnel Association. Retrieved October 1, 2009, at http://www.learningreconsidered.org/

Kemer, F., Baldrige, J. V., & Green, K. (1982). *Strategies for effective enrollment management*. Washington, DC: American Association of State Colleges and Universities.

Kotter, P. & Fox, F. A. (1985). *Marketing strategies for educational institutions*. Englewood Cliffs, NJ: Prentice-Hall.

Massa, R. (2001). *Developing a SEM plan*. In J. Black (Ed.), The strategic enrollment management revolution, 149–171.

Washington, DC: American Association of Collegiate Registrars and Admissions Officers.

Norris, D., Baer, L., Leonard, J., Pugliese, L. & Lefrere, P. (2008, January/February). *Action analytics: Measuring and improving performance that matters in higher education.* EDUCAUSE Review, 43 (1) 42–67. Retrieved from http://www.educause.edu/EDUCAUSE+Review/EDUCAUSEReview MagazineVolume43/ActionAnalyticsMeasuringandImp/162422

Quinn, R. (2004). *Building the bridge as you walk on it: A guide to leading change.* Jossey-Bass. John Wiley & Sons, Inc.

Sandmeyer, L. E., Dooris, M. J., & Barlock, R. W. (2004). *Integrated planning for enrollment, facilities, budget, and staffing: Penn State University.* New Directions for Institutional Research, 2004 (123), 89–96.

Wallace-Hulecki, L. (2007). *Creating the conditions for shared responsibility of enrollment outcomes: Reframing strategic enrollment management (SEM) from the academic lens.* Unpublished master's thesis, University of Nebraska-Lincoln, Nebraska.

# CHAPTER FIVE
## INSTITUTIONAL REPUTATION AND POSITIONING

The two authors of this chapter examine the twin challenges of, firstly, defining an effective and distinctive institutional position in the current higher education landscape, and secondly, ensuring congruence between promotional claims and the experiences of stakeholders, particularly students. Part I of this chapter, written by a seasoned marketer and higher education branding consultant, Ken Steele, examines the growing importance of effective institutional positioning for Canadian colleges and universities, and describes the challenge of distilling the complexity and multiplicity of a campus to a clear, concise institutional brand. Part II of this chapter, written from the perspective of an experienced campus leader and noted strategic enrolment management consultant, Dr. Jim Black, describes the creation of a differentiating brand promise, approaches to ignite the passions of internal stakeholders, and the ingredients necessary to deliver on an institution's promise consistently.

## PART I:
# DEFINING AN EFFECTIVE INSTITUTIONAL BRAND

**BY KEN STEELE**

### THE MARKETING IMPERATIVE

In the face of demographic, economic, and competitive forces (see Chapter Two), most Canadian colleges and universities have long since accepted marketing as a necessary evil, to attract enrolment outside traditional catchment areas or in a highly competitive urban environment, to secure alumni loyalty and donor support, to enhance town-gown relations, or to attract prospective faculty members. The senior leadership at most institutions I have visited openly desire national or even international awareness and reputation, almost always for the same fundamental qualities: academic excellence, a comprehensive range of quality programs, outstanding research, and/or a student-centred campus culture. Hundreds of Canadian colleges and universities (and thousands of international institutions) are simultaneously trying to communicate very similar messages, in a very similar tone of voice.

Although most institutions of higher education now acknowledge the importance of so-called "marketing" to advance their missions, very few actually practice true marketing at all. The discipline of marketing entails the management of the so-called "Four Ps": Product (design and offering of courses, programs, majors, degrees), Price (tuition, scholarships, bursaries, work terms), Place (classrooms, residences, recreational facilities, instructional delivery, class timetabling), and lastly—and arguably least critical to enrolment success—Promotion (Web and print communications, media relations, advertising). (Some marketing theorists have added a "Fifth P"—People—which is explored in the second part of this chapter.) Typically, these responsibilities are scattered across campus and beyond: academic leadership is responsible for "product" decisions and innovations, either centrally or at the department level; offices of student awards, financial aid, and the provincial ministry of advanced education determine "price"; campus planners, the registrar's office, and individual faculty members determine "place"; and "promotion" is often carried out by dozens of decentralized and largely uncoordinated offices. In many ways, it is unfair and unproductive to hold campus recruitment marketers solely accountable for enrolment results, when they have little or no control over three of the most important "Ps" of marketing.

When an institution is founded on marketing principles, like Royal Roads University in British Columbia or Athabasca University in Alberta, decisions about all "Four Ps" are coordinated strategically, based on consumer research, and institutional structures and policies evolve to serve the marketing strategy of the institution. Royal Roads was established from the outset to provide degree completion and professional graduate-level credentials to mid-career professionals working in select sectors of the economy, and therefore the institution developed degrees and a unique blended learning model, to meet the needs of that target market. Athabasca offers distance learning courses to students with greater convenience of time and place than conventional universities, and many of their students are in fact full-time undergraduates at other institutions that have inadequate variety or capacity in their course offerings. Both institutions make strategic investments, program decisions, faculty hires, and marketing decisions based on a clear focus on their defined target market.

These two universities are the exceptions that prove the rule: many academics at traditional institutions still harbour misgivings about universities that cater consciously to their markets. Yet while marketing and branding may seem out of place on many campuses, few would disagree that institutional reputation is a valuable asset to any college or university. Faculty members take pride in their institution's reputation, and prospective faculty members can be attracted by a strong national or international profile. For years, applicant studies have shown consistently that prospective students consider the academic reputation of an institution or program to be the most compelling factor in their decision process (UCAS™). Campus marketers, seeking to establish national profile and sustain a positive reputation for their institutions, are increasingly turning to the proven disciplines of corporate branding to achieve their goals.

## THE BRANDING IMPERATIVE

Higher education institutions must compete for attention from prospective students, donors, faculty members, and various influencers in an increasingly crowded marketplace, with infinitesimally small budgets compared to national and multinational commercial advertisers. (One notable exception is the for-profit University of Phoenix, with an international marketing budget in excess of $500 million.) To maximize marketing effectiveness, most institutions have come to understand the necessity of a consistent "look and feel" in both online and offline promotions: a consistent visual identity, tagline, colour scheme, page layout or site navigation, and perhaps even consistent photographic style or tone of voice. The challenge on a decentralized campus is building support for a consistent visual brand among diverse faculties, schools, institutes, and service units, and frequently such internal wrangling consumes all the energy of marketing communications professionals, who become known pejoratively as the "logo cops." On many campuses, mere consistency in marketing is mistaken for "branding": a set of guidelines for copywriters, graphic designers, and Web developers to follow. As a result of this misconception, faculty, staff, and many students on these campuses regard the institution's "brand" as slick but superficial marketing techniques that are irrelevant to their working lives.

Properly understood, however, an institutional brand should be much more than mere promotional window dressing (Aaker, 1991): a college or university brand is a concise, compelling expression of campus identity, a distillation of institutional mission, vision, and values that focuses passion and enthusiasm among stakeholders, attracts external audiences, and drives strategic decision-making at every level of the organization. An institutional brand, in this fuller sense, is an organizing principle that attracts and guides faculty, students, and supporters; that positions the institution among its competitors; and that reflects the unique and distinctive value the school brings to its constituents. To be effective, such a positioning strategy must be championed by the president and led by senior administration, and should be integrally connected to the institution's academic plan, strategic plan, business plan, enrolment plan, and marketing (promotion) plan. Ideally, the positioning strategy is carefully developed with solid market research, thorough stakeholder consultation, and careful competitive analysis, and can, in fact, survive as a long-term, multi-decade strategy.

The University of Western Ontario exemplifies a strategic approach to institutional positioning. In its student recruitment marketing, Western promises "Canada's best undergraduate student experience" (although the university's full mission statement elaborates, "the best student experience among Canada's leading research-intensive universities"). Western's "student experience" position in the higher education market is made credible by a long tradition of school spirit and extracurriculars, varsity athletics, and off-campus nightlife. The "experience" position appeals to prospective students, who imagine a lively social life and party atmosphere, and also to their parents, who imagine their child reading a textbook on the campus green or participating in a campus club. It suits the institution's enrolment strategy, which appears to focus on attracting full-time residential students from the Greater Toronto Area, located an optimal two hours away up the nation's busiest freeway. (And though faculty might have worried about attracting less studious students with an "experience" brand, the heightened competition for admission to Western has actually increased entrance averages.) But Western's brand is more than a marketing statement that reflects reality and attracts great students: it is embedded in the mission of the institution, and guides decisions on policy, procedure, and budget. The campus master plan allocated significant funds to construct appealing modern residence halls, and to relocate administrative offices from the centre of campus to the outskirts—creating a literally student-centred campus. Over time, Western's succinct declaration of its mission and focus—its brand—will attract donors who share the vision, and faculty and staff committed to fulfilling the mission on the front lines. This is how an institutional brand can help advance institutional strategy, and if Western stays the course for a decade, they will likely be synonymous with the "experience" position in Canada.

## THE IMPACT OF INSTITUTIONAL POSITIONING

Positioning is a brand discipline defined thirty years ago in the seminal book, *Positioning*, by legendary marketers Al Ries and Jack Trout (Ries & Trout, 1981). They argue that consumers in our prosperous society do not simply buy quality products, they choose between competing products based on the distinctive features or values those products offer. Since consumers are deluged with thousands of marketing messages every day, their mental map for any given brandscape is simplistic, and ultimately positioning amounts to a battle "to own a word in the prospect's mind." Automotive brands may be the clearest examples of positioning: Volvo = safety, BMW = excitement, Mercedes = prestige, Kia = practical value. Each automotive brand owns a distinctive position, and when it ceases to be unique, or loses the clarity of its brand focus, it loses market share. The same sort of positioning occurs in much lower price categories too: Coca-Cola sells its heritage, while Pepsi sells to a new youthful generation (even though the brand dates back to 1898).

Postsecondary recruiters know all too well that prospective students are weighing their alternatives carefully: most university applicants visit six or more Web sites, visit two or three campuses, and even apply to three or more institutions that make their shortlist (UCAS™). For applicants, how a college or university differs from other institutions is far more critical than all the many things those institutions have in common.  Canadian consumers assume that all public institutions will offer quality, accredited programs, a safe campus environment, reasonable tuition prices, and generally satisfied students. Yet students feel immense pressure to make the right choice, since they are making a major investment in an abstract intangible that will define them and their career opportunities for years to come. In dozens of focus groups, I have heard young people repeatedly express frustration at how similar all institutional viewbooks look and sound: "How am I supposed to choose when they all look the same? It's like they just slap a different logo on!" If a geographically remote college or university hopes to attract students across hundreds of miles, past dozens of competing institutions, it needs to offer something truly compelling, credible, and distinctive.

## EMPTY CLAIMS TO EXCELLENCE

Almost without exception, faculty and administration on every campus believe their institution is fundamentally about academic excellence, and perhaps also world-class research. Academic culture is extraordinarily focused on excellence: once campus stakeholders grasp that institutional positioning is about "owning a word," the first word they all want is "excellence" of some kind. Unfortunately, claims of quality almost always ring hollow in any product category (Ries & Trout, 1981), and certainly they cannot be distinctive when hundreds of competitors echo identical claims. "Quality is important, but brands are not built by quality alone" (Ries, 2002). Ries and Trout maintain that only one brand can occupy a given position in the minds of consumers, and that usually the first brand entering a market holds that position permanently—unless a competitor outspends them significantly on marketing: "the easy way to get into a person's mind is to be first" (Ries & Trout, 1981). Every product or service category can be understood as a "little ladder in your head" on which consumers rank competing options—a concept quite familiar to higher education, thanks to the Maclean's University Rankings and the Globe & Mail University Report Card.

Academica Group's applicant research seems to bear out the theory that the first institutions to enter a prospective student's mind wind up owning the top position for quality. Over more than fourteen years conducting the UCAS Applicant Study, university applicants have perceived institutional reputation with remarkable consistency year over year. They are able to rate institutions on "reputation for academic quality" and "reputation for student life experience," and the two tend to correlate, although the exceptions are naturally interesting (UCAS). Generally, institutions are rated more highly if they are older, larger, or in closer geographic proximity to the respondent: in effect, the first institutions to enter students' minds, often in elementary school, own the highest positions on these two axes of reputation. While applicants overall perceive perhaps half a dozen universities in Canada to inhabit a top tier for academic quality, the vast majority of institutions are clustered in an undifferentiated mass— essentially occupying a relatively neutral position in the marketplace (see Figure 1). This is what broad claims of academic excellence will earn an institution: an undifferentiated reputation as "average."

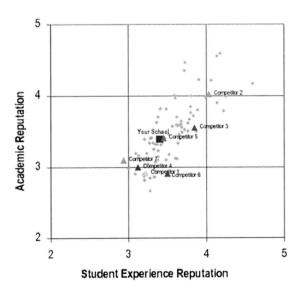

**Figure 1:** *Reputations of Canadian universities for academic quality and student life experience, as perceived by university applicants (UCAS, 2005).*

Instead of competing directly over identical market positions, Ries and Trout emphasize that strategic positioning often involves discovering a specific niche or a novel position—or, sometimes, involves repositioning a more established competitor (Ries & Trout, 1981). It is hardly surprising that prospective students, parents, guidance counselors, and even peer academics would be highly skeptical of claims from a regional college to academic excellence on par with Harvard. It might be possible, however, for that same regional college to establish an international reputation for excellence in a particular discipline (such as Grande Prairie Regional College has in Harley-Davidson motorcycle repair), or for a unique pedagogical approach (such as Colorado College or Quest University have with their modular block system for one-at-a-time courses). Instead of a bland, undifferentiated, and ultimately less than credible claim for academic excellence in the abstract, a more focused claim is more credible, more distinctive, and can become the basis for a successful national profile and reputation.

Institutions that leverage a focused position will find that, over time, a "halo effect" will in fact raise the credibility and reputation of the entire institution. Albeit without conscious strategy, this is how McGill University's reputation for pioneering neuroscience in the early twentieth century developed into an all-encompassing reputation for academic quality that persists to this day, despite decades of underfunding. This is how the University of Waterloo's reputation for mathematics and computer science—amplified by connections to RIM, Open Text and Microsoft—has translated into a remarkably strong institutional reputation for a relatively young university. The University of Saskatchewan's overall reputation benefits from massive federal research investments in its synchrotron. MIT's Web site has become the most trafficked university site in the world, thanks to its OpenCourseWare initiative. McMaster University has occasionally used the tagline, "Canada's premier health university," but can leverage that strength to promote humanities and business programs. Building an institution's reputation for something in particular, making strategic investments to grow and enhance that "something," and communicating that "something" succinctly, memorably, and consistently for years, will gradually differentiate an institution from its competitors, and raise perceptions of quality among a broad range of audiences.

## THE THREE C'S OF SUCCESSFUL BRANDING

An institutional position could conceivably be constructed around almost anything, from an academic discipline, a research institute, a prominent professor, or a prominent graduate, to a corporate partnership, a pedagogical approach, a style of architecture, an athletics team, a provincial stereotype, or an implementation of technology. To be successful, however, an institutional position needs to be built at the intersection of what I like to call the "three C's" of branding: the institution's brand position must be simultaneously Credible, Compelling, and Competitively Distinct. In many ways, these align with the three intersecting circles of corporate strategy: company capabilities, customer needs, and competitor offerings (Collis & Rukstad, 2008). The "sweet spot" for institutional strategy is found in the overlap between student needs and institutional strengths, where it is distinct from competing institutions' positions (see Figure 2).

**Figure 2:** *Successful institutional brands arise from the intersection of the "Three C's" of branding (Ken Steele).*

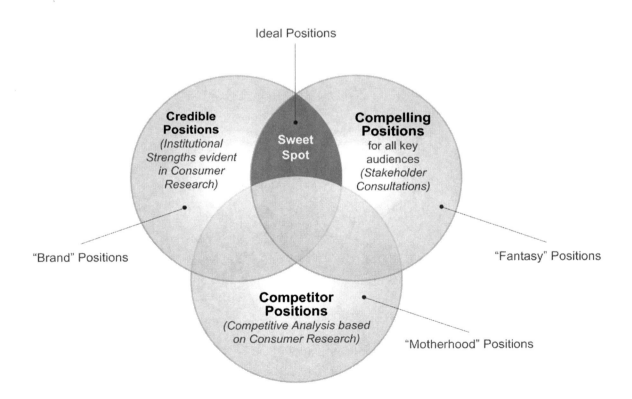

## CREDIBLE POSITIONS

An institutional brand position must first of all be credible to all stakeholders: in the context of what they know or have heard, prospective students must regard the claim as believable, faculty and staff as achievable, and education professionals as reasonable. In other words, the brand position must reflect reality—and perceived reality—both to be believed and to ensure there is no major disconnect when students arrive on campus. Rightly or wrongly, if prospective students perceive an institution as having lax academic standards, any brand messages celebrating academic excellence will be met with incredulity and derision. If faculty believe an institution is committed to research, but students expect it to be student-centred, one or both parties will be severely disappointed, and strategic planning will be contentious. If students know little about an institution aside from its geographic location, the brand position needs to fit credibly with what they already believe about the location, whether urban nightlife, cosmopolitan culture, outdoor recreation, or sleepy college town. If a brand positioning strategy fails to incorporate attributes that are perceived as credible by stakeholders, I call it a "fantasy" position (or less kindly, a "delusional" position), and it is doomed to failure.

Solid market research is the best way to objectively establish and measure existing brand perceptions, and help to define the credible "brand footprint" for an institution in the near future (see Chapter Three). For example, if consumer research clearly shows that an institution is a well-known "party school," a credible brand position might encompass school spirit or a "work hard, play hard" message, but it would be a stretch to position the institution's brand on academic rigour or quiet study.  An institutional brand can certainly be aspirational in nature, but it must be sufficiently elastic to appear credible to stakeholders in the present reality. If the campus reality needs time to catch up with the vision, a branding campaign must either be delayed, or phased in so that credibility is always maintained.

## COMPETITIVELY DISTINCTIVE POSITIONS

An institutional brand position will not be effective if it is not distinct from the perceived positions of key competitor institutions. (The only way to supplant an established competitor in a given market position is by significantly outspending them in marketing communications, consistently and memorably.)  Whether writing a mission statement or brainstorming for an institutional branding project, campus stakeholders have a stubborn tendency to focus on traditional academic principles that are common to virtually every college or university: the most vital aspects of higher education tend to be such "motherhood" statements, which fail to differentiate an institution.

For example, over the past decade environmental concerns have swept across every campus in North America, so the University of Northern British Columbia's tagline, "Canada's Green University," may not be particularly strong as a differentiator. The University of British Columbia has a credible claim to this title, thanks to its highly successful EcoTrek sustainability programs, and other institutions certainly focus on environmental programs and LEED gold or platinum campus buildings. However, at this point only UNBC is attempting to stake out the "Green" position in Canadian higher education, so despite a modest marketing budget, they might be successful in the long term at owning the word "Green."

When multiple institutions are simultaneously pouring their limited marketing budgets into identical brand positions, however, most of those marketing dollars are wasted. In 2007, as globalization and international student recruitment became a priority for almost all Canadian institutions, their positioning strategies (as exemplified in their positioning statements or taglines) converged on a collision course. UBC proudly proclaimed it was "Canada's Global University." Nearby Simon Fraser University was "Thinking of the World." On the other coast, Saint Mary's University was attracting students with the slogan, "One University. One World. Yours." and Nova Scotia Agricultural College invited prospective students to "Embrace Your World." Trent University assured applicants that "The World Belongs to those Who Understand it." Sadly these were by no means all of the institutions jockeying for the "global" position in the higher education marketplace. Internationalization is a virtue, an attractive revenue model, and reflects student interest in a new global economy, but it is not tenable as a distinctive position in the higher education landscape.

At the time of writing, a series of institutions are competing head-to-head to own the position as Canada's university. Carleton University in Ottawa was first into the fray some years ago, with their tagline "Canada's Capital University." They were followed very shortly by the University of Ottawa, who declared itself "Canada's University." In 2010, the universities in Nova Scotia launched a collective campaign to position the maritime province as "Canada's University Capital." The competing claims to such similar territory, in such similar language, undermine the effectiveness of all three brand campaigns, and leave prospective students even more confused and frustrated.

Quantitative research can help build campus consensus and focus branding efforts on the credible, distinctive, and compelling qualities of an institution. The UCAS™ survey asks

300,000 applicants to universities and colleges to gauge the impact, positive or negative, of fifty different features on their choice of institution (UCAS™). Academica Group often poses the same question to current students, faculty, and alumni to measure the perceptions of a range of stakeholder groups. (In effect, the push-pull gaps measure simultaneously how compelling a factor is, how credibly it is associated with a given institution, and how distinctive it is from competitor positions.) When the scores given to competing institutions are compared in a "push-pull" graph (see Figure 3), it often becomes clear that the schools are differentiated most strongly on only a handful of decision factors: in this example, the strongest distinctions are that School A offers a small student population, small surrounding community, and small class sizes, while School B is perceived to offer greater student diversity, relevant industry in the area, and relative ease of acceptance. If other stakeholders and other competitor comparisons yielded corroborating evidence, School A could reasonably proceed with a positioning strategy emphasizing nurturing qualities in some way. It would be unwise, on the other hand, to attempt to distinguish School A on the basis of financial costs or institutional reputation.

**Figure 3:** *Compelling, credible, and distinctive qualities of institutions, as perceived by prospective students, measured in a "push-pull" graph (UCAS™).*

| DECISION FACTORS | | Competitor | Your Institution |
|---|---|---|---|
| **Academic Factors** | Academic reputation of institution | | |
| | Academic reputation of program/major | | |
| | High admission average | | |
| | High-profile research | | |
| | Institution rankings/guidebook ratings | | |
| | Investments in latest technology | | |
| | Library collections/facilities | | |
| | Quality of faculty | | |
| | Special programs for academically gifted students | | |
| **Campus Factors** | Attending the school your parents attended | | |
| | Attractive campus | | |
| | Availability of off-campus housing | | |
| | Campus cafeteria/food service options | | |
| | Campus housing/residences | | |
| | Clubs and social activities | | |
| | Diversity of student population | | |
| | History/tradition of school | | |
| | Large student population | | |
| | Off-campus urban life | | |
| | Recreational sports/fitness facilities | | |
| | Reputation for student experience | | |
| | Successful teams/varsity athletics | | |
| **Financial Factors** | Availability of childcare | | |
| | Availability of merit-based scholarships | | |
| | Availability of needs-based financial aid/bursaries | | |
| | Costs of attending university/college (excluding tuition) | | |
| | Flexible course delivery (evenings, weekends, online, etc.) | | |
| | Institution is close to home | | |
| | Part-time job opportunities or work-study options | | |
| | Tuition costs | | |
| **Outcome Factors** | Ability to transfer credits earned to another school | | |
| | Acceptance of my previous credits | | |
| | Co-op programs/internships | | |
| | Easy to get accepted | | |
| | Graduates get high-quality jobs | | |
| | Graduates get into top professional and grad schools | | |
| | International exchange options | | |
| | National/professional accreditation | | |
| | Opportunities for student leadership | | |
| | Relevant industry in the area | | |
| | Undergraduate research opportunities | | |
| **Nurturing Factors** | Campus safety/security | | |
| | Faculty-student interaction | | |
| | Friends attending | | |
| | Personal attention during application/admission process | | |
| | Religious considerations | | |
| | Small class sizes | | |
| | Small student population | | |
| | Small surrounding community | | |
| | Student evaluations of professors | | |

107

## COMPELLING POSITIONS

Finally, perhaps it seems obvious that a successful brand position for a college or university must also be compelling—but it may not be so obvious that it should be compelling not only for the primary target market (usually prospective undergraduate students), but also for graduate students, faculty and staff, prospective faculty, alumni and donors. If the strategic positioning process has been sufficiently inclusive and consultative, all stakeholders will be engaged in the process of uncovering the core of the institution's mission and vision. Market research can measure the appeal and impact of the most compelling brand promises, and help identify the language that can clearly communicate the concepts to various audiences. Student recruitment marketing will express the brand in language, visuals, and terms that are most compelling and memorable for the primary target market, but the underlying brand position must be compelling to other campus stakeholders as well.

Many colleges and universities undertake expensive branding or positioning exercises, yet ultimately fail to arrive at a sufficiently compelling brand promise: they instead arrive at what I call a "bland position." Bland positions often result from a lack of leadership or authority in the strategic positioning process: if the institution's president does not champion the brand strategy, if the task force or committee is trying to satisfy too many masters, if the process has a lack of clarity about the primary target market or a lack of research evidence to focus its efforts, the result will be a brand "camel" (to adapt the old adage that a camel is a horse designed by committee). Effective institutional strategy is all about making tough choices; bland strategy results from a failure of will to make choices at all. Instead of focusing the mission of the institution, and its marketing messages, on a single word or concept, colleges or universities with a bland position are typically trying to "own" six or eight different concepts simultaneously.

## FINDING THE GRAND OVERSIMPLIFICATION

Ries and Trout warn that "most positioning programs are nothing more or less than a search for the obvious," and state memorably that "the essence of positioning is sacrifice" (Ries & Trout, 1981). In other words, "the most important aspect of a brand is its single-mindedness" (Ries, 2002). The biggest challenge to university marketers is that scholarly training and the liberal arts tradition of a "multiversity" are diametrically opposed to the simplification of a single unified brand. With good reason, faculty members are committed to academic freedom and intelligent debate: a coherent, consistent message from the entire institution runs counter to the academic mindset. On community college campuses, it can be equally difficult to achieve consensus on a singular brand focus because the faculty are fundamentally committed to breadth of programming and providing access to education for all students, not a specific target market. Academic program reviews on every campus in the country find it easy to launch additional programs to expand the breadth of offerings at the institution, but face public outcry from faculty and students, and often legal opposition from faculty associations, when they attempt to narrow program offerings in any way.

It seems to be the natural inclination of postsecondary institutions to seek breadth, not focus, and this makes the strategic positioning process particularly sensitive and often politically explosive. The objective of a strategic branding process is definitely not to fabricate an unrealistic or untrue fiction, but it does absolutely require the distillation of the essence of the institution to a singular concept—a grand oversimplification—in order to cut through the media clutter and communicate meaningfully with audiences. Effective institutional marketing must identify what is credible, compelling, and truly distinctive about an institution, and express that kernel of truth creatively in language that resonates with the target audience—usually high school seniors.

Even in the simplest consumer categories, "the human mind tends to admire the complicated and dismiss the obvious as being too simplistic" (Ries & Trout, 1981). Academic minds take this reverence for sophistication and complexity to a whole new level. With a few notable exceptions, institutions of higher learning are very reluctant to stand for something concrete, focused, or specific in the marketplace. They must overcome particularly strong internal pressure if they are to arrive at a brand position that is comprehensible to teenagers, let alone one that is expressed in terms teenagers will find attention-getting and appealing.

But if an institution fails to express its brand position credibly, distinctively, and compellingly—if it attempts to stand for too many things simultaneously—the institution ultimately stands for nothing in particular at all in the minds of the public and the marketplace. And if a college or university abdicates responsibility to define and communicate its essence, the marketplace will fill that information vacuum by inventing a position for the institution, through rankings, word of mouth, gossip, perceptions, and misperceptions.

## THE "WISDOM" OF THE MASSES

When thousands of twelfth-graders decide what your institution of higher learning is really all about, the simplification will almost certainly displease more campus stakeholders than a carefully managed branding strategy. The UCAS survey asks postsecondary applicants to provide a top-of-mind word or phrase that they associate with particular Canadian institutions; analysis of the results for hundreds of institutions reveals the sort of brand positions the marketplace invents on its own. (Quotations that follow are taken verbatim from open-ended responses by university applicants to the 2006 UCAS™ applicant survey.)

The most frequent response, naturally, is some variation on the word "nothing" (UCAS™)—either students have never heard of the institution, or cannot provide any association whatsoever; this is brand position purgatory. The risk of attempting to be all things to all people, is that in fact an institution becomes nothing to anyone. To achieve an effective brand position, an institution must first seek awareness (or at least name recognition), then cultivate interest through a clear position, and only thereafter can it attempt to communicate a more complex and comprehensive understanding of all that the institution has to offer.

The next most frequent brand associations applicants offer are fairly obvious associations with geographic locations. The implication, obviously, is that an institutional brand can be tightly connected to its provincial or municipal namesake, and all the positive and negative connotations that may entail. Many applicants are miles off target when they ascribe a location to a college or university, adding insult to injury when this is the top-of-mind association they have with the institution.

When an association with academic quality comes to mind for applicants, it is typically polarized into extremely positive or relatively negative terms. Institutions are perceived as either "extremely good," "challenging," "excellent," and "tough," or they are perceived as "average," "not bad," "so-so," or "not good." Applicants are often explicit that their top-of-mind association with the institution is solely about reputation and prestige: "famous," "recognized," "well-reputed," "top-ranked," or "the Harvard of Canada." The opposite of such reputation is, naturally, obscurity. Applicants also ascribe academic quality to institutions in terms of the difficulty of admission: schools are either "competitive," "intimidating," with "high admission cut-offs" and "high achievers," or they are "mediocre" and "accept anybody"—or even accept "rejects from elsewhere." These institutional positions based on perceived quality shift very little over years or even decades.

Applicants also associate institutions with their size, usually in a pejorative sense. Small schools are "quaint," "UofT junior," or a "high school." Large institutions are "crowded," "overpopulated," and "suffocating," where students will get lost in a "maze" and be treated as "just a number." Applicants' top-of-mind associations for some institutions are focused on the student social environment. Schools with strong campus spirit bring to mind "Homecoming," "Frosh Week," "fraternities," "fun," "parties," "porn," "girls," and "drinking." Welcoming campuses are "close-knit," "people-oriented," "friendly," or even "student-centred." And commuter campuses are often perceived as places with "no social life," where students go "to study and that's it."

Many applicants associate particular postsecondary institutions with a specific subject or faculty, often a professional school like business, medicine, engineering, law, or veterinary medicine. Many respondents are conscious of the brands of named professional schools like Osgoode Hall Law School, the Schulich School of Medicine and Dentistry, the DeGroot School of Business, or the Ivey School of Business. Some faculty-specific associations are obviously pejorative, such as "Moo U" (for agriculture) or "Skule" (for engineering). Although specific programs come to mind for the marketplace when they think of particular postsecondary institutions, these programs are seldom dominant brand associations. Positioning an institution on the basis of unique, respected, quality programming—sometimes called "pillar programs" or "centres of excellence"—can be both difficult and dangerous. Difficult because politically, faculty and staff tend to resent the "tall poppies" and prefer equitable exposure for the work being done across the institution. Dangerous because unique programs can quickly be imitated by competing institutions, or fall out of funding or market demand. Positioning should be solid ground you can claim and defend for years to come, not an everchanging race to be first to market with new programs. It can be highly effective to develop strategic recruitment programs and public relations initiatives at the program level, but an institution's brand position usually needs to surpass individual program areas.

Although the UCAS data demonstrates some minimal recall of marketing slogans and taglines, generally these are cited by very few respondents when providing top-of-mind associations with a college or university. (The applicants do, however, ascribe a variety of interesting brand attributes to institutions, from "innovation" and "discovery," "huge history" and "castles," to "nerds," "Brains," and "Brainiacs" or "successful grads.") Taglines and positioning statements, however clever they may be, do not have a significant lasting impact on campus stakeholders or target markets, but positioning strategies that are integral to institutional mission and vision, that guide strategic planning and resource allocation, and that are communicated clearly and compellingly to all audiences, have the power to shape institutional reputation and create a shared sense of direction. Taglines are important as tools to crystallize the brand position in a few words, particularly for internal audiences, but prospective students are likely to retain only a general impression drawn from the tagline, photography, and perhaps news headlines.

## A CONCEPTUAL FRAMEWORK FOR POSITIONING

Over the past two decades, we have developed a new conceptual framework for positioning colleges and universities in the higher education landscape, based on quantitative research data, hundreds of focus groups, and working with dozens of institutions on rebranding and positioning strategies. The remainder of this section will outline our approach to institutional positioning.

We believe that a complete institutional position is formed by identifying and presenting three levels of differentiation: in our terminology, a broad institutional Category is then defined by institutional Style, and uniquely positioned with Focus. The distinctiveness of the position required is established by the Scope, which defines the institution's competitive set. Once the positioning focus is identified, creative executions of the brand find the language and imagery to convey that position to key target markets.

## CATEGORY:

Statistics Canada classifies Canadian postsecondary institutions into four broad categories with nineteen sub-types (Orton, 2009):

| University and Degree-Granting | Primarily Undergraduate | |
| :--- | :--- | :--- |
| | Comprehensive | |
| | Medical Doctoral | |
| | Special Purpose | |
| **College and Institute** | Degree-Granting College and Institute | |
| | Multi-Purpose | |
| | Special Purpose | |
| **Career College** | Degree-Granting Career College | |
| | Multi-Purpose | |
| | Special Purpose | |
| **Apprenticeship/Adult Education** | Art | Immigration Centres |
| | Language | Literacy, Upgrading, ESL |
| | Medical/Health | Native Friendship Centres |
| | Professional | School Board Adult Ed |
| | Other | |

Generally, prospective students are relatively clear about the category of institution to which they are applying, and provincial governments are explicit about the mandate of each institution. Applicants to each Category of institution are demographically and psychographically different; although roughly one-quarter will cross-apply, this is generally between adjacent categories. Institutional evolution between Categories, such as when a college is granted university status, inevitably shifts the institution's applicant pool, although adjacency may retain some portion of the market.

**STYLE:** As noted previously, applicants consider about fifty key decision factors, to some extent or another, when comparing their postsecondary options. Applicants perceive most Canadian institutions as satisfactory on all fifty factors, but when making final choices from their consideration set, applicants distinguish between institutions in five key areas: academic quality, outcomes, campus experience, nurturing environment, and financial considerations (Steele, 2008). To simplify the complexity of a life-changing decision, applicants generally ascribe each institution to a single Style, which can be roughly aligned with four quadrants of institutional reputation for academic quality and student experience.

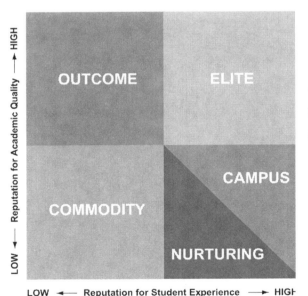

***Figure 4:*** *A conceptual map of possible institutional positioning "Styles" (Ken Steele).*

Internal stakeholders are likely to see their own institution as comparatively strong in many of these Styles, but measurement of applicant decision factors and top-of-mind brand associations confirms that the marketplace mentally positions most institutions more simplistically. Complexities and subtleties that are important and readily apparent to internal stakeholders are not always evident to casual observers in the marketplace. Moreover, the danger of attempting to position an institution in multiple quadrants simultaneously is that the position instead is watered down to a central, neutral position, not perceived as particularly strong on any aspect. Over time, a bland position can gravitate downward into a commodity position, attracting only local or regional students.

**FOCUS:** Focus is the narrowing of the institutional positioning yet further, within a Style, to a singular, unique focus. There are potentially thousands of distinctive Focus positions for an institution, and multiple universities can possess unique positions within the same general Style. For example, the University of Toronto, McGill University, and Queen's University, are all Elite universities, but can be ascribed distinctive foci: Toronto is known for its sheer magnitude, McGill for its international prestige, and Queen's for its historical traditions. The outcome of a strategic positioning exercise is to identify the focal point, the precise spot in the higher education landscape on which to plant the institution's flag. Ideally, that focal point will also serve as a star to guide the institutional vision and strategic plan. Institutional resources, energy, and talent must necessarily continue to be directed to ensure that an institution remains competitive on all fifty points of comparison, but additional capital investments, resources, strategic thinking, and marketing emphasis need to be channeled to ensure that the positioning focus truly outshines all other institutions within the scope of its marketplace.

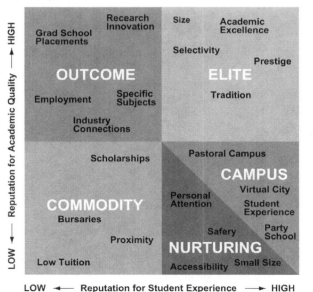

***Figure 5:*** *A conceptual map of some possible institutional positioning "Foci" (Ken Steele)*

**SCOPE:** Postsecondary institutions can also be classified by the geographic scope of their marketplace, their historical or aspirational catchment for student recruitment: institutions typically have local, regional, national, or international scope. Where brand strategy is concerned, Scope denotes the competitive landscape in which an institution must establish a unique and attractive position. If students nationally are to consider an institution, it must stand out nationally. By comparison, a commuter university may be successful in its local market without ever clearly defining its position or brand, and a regional university may need only to define a broad Style in order to be distinctively positioned in its region.

There is, however, a risk in setting one's sights too low. Greater globalization is reducing the barriers between regions, widening the playing field with more competition coming from across the country and around the world. The growth of the University of Phoenix and other for-profit multinational distance education providers may continue in Canada, and many institutions will be attempting to establish national brands. The risk of defining an institutional position relative only to local competitors is that the position may not be credible or distinctive in a broader competitive field. Claiming a fully defined and unique position (on a national or international scope) will better insulate an institution from encroachment into its region, and prepare it to extend its brand to a wider marketplace in future.

## CREATIVE EXPRESSION OF THE BRAND

The process of developing an institutional positioning strategy, taking into consideration Category, Type, Focus, and Scale described above, typically takes six months to a full year to complete thoroughly. Institutions must amass solid consumer research, if it is not preexisting; conduct a thorough competitive analysis; and undertake wide-ranging and repeated consultation with campus stakeholders to gather their input and perceptions and inform them of the process as it unfolds. By the end of the process, the university or college has reached a shared understanding of its unique mission, and its credible, compelling, and competitively distinctive position in the higher education landscape. Yet, in many ways the branding process is only halfway complete. Once an institution understands its unique Focus, it still needs to find the words, images, and tone to express that Focus—to communicate it to key target markets, and to engage and motivate campus stakeholders to become true ambassadors of the brand.

Although some larger universities have well-staffed graphics or creative communications departments, in general the design teams on most campuses are already working flat out to keep up with regular online and print communications needs for the institution. In many cases, internal staff do not have the creative experience to convert an institutional positioning strategy into a truly effective visual brand. Most institutions will turn to external brand expertise to develop a memorable, creative, attention-getting, and sustainable creative framework for messaging, visuals, and content—usually with a teenage market in mind.

For a successful brand positioning exercise, it is critical to have widespread input and engagement in the process leading up to the development of the institutional positioning strategy. Senior administration from the president on down need to champion the positioning exercise, and input needs to be sought from faculty and staff, students, alumni, and the governing board. But it is often equally important that senior campus leadership adopt a "hands-off" attitude when it comes to the tactical level of brand execution. Talented, experienced creative agencies can develop a powerful expression of the institutional brand for particular target audiences, and research firms can test those concepts through focus groups and online panels.

Senior administrators and faculty are almost never the primary target market for institutional branding campaigns. The central purpose of university recruitment marketing is to attract the attention of prospective students with very little true comprehension of higher education. Marketing aims to resonate with its target audience, addressing their current concerns and priorities with a simple, focused, and often emotional appeal. Brand campaigns do not and cannot challenge the intellect, open minds, or expand horizons—that is the transformative role played by faculty, once applicants become students at your institution.

# DELIVERING ON THE BRAND PROMISE

## BY JIM BLACK

Often institutional positioning efforts are confined to marketing strategies. While there is value in this approach, a marketing focus alone simply does not leverage the opportunity to align the campus culture, practices, policies, and behaviours with the promises inherent in the brand. Alternatively, a combined focus on marketing strategies and promise delivery can redefine an institution and thus, secure its reputational position.

## DEFINING BRAND PROMISE

A brand promise is essentially the point of difference the brand commits an institution to delivering consistently to its constituents (Krueger, 2007, March). Through focus groups with thousands of students in Canada and the U.S., our consultants have found that these informants have very specific perceptions of institutional promises. Some articulate these promises as expectations while others view them as guarantees. Regardless of how they articulate the promise, students universally see themselves as educational consumers with certain rights and privileges. When promises are kept, student commitment and loyalty to an institution grows. Conversely, when perceived covenants are broken, student dissatisfaction, attrition, and negative word-of-mouth become natural consequences.

This author concurs with the findings of Westervelt (2007) that most brand promises in higher education are abbreviated versions of institutional mission statements. This approach represents a flawed mental model of what a brand promise should be. Mission statements are purpose statements that convey why an institution exists. Mission statements usually fail to differentiate schools from their competitors and seldom reflect a promise of what institutions will deliver to students and other constituents.

With that said, a school's mission statement, vision, and core values should be the foundation for the brand promise (Ehret, 2008, July). The challenge in creating a brand promise is to design a concise statement that reflects these foundational elements while differentiating the institution among its competitors and identifying a promise that employees and others can become passionate about, and constituents can experience with every encounter they have with the institution. To illustrate, one Canadian college we have worked with has defined their promise in one word, "Inspire." For this institution, the promise is intended to focus the campus community on inspiring students in every encounter they have with students—inspirational teaching, service, communications, facilities, etc.

## A BRAND PROMISE THAT DIFFERENTIATES

To differentiate effectively, the brand promise must be bold yet credible. The higher education marketing landscape is replete with brand messages using words like excellence, quality, and learning. Few, however, claim something profoundly different or life changing. In developing a brand promise, consider an element of the institution's personality that goes beyond what students and others expect. Ideally, the promise should create a "WOW" effect. Think about a relationship or an experience you want to create for all students.

The brand promise should "catapult" your institution over its competitors. What is the next "big thing" in the university or college sector? It could be an innovative approach to curriculum or pedagogy, a unique integration of the living and learning experience, a study abroad experience for every student, or simply packaging what you already do in a way that makes it distinctive. It is what marketing guru Seth Godin refers to as the "purple cow"—it's different from all the other cows and thus is memorable (2002). The magic in creating a "purple cow" is providing your constituents with something they don't know they yet need—just when they are ready for it (Kerner & Pressman, 2007). Whatever distinctive position you claim, you must be prepared to deliver on its promise 100% of the time.

## A BRAND PROMISE THAT INSPIRES PASSION

Brand promise statements are powerless unless everyone on campus passionately embraces and lives them. Certainly, college and university employees do not come to work each day with the intention of undermining the institution's brand. More likely, they are not necessarily even cognizant of the brand or its importance to the school's vitality. Generally speaking, employees are not "wired" to deliver experiences that align with the brand promise. They naturally respond to teaching, advising, and service encounters in ways that are largely driven by their personalities and styles (Lebard, Rendleman, & Dolan, 2006).

To help faculty and staff transition from a state of minimal brand awareness into brand enthusiasts, institutional brand champions must facilitate the metamorphosis. The following is an adapted excerpt from a white paper I recently published titled, "The Branding of Higher Education" (2007). The five steps outlined here provide a road map for actualizing a brand promise.

1. **Define the brand promise.** The definition must be based on the institution's personality—congruent with what the institution espouses to be and more importantly, consistent with institutional behaviour. Most colleges and universities have clearly articulated core values, which should be fundamental elements of the brand promise definition. These values and thus, the brand promise must be relevant both to internal and external constituents. Relevancy does not equate to standardized adoption, but instead it translates to individualized interpretations and behaviour associated with the promise. Hence, the promise must be malleable enough to be accepted and practiced by different subcultures within an institution as well as individuals with their own unique beliefs and values. In the academy, this is the only practical way to strike a balance between the objective of universal adoption and maintaining a modicum of autonomy. Collectively, the college or university community must define desired expectations and behaviours associated with the promise.

2. **Live the brand promise.** Consider the role of all faculty, staff, and administrators as "institutional trust agents." Whether encounters with students occur in the classroom, in an administrative office, through a campus event, online, in person, or on the phone, each experience either fosters or diminishes institutional trust. Think for a moment about your own personal and professional relationships. Is there a single valued relationship in your life that is not built on a foundation of mutual trust? Our students, their families, the school's alumni, and others we serve are fundamentally the same. They will desire a relationship with the institution only if they trust you.

3. **Operationalize the brand promise.** The promise must be personified through your services, business transactions, human interactions, information delivery, and learning experiences. It must be embedded in the culture and become a part of your institutional DNA. It must be viewed as a covenant between the institution and those you serve—never to be broken. Finally, it requires an unfaltering focus on identifying and eradicating promise gaps using some combination of people, processes, pedagogy, and technology.

4. **Deliver the brand promise consistently.** To achieve consistency, institutions must 1) clearly define the desired constituent experience and 2) ensure the employee experience is aligned with the desired constituent experience. For instance, if a staff member feels mistreated by the institution, it will be virtually impossible for that individual to effectively represent the brand promise to the students they serve. So, to improve consistency of promise delivery to your constituents, you must first create an environment for employees that is conducive to

feeling passionate about the organization and its promise. The campus environment must be one that values the contributions of individuals and proactively enhances human capacity.

**5. Convey the brand promise.** Too often, higher education organizations permit their constituents to form impressions of the institution in an information vacuum—usually based on anecdotes, media coverage, and the negative experiences of the few. Effectively conveying the promise requires an ongoing internal and external campaign. It requires careful management of constituent expectations, the promotion of promise delivery successes, as well as intentional efforts to build institutional loyalty over time.

In forming a brand promise, you must engage the campus community in the process. Gain an understanding of what your people already are passionate about, or could be if a promise reflected their values and the values of the institution. While it is unrealistic to expect to find unanimous consensus, look for themes that can be woven together to create a single brand promise that the community will actively support (Lull & Thiebolt, 2004). In order to identify a brand promise that will be fervently believed and practiced, you will need to sacrifice other alternatives.

## A BRAND PROMISE THAT DELIVERS

Carlson (1987) coined the phrase, "moments of truth" in his book by the same name. The application of this phrase to higher education simply means that colleges and universities have thousands of "moments of truth" with those they serve every day—both in and outside the classroom. Each of these "moments of truth" is a measure of how well an institution is delivering on the promise of its brand. With each encounter, trust in the brand is either enhanced or eroded. Failure to carefully manage these "moments of truth" renders a brand and its inherent promise worthless—often with severely negative consequences to the image of the institution.

Though they never used the jargon marketers espouse, academics were the first to shift the focus from the institution (or faculty) to the students. In November of 1995, the cover article in *Change* initiated discourse in the academy over a paradigm shift from instructor-centred teaching to student-centred learning (Barr & Tagg, 1995, November). Admittedly, it has taken years for this seismic shift to infect academic culture, but the metamorphosis that has transpired is revolutionary. The "sage on the stage" has gradually been supplanted by faculty who engage their students in active learning; coach and facilitate rather than lecture; customize the learners' experience based on their needs and learning styles; and leverage technology to enable learning. By fostering a learning environment where students are encouraged to collaborate, create knowledge, synthesize and apply information, strategize, and even find entertainment in the learning experience, faculty have created the conditions for managing "moments of truth" (Tapscott, 2009).

In the service sector of higher education, the movement gained momentum with a collaborative effort among a handful of "best practice" institutions, IBM, and the Society for College and University Planning. This group produced the first book dedicated solely to student services (Beede & Burnett, 1999). However, it was the second book published by these organizations that directly addressed the notion of delivering on the promise of the brand. In that book, *Innovations in Student Services: Planning Models Blending High Touch/High Tech,* a rising star at Disney, Cynthia Wheatley, wrote vividly about the importance of delivering service reflecting an organization's brand (Wheatley, 2002). She focused on the areas of engineering the service experience; having reliable delivery systems; utilizing a service lens that considered three dimensions of service delivery: people, processes, and place; mapping the service; aligning the employee's experience with the student's experience; as well as reaffirming the value of active participation of the student in his or her own learning experience.

Although the learner-centred model of delivering education and services has been embraced by most institutions—in theory by virtually all and in practice by a growing number—it is just now being adopted as part of the brand strategy by colleges and universities. Until recently, branding on most campuses has been viewed as purely a promotional endeavor and thus, has been relegated to a marketing department or a division of institutional advancement or enrolment management to implement. Arguably, brand positioning, promotion, and the other facets of brand development are essential to any institution that competes for students and external funding. However, successful brands deliver on the claims they promote.

The delivery component of a brand strategy is significantly more difficult to engage in than the promotional dimension. As illustrated in the following graph, Lebard, Rendleman, and Dolan outlined a two-year, four-stage process to creating brand enthusiasts throughout an organization (2006). The process begins with promoting brand awareness among employees, followed by teaching brand knowledge, then developing brand believers, and lastly delivering consistently on the brand promise. It is important to note that the frame of reference for these authors is business, not higher education. In my experience, this is a protracted evolutionary process in the academy, which unlike business is not a command and control environment.

## CHANGING EMPLOYEE BEHAVIOR DOESN'T HAPPEN OVERNIGHT
### Path to brand enthusiasm

*Develop to Change Attitude*

*Inspire to Affect Behavior*

| | 6 months | 12 months | 18-24 months |
|---|---|---|---|
| **BRAND AWARE** | **BRAND KNOWLEDGEABLE** | **BRAND BELIEVER** | **BRAND DELIVERER** |
| • Understand what brands are<br><br>• Understand the role and the benefits of brands<br><br>• Understand the company's emphasis on delivering brand experience | • Is familiar with brand positioning components and features<br><br>• Is familiar with examples of excellent brand experience delivered through employees<br><br>• Know what is expected of them in terms of behavior | • Believe can personally make a difference<br><br>• Believe can be a brand ambassador<br><br>• Believe it is in their interest to deliver the brand | • Actively and enthusiastically deliver branded promise to customers<br><br>• Is recognized and rewarded for success in the brand delivery<br><br>• Convince other employees to become brand ambassadors |

**ORGANIZATION LEVELS**

| • Culture<br>• Soft skills<br>• Structure | • Culture<br>• Hard skills<br>• Structure | • Skills<br>• Measurement systems | • Compensation systems<br>• Processes<br>• Information systems |
|---|---|---|---|

**MEDIUM**

| • Events<br>• Indirect communications<br>• Top management | • Training<br>• Face-to-face internal communications | • Training<br>• Face-to-face internal communications | • Cascading<br>• Face-to-face internal communications<br>• HR policy |
|---|---|---|---|

*Source: Lebard, Rendleman, and Dolan, 2006.*

Any culture that values collegiality and a degree of autonomy may find such an organizational transformation to take five years or longer. So, for institutional leaders, such an endeavor requires patience, focus, and the will to stay the course. According to Heaton and Guzzo, aligning a human capital strategy like the one proposed by Lebard, Rendleman, and Dolan with brand strategy has one overarching organizational benefit that makes the effort worthy of such a prolonged investment of time and resources—constituent needs end up driving the entire enterprise (2007).

Beyond the time and resources required to create a brand-oriented, learner-centred culture, common barriers to delivering on the promise are substantial and include:

- Inadequate staffing
- A lack of investment in organizational learning
- Inadequate technology to support the delivery of services and education
- Inefficient business processes
- Inaccurate or inaccessible information
- A lack of employee incentives as well as accountability for adherence to brand promise principles and values
- Poor communications, particularly across functional and organizational boundaries
- Organizational structures that inhibit the support of a holistic approach to brand delivery

Daunting as it may be, the Herculean effort to deliver what is promised is a requisite to a successful brand strategy. Without it, institutional branding will be an exercise in futility.


## CONCLUSION

In an increasingly competitive student recruitment environment, institutional positioning and strategic marketing are becoming vital techniques to advance the mission of Canadian colleges and universities. Effective institutional brand positions must arise organically from the intersection of the "Three C's" of branding: positioning claims must be Credible in the marketplace and reflect the reality of campus experience for all stakeholders, they must be Compelling not only to prospective students but also to faculty and staff, and they must be Competitively Distinctive or the institution will fade into a neutral, commodity position in the marketplace. The campus community will need to accept a "grand oversimplification" to create a concise message that can be delivered clearly to an indifferent public, and creative executions that appeal more to teenage prospective students than to middle-aged faculty members.

Effective marketing strategy entails an alignment of all the "Five P's" of marketing: differentiating a Canadian college or university among its competitors is as much a product, place, and people exercise as a promotional one. (As tuitions rise and greater disparities appear, even price will become an important aspect of the postsecondary marketing mix.)

Even the best promotional efforts will not overcome lackluster or low-demand programs, unreasonably large class sizes and outdated lecture techniques, or cumbersome and inefficient student services.

Higher education is above all else a people business: campus communities are comprised of intelligent, questioning, and independent faculty and staff, and the education process is very much a collaborative one between faculty and students. An institutional brand that fails to inspire its leadership, faculty, staff, and students has little chance of receiving broad-scale adoption—and campus constituents need to "live the brand" for it to become real at all. A branding effort that is not personified internally is "full of sound and fury; signifying nothing" (Shakespeare, 1605–06): there will be obvious incongruence between the expectations created with external constituents through related marketing activities and their experiences with the institution. Campus master plans, academic plans, budgets, and strategic decisions all need to be aligned with the institutional brand position and contribute to the fulfillment of the brand promise. All stakeholders must experience, and exemplify, the brand promise consistently with each interaction, or the immense potential of a strong institutional brand is squandered and becomes merely a marketing slogan.

## REFERENCES

Aaker, David A. (1991). *Managing brand equity: Capitalizing on the value of a brand name.* New York: Macmillan.

Barr, R. B. & Tagg, J. (1995, November). *From teaching to learning—A new paradigm for undergraduate education.* Change. Washington, D.C.: Heldref Publications.

Beede, M. & Burnett, D. (1999). *Planning for student services: Best practices for the 21st Century.* Ann Arbor, MI: Society for College and University Planning.

Black, J. (2007). *The branding of higher education.* Retrieved from: http://www.semworks.net/white-papers.php

Carlzon, J. (1987). *Moments of truth.* Cambridge, MA: Ballinger Publishing Company.

Collis, David J. & Michael G. Rukstad (2008). *Can you say what your strategy is?* Harvard Business Review April 2008.

Ehret, J. (2008, July). *The brand promise. The marketing spot.* Retrieved from: http://themarketingspot. blogspot.com/2008/07/brand-promise.html

Heaton, C. and Guzzo, R. (2007). *Delivering on the brand promise: Making every employee a brand manager.* Lippincott. Retrieved from: http://www.lippincott.com/insights/a_heaton01.shtml

Kerner, N. & Pressman, G. (2007). *Chasing cool.* New York: Atria Books.

Klein, Naomi (2000). *No logo: Taking aim at the brand bullies.* Toronto: Vintage Books.

Krueger, J.R. (2007, March). *Brand promise: Providing the "second wow."* JCK Magazine. India: Reed Business Information.

Lebard, P., Rendleman, K., & Dolan, K. (2006). *Delivering the brand promise through employees.* Viewpoint. Retrieved from: http://www.mmc.com/knowledgecenter/viewpoint/ archive/lebard2006.php

Lull, C. & Thiebolt, B. A. (2004). *Creating the institutional marketing statement*. In R. Whiteside (Ed.), Student marketing for colleges and universities. Washington, D.C.: American Association of Collegiate Registrars and Admissions Officers.

Godin, S. (2002). *Purple cow: Transform your business by being remarkable*. New York: Penguin Group.

Ries, Al and Jack Trout (1981). *Positioning: The battle for your mind*. New York: McGraw-Hill.

Ries, Al and Laura (2002). *The 22 immutable laws of branding: How to build a product or service into a world-class brand*. New York: HarperCollins.

Shakespeare, W. (1605–06). *Macbeth*.

Orton, Larry (2009). *Statistics Canada's definition and classification of postsecondary and adult education providers in Canada*. Ottawa: Ministry of Industry. Retrieved from: http://www.statcan.gc.ca/pub/81-595-m/81-595-m2009071-eng.pdf

Steele, Ken (2008). *Classifying universities: Institutional brands from the market's perspective*. Toronto: Academica Group White Paper. (Available at www.academica.ca )

Steele, Ken (2009). *Selling the academy without selling out*. Ontario Confederation of University Faculty Associations Academic Matters, Feb-Mar 2009.

Tapscott, D. (2009). *Grown up digital*. New York: McGraw-Hill.

Westervelt, R. (2007). *A brand statement? Ubrander: The wild west of higher education marketing*. Retrieved from: http://ubrander.wordpress.com/2007/08/30/a-brand-promise-statement/

Wheatley, C. (2002). *Delivering the brand experience: Keeping the promise*. In D. Burnett & D. G. Oblinger (Eds.). Innovations in student services: Planning models blending high touch/high tech. Ann Arbor, MI: Society for College and University Planning.

# CHAPTER SIX
## CREATING A CULTURE OF STUDENT SUCCESS

**BY BRYANT HUTSON & ROD SKINKLE**

Traditionally, higher education executive leaders rely on a number of useful key performance indicators (KPIs) such as application and admissions rates, retention rates, and graduation rates, to help gauge student success. As indicated in Chapter Three, this type of throughput data is essential; however, there are two limitations particularly relevant to this discussion: 1) By the time these data reveal problems, the antecedent conditions may be quite entrenched; and 2) These KPIs do not reveal the underlying causes and conditions associated with student success. Efforts to enhance those "bottom-line" numbers often focus on programs for specific student populations that have been identified as "at risk." The logic behind the design and delivery of such programs is that as long as we identify what our problems are (i.e., at-risk student population), and introduce solutions to fix the problems (i.e., retention programs), we will improve retention or graduation rates. In reality, however, the retention and academic success programs designed with this logic in mind tend to have only short-term impact. Even though some programming may show encouraging immediate results and contributes to retention efforts, the impact of these programs is not sustainable. The reactive nature of this approach, through which "problems" are "solved," also prevents the institution from initiating efforts to promote student success proactively and gaining momentum to reach comprehensive, long-term, campus-wide student success. In order to establish and maintain proactive and sustainable retention efforts, we need to focus on the creation of a campus culture for student success. The primary role of the chief executive is to create this culture.

All institutions have their unique cultures. Culture represents the shared beliefs, values, customs, and traditions that impact our actions and interactions. We cannot simply declare an institutional culture. It needs to be cultivated, shaped, and maintained by leadership with a visionary outlook and strategic mindset. In this chapter, we will explore features that constitute a positive institutional culture that supports student success, and examine how institutional leaders could be proactively involved in cultivating and maintaining a culture for student success. We also discuss strategies to develop a culture of evidence to support a culture of student success.

## ESSENTIAL FEATURES OF AN INSTITUTIONAL CULTURE OF STUDENT SUCCESS

National studies identify executive leadership as indispensable for communicating commitment and for developing a results-oriented institutional culture in which academic and student affairs collaborate to provide programs and services that engage students, build a strong sense of community, and track internal data to inform ongoing improvement (Engle and O'Brien, 2007; American Association of State Colleges and Universities, 2007; Carey, 2005). In order to support student success, executive leaders must understand their institutional culture, and leverage—or change—that culture to have an impact. Your particular institution may already have a strong student success oriented culture; in which case, your objective is to build on this and ensure that it is sustainable and capable of continuous improvement. Alternatively, and more commonly, your institution includes a mix of positive and negative student success procedural and cultural features. A culture of student success involves many components, including a shared vision, a student-centred attitude across campus, strategic and coordinated programming, a well-trained staff, and the use of "champions" to make all this happen. Below, we detail these components and adopt the position that student success can always be improved and should start with a realistic appraisal of your environment.

## A SHARED VISION

For any organization, a shared vision is key to establishing "a shared picture of the future we seek to create" (Senge, 1990, p. 9). Such a vision not only encourages effort and innovation to improve institutional culture, but more importantly, it ensures congruency in such efforts. Since postsecondary institutions tend to have different units with varying purposes and goals, providing and reinforcing a shared vision becomes especially critical. In addition to having an institution-wide vision, it is critical to ensure that all stakeholders be aware of the vision and attentive to potential inconsistencies that may exist. For example, if the institution adopts a goal of improving retention rates through long-term programs that may impact students beyond their first-year, yet many departments maintain a culture in which the first year is used to cause "less able" or "less committed" students to "wash out," there is an apparent misalignment between the institutional vision and departmental practice. Increased clarity of the vision, and congruent commitment from all units on campus would be the critical first step in establishing the foundation for the culture of student success.

## COORDINATED COLLABORATION

Related to the shared vision is the involvement of both faculty and staff in working toward the common goal of student success. Faculty from academic units and student support specialists all work with students simultaneously, and bring different expertise to the student experience; however, it is common to find that these different campus units are disconnected and are unaware of or have misconceptions about each others' student success efforts. This is somewhat ironic, since students tend to see the institution as a single entity, and may be frustrated to find lack of communication across the various institutional components. Institutional leadership must develop mechanisms to make each unit on campus aware of each others' work with students and develop methods to avoid academic departments and offices working at cross-purposes and duplicating efforts. Additionally, improved communication will uncover opportunities for collaboration across different stakeholders on campus. The "retention champion(s)" described in detail later on will often find themselves in the role of coordinating these efforts.

## STRATEGIC AND SYSTEMATIC EFFORTS TOWARD A COHESIVE STUDENT EXPERIENCE

Contrary to the findings of most withdrawal surveys, there is usually no single event or problem that pushes a student past the tipping point—where the costs of staying exceed the benefits. More often, it is the cumulative effect of various pressure points over time that leads to a student's premature departure (Gladwell, 2002; Black, 2010). Therefore, it is clear that one-size-fits-all interventions seldom address the root causes of attrition, which are often masked by the obvious symptoms (e.g., poor grades, class absences, or a lack of social integration). Effective interventions are customized, directly related to the individual's attrition causation factors, and administered over a period of time.

Many institutions provide a fragmented approach to student success programming, typically exemplified by a collection of program-level initiatives that are disconnected and which have been identified through a review of best practices from other institutions. For that reason, as will be described in detail later in the discussion of a "culture of evidence," data must be collected about the students who are currently enrolled and programs should be developed that respond specifically to their needs. To achieve a culture of student success, we must create organizational structures and policies that provide a comprehensive, integrated, and coordinated approach to the student experience, which reflects the needs, challenges, and goals of your students.

## A CAMPUS "CHAMPION"

While there may be buy-in and commitment to a culture of student success among faculty and staff, there still needs to be someone who is in the campus community who is coordinating all these efforts, organizing data collection, advocating for policy changes, driving consensus-building, and addressing conflicting or duplicated initiatives. As Black (2010) has pointed out, building and sustaining a success-oriented culture requires the identification of a "retention champion" who defines expectations for the college and consistently reinforces them. At their most effective, these champions clarify the best practices and programs that enhance students' opportunities for degree completion, and they allocate money and staff to achieve the goal of graduation. They then assess their progress and change course where necessary. Just as no single individual or group can tackle every issue, the retention champion creates opportunities for team-building and collaboration among individuals and departments that lead to improved student success. Finally, they recognize all contributors—faculty, department heads, administrators, students—who sustain this environment.

In order to be effective, this champion should be given the authority to influence policies, procedures, strategies, and employee behaviour. For example, this individual would serve as an advocate for student-centred policies and curricular changes in faculty assemblies, which may require that the role be at a dean or associate provost level. They will likely need to devise training opportunities and implement incentives for staff to pursue outstanding service to students, which would necessitate a permanent budget and the authority to put into practice new human resources policies.

The introduction of a retention champion may require some organizational changes. As an executive leader, you should consider the organizational alignment of retention programs and services under the retention champion. For example, should academic advising be centralized under the retention champion's leadership, or is it best to maintain a decentralized advising model led by a faculty committee that works closely with the retention champion? Similarly, does it make sense for enrolment management functions such as the Registrar's Office and Admissions Office to be aligned with services such as career counselling, first-year experience programming, and at-risk student initiatives under the retention champion? Such questions need to be carefully weighed by the institution's executive leadership, with the strategic goals of the institution, the needs of students, and the institution's readiness for change in mind. The organizational changes that are implemented with the introduction of the retention champion will reflect the direction of the institution and will impact its current culture. Executive leadership should therefore be able to anticipate and envision how these changes will play out over the long term.

## ONGOING PROFESSIONAL DEVELOPMENT

Key to the success of retention initiatives is a well-trained frontline staff. Members of the campus community who work with students on a daily basis such as academic advisors, career counsellors, financial aid personnel, and even faculty should be knowledgeable of retention theory and how it applies to their interaction with students. They also should understand the institution's retention goals and objectives, how their work with students supports these goals, and how they can partner with other campus stakeholders to better support students. One role for your champion is to identify and provide appropriate training to campus personnel on retention theory and practice, as well as how this information will support the institution's student retention goals. Further, your retention champion should develop and offer training in the campus resources and how to make the most effective referrals.

## STRATEGIC ALLOCATION OF RESOURCES

If there is to be any serious improvement of retention, executive leadership should secure a permanent budget to support the efforts of the retention champion. Long-term funding must be obtained for retention efforts to be successful; new initiatives not linked to the budget process will die and thus increase campus scepticism about efforts to improve retention. It is easy to find examples of how campuses offered programs based on a pilot model that achieved short-term success, but that eventually declined in impact because of lack of long-term support. While one-time funds and grants can launch initiatives, the most successful programs in terms of impact and longevity have a permanent budget line. Without funding, any efforts by your retention champion will be hamstrung. Given the financial constraints that institutions face, one of the retention champion's roles will be to examine the impact of programs, and eliminate or scale back less effective retention initiatives and replace them with strategies with greater potential to impact student outcomes.

## USING A CULTURE OF EVIDENCE TO SUPPORT A CULTURE OF SUCCESS

A culture of student success is widely engaging and evidenced based. It engages faculty, student services staff, and administrators on a wide scale in using data to 1) understand where their students are experiencing success and problems, 2) design strategies to enhance success and address problems, 3) evaluate the effectiveness of the strategies, and 4) make revisions based on evaluation findings. The overarching objective is to build a culture of shared responsibility for student success, a readiness to accept both positive and negative evidence of student success, and the will to act on the evidence.

Initial discussions often begin with questions such as:

- How well do our programs work, and how do we know they are working?

- How many students do our efforts reach in meaningful ways, and how do we know?

- How many students do not complete their program of choice (attrition rate), and why?

- What is an acceptable attrition level?

- Which, if any, of these attrition drivers could be influenced, and how?

- Are there substantial differences across programs/departments/faculties, and why?

Note that the above questions require us to have already addressed the strategic questions concerning how the institution defines "success." These questions also require stakeholders to identify the data that would be necessary to answer these questions. This is more challenging than it sounds. Even when buy-in exists among campus stakeholders, many faculty and staff are not accustomed to analyzing data to devise improvements, or even knowing what questions to ask. It may require some investment in educating faculty and staff about how to use (i.e., gather and interpret) data to identify student support considerations. In our view, it is important to invest in collecting data about your specific campus, rather than relying exclusively on a review of the literature and "best practices" from other institutions. While these sources offer a starting place, they are not a substitute for carefully examining your own institution's practices, students, and opportunities.

The overall objective is to identify and then align your institutional goals with programs and services and insist on a culture of evidence including articulated program logic and evaluation criteria. To assist with this we recommend the use of Program Logic Modelling techniques. Program logic modelling is a well-established and powerful approach to mapping your particular institutional programs/services to goals and evaluation criteria (Wholey & McLaughlin, 1998). This approach requires that you break your program into its different components, including the specific inputs (such as staff, funding, and materials), the program activities (i.e., training, curriculum, workshops), outputs (i.e., the number of students served each week, hours of service provided), and more long-term outcomes (i.e., longitudinal goals for participant change, retention rates, etc.). It also requires that you identify how to measure the value and impact of each component. This is a very powerful approach for finding where programs have the greatest impact and for understanding the return your institution is receiving on its investment in different retention efforts.

Once you have mapped your program/services, goals, and evaluation criteria, there are several tactical steps that campus leadership can take to promote a culture of evidence:

- Allocate a research analyst position dedicated to analyzing the causes for student attrition and the effectiveness of retention initiatives.

- Invest in the appropriate infrastructure, such as current and user-friendly information systems and data-management technology. Integrated data dashboards that are shared across the student support community can be particularly useful in this regard.

- Note that evidence should not just flow upward. Useful evidence should be available for stakeholders at all decision-making levels. Not only will this help promote student success, it also assures buy-in among faculty and staff. In fact, incentives should be provided for using and applying evidence in decision-making and program development.

- There should be clear alignment between the data collected and the goals and strategic plans of the institution.

In order to successfully integrate the data collection and review process with student success efforts, the retention champion will need to have significant involvement. This individual may chair the committee and may coordinate the overall effort.

The importance of collecting current data cannot be overemphasized. Recommendations from the current academic research may not necessarily be helpful to your institution, as they are generalized from data drawn from institutions that may be dissimilar to yours. Student success is a localized concern, and data from past student cohorts are not helpful. Padilla (2009) notes that policy, practice, and programs that improve student success are driven by data that is collected locally and is provided by current students and other stakeholders. Efforts to improve student success must be supported with timely local data that can point the retention champion to the policy challenges that are most salient for student success on their particular campus. Additionally, faculty and staff, using local data, can identify the unique barriers that impact specific segments of the student population with whom they work, and devise focused responses accordingly.

Additionally, localized data collection can assist student services in addressing the barriers that current student are actually facing. Too often, student services on campus are designed to address barriers for students who once attended the institution but who are no longer the dominant type of student on campus. With most campuses facing rapidly changing demographics, new students often enrol with different needs that are left underserved. One way to realign student services with actual student needs is to make sure that all student services are addressing the barriers identified by their current students. For example, at least once a semester students may be surveyed to identify the needs that they have and the barriers that they face. Then, a comprehensive self-assessment of each student service is conducted to see to what degree these student needs are being addressed. Finally, an action plan is developed to refocus student services so that the services are responsive to current barriers on campus. Such an approach uses data to keep student services targeted and responsive to student needs.

## CAMPUS-WIDE ENGAGEMENT

You can have all the right services, resources, and data, but if you do not have the right people in the right roles, any effort at creating a culture of increased student success will struggle. Jim Black (2010) notes that the mantra "retention is everybody's business" does not work. Rather, you need to identify and support campus champions for the key student success issues. There needs to be someone who is in the campus community telling the success stories, advocating for policy changes, coordinating efforts, and driving consensus-building. More than any other single factor in organizational life, a well-motivated, well-managed staff is the key to the execution of student success initiatives, and the retention champion can play a key role in bringing this about. As described earlier, by maintaining constant and consistent communication with campus stakeholders about best practices and the best use of institutional policies to support student success, providing professional development opportunities, putting systems in place for collecting and distributing meaningful data, and recognising the impact of faculty and staff on student achievement, the retention champion can help bring about a greater level of campus-wide engagement.

Still, it is self-evident that this type of meaningful intervention is not really possible without broad, multidisciplinary engagement across academic and student support services. To lead an overall retention improvement process, many institutions find it effective to combine the champion and taskforce approaches. The retention champion can provide leadership and continuity in the development of retention task forces or committees with the goal to design a master plan for retention. Just as no single individual or group can tackle every issue, the retention champion creates opportunities for team-building and collaboration among individuals and departments that lead to improved student success. For example, the most effective plans focus on academic achievement, which requires the insight and support of academic leaders from among the faculty in addition to student support specialists. This approach recognizes all contributors—faculty, department heads, administrators, students—who sustain this student success environment. This approach is also invaluable in that it offers an opportunity for input and buy-in from a range of campus stakeholders, and it takes advantage of the range of experience and knowledge that these individuals possess.

## STUDENT CHARACTERISTICS

To this point we have concentrated on the institutional side of the student success equation. However, like all equations, there are two sides and we cannot solve the equation by looking at either in isolation. It is important to acknowledge that the characteristics of the student, including academic preparedness, study habits and values, expectations, past experiences, goals, and aspirations interact with the culture and programs of the institution to define the nature of student experience (i.e., student success). Thus, there is merit in considering some of the most important factors and recent trends that have influenced student population characteristics—in so far as they relate to student success.

In Canada, it is safe to say that the landscape of higher education has changed more in the past 50 years than in the combined total change of the preceding 400 years. As Ken Steele makes abundantly clear in his chapter on trends in higher education, there is a multitude of factors converging to drive this unprecedented level of change. One of the most significant themes associated with this (r)evolution in higher education, is the increase in the proportion of the population now participating, and the concomitant increase in the "heterogeneity" of the student population. Gone is the largely homogeneous (mostly male, wealthy class) 5–10 percent of youth cohort that once populated institutions of higher learning. In Canada, Côté and Allahar (2007) have described many aspects of this growth in the face of shrinking resources and what they see as increasingly negative outcomes for the quality of student experience, engagement, and learning outcomes. While the debate concerning this growth, shrinking resources, and implications at the system level is beyond the scope of this discussion, it is not irrelevant. We think this issue is extremely important to higher education quality generally and, moreover, that there are clear implications for student experience (i.e., student success). There are both positive and negative implications associated with these macro-level changes; the challenge for institutional leaders is to understand these at the micro (classroom) level in order to direct student success initiatives for maximum impact (ROI)—with existing resources. Below, we highlight a few of the most significant factors and consider implications for student success intervention planning.

## STUDENT DIVERSITY

As noted above, with increasing participation comes greater heterogeneity of incoming student populations. Heterogeneity is synonymous with diversity and it is this "diversity" that has the most important implications for student success planning. When we think of diversity we tend to think of ethnic diversity, which can include race, religion, and language, all of which are important. However, we are at the same time experiencing unprecedented change in accompanying areas important to postsecondary pedagogy, including for example, age, experience, and lifestyle (e.g., family, income, employment). Clearly, this increased diversity has the potential to improve the quality of student experience and is consistent with some of the highest ideals of education, (i.e., multicultural exposure, tolerance, and benefiting from learning of students with more life/work experience) (Light, 2001; Kuh et al., 2005); however, it behooves us to also acknowledge the flipside; this diversity includes corresponding diversity in all of the critical student success characteristics noted above (academic preparedness, study habits and values, expectations, past experiences, goals and aspirations). Moreover, this increasing diversity of student success characteristics has been accompanied by decreasing per student funding levels and related challenges, including increasing class sizes (student/faculty ratios), and use of part-time faculty.

## A FOCUS ON STUDENT NEEDS AND MOTIVATION

In order to support their success, it is important to assess the needs and strengths of your students at regular intervals, beginning with the pre-admission stage. Incoming student assessments can be administered with incoming students to learn more about their developmental and cognitive needs, as well as their academic and social motivations. There are a range of assessments that might be used, depending on the goals of the institution. For example, there are several instruments that measure emotional intelligence—i.e., the ability to recognize and interpret emotions and their relationships, and to reflectively regulate emotions so as to promote emotional and intellectual growth—which has been examined as a predictor of student achievement (Mayer, Salovey, & Caruso, 2004). These include the EQ-I, Multifactor Emotional Intelligence Scale, and the Emotional Competence Inventory. Additionally, instruments based on the Holland Codes, such as the Strong Interest Inventory, can help students find alignment between their academic pursuits and career goals. More qualitative instruments also may be useful. For example, Oregon State University has adapted Sedlacek's (2004) model of eight noncognitive variables that predict student success into a qualitative instrument called the Insight Resumé, in which applicants respond to six prompts, with only 100 words for each section. The institution has also discovered a direct correlation between higher scores on the Insight Resumé and retention rates, and has experienced a slight increase in mean GPA (Jaschik, 2007). Assessments such as these can help create a student profile that academic and student support staff can use to assist incoming students in developing a first-year experience that best fits their academic needs and personal goals.

Similarly, predictive modeling can help identify newly admitted students who may be more at risk. In this process, a model is created to try to best predict the probability of an outcome based on the analysis of patterns found in the large sets of data that institutions collect about students, such as demographics, previous education, registration patterns, and other information. These models can assist in identifying what kinds of programming and support would be most effective for the different types of students who enroll in your institution.

Student-centred retention efforts start with the enrolment process, well before students are admitted into the institution. Given an understanding of student motivation, we are in a position to shape the student population through a) sending the right messages to the market (branding, etc.), attracting students whose motivations/expectations will be aligned with the institution's; and b) building on and nurturing this messaging throughout the student experience. Black (2010) notes that, whether it is intentional or not, institutions make promises to their students. Central to student academic success and retention is finding alignment between students' motivations and what the institution has to offer. When students perceive their expectations as having been met or exceeded, they are far more likely to stay. Note this is not to suggest the institution should change its goals to match incoming student needs/expectations, rather, that the institution should articulate clearly and deliver consistently. Black (2010) suggests two methods for ensuring the alignment: communicating clearly institutional expectations including limits for addressing student needs and wants, and ensuring that all realistic student expectations, such as class availability and quality instruction, are met. This is a process that can begin even before matriculation with the right marketing and communication toward prospective students. Similarly, investing in pre-enrolment academic counselling and advising can ensure that students enrol in programs of study that reflect their interests, goals, and values before their first term even begins.

According to Feldman (2005), fostering the career development of incoming freshmen increases student satisfaction and has the added benefit of aiding the institution's retention efforts. Indeed, in a study of university alumni, Skinkle and Dawson (1996) found that perceived career competency and program satisfaction were positively related even after graduation. In addition, career development interventions present opportunities for students to connect college activities with a future career path (Niles & Bowlsbey, 2005). Tinto (1987) indicated a lack of clear academic focus and career goals as factors for students stopping, or dropping, out. This is supported by recent Canadian data that show that a majority of students that leave a PSE institution go on to eventually attend a different PSE institution (Parkin & Baldwin, 2009). Targeting, tracking, and engaging students as they identify their course of study can be a useful way to institutionally support students exploring majors and thus serve as a means of retaining these students. We refer to this as "education and career goal development" to help distinguish it from basic career or vocational counselling. In another recent Canadian study at the University of Toronto, investigators showed that a program as simple as having students write about their education and career plans among at-risk students, resulted in significant improvements in academic performance compared with a control group (Morisano, et al., 2010).

The social aspects of integration are of as great a concern as the academic dimensions. It is vital that orientation programs facilitate both social and academic integration, and that the institution provides opportunities for students to establish social networks throughout their enrolment. Examples include facilitating social networks through special programming such as clubs, cultural groups, and sporting activities. While there is some evidence that too much social activity may negatively affect academic outcomes, their value should not be underestimated. These social networks present the higher education experience to students in a more comprehensive way that goes beyond academic studies. They prepare students for future social interactions in their works environment, among other things. Additionally, social networking helps students establish support groups for their academic pursuits, and offers opportunities to develop interdependence strategies for overcoming academic challenges. In fact, a key role for the institution should be to coach students in the skills required to take advantage of these social networks (Kuh, et al., 2005).

Orientation programs afford students the opportunity to start developing these social networks prior to enrolment. Such efforts not only help students overcome problems with course selection and the transition from high school, these programs also assist students in anticipating the values, norms, and behaviours they will encounter at the institution. As a case in point, the University of Victoria offers "Experience UVic," a campus visit program that offers prospective students campus tours, classroom experiences, course registration information, opportunities to meet students, staff and faculty members in an effort to help students decide whether the institution is a good "fit" for them. Programs such as these, which help students find alignment between the institution's expectations and values and their own before the first semester begins, can assist with improving student retention. In addition to programs designed to offer a series of experiences that are representative of the institutional culture, the use of self-assessments or reflection questions that students can do at home prior to orientation events may also help anticipate the culture of the institution.

While institutions often hope that students will adapt to the institutional culture, it is not a matter of simple assimilation. Many students have only intermittent contact with their institution, as work and other aspects of their lives take precedent. Additionally, there is much evidence to suggest that student departure is influenced by their perceptions of how well their own cultural attributes are valued and accommodated, and how differences between their cultures of origin and those of the campus are bridged. Students should sense that they are valued for individuality and uniqueness, and that they do not struggle with discrimination (Kuh & Love, 2000). In addition to assisting students with transitioning into the institution and finding alignment between their own values and those of the institution, the institutional social and academic culture should welcome diverse cultural capital and make efforts to adapt to diverse students' needs. A key challenge for the institution is to strike a balance between defining and communicating an institutional culture in which students feel at home, and recognizing, accommodating, and celebrating student individuality and difference. Increasingly, institutions are recognizing and accepting learners' goal and cultural capital, and are adapting their mores and practices to accommodate these in a learner-centred way (Zepke & Leach, 2005).

## THE ROLES OF INSTITUTIONAL LEADERSHIP

Kuh and Whitt (1988) noted that efforts to enhance student success often falter because too little attention is given to understanding the properties of the institution's culture that reinforce the status quo and perpetuate everyday actions. Fullan (2001) observed in his studies of school performance that culture is the single most important element that must be altered and managed in order to change what an organization or institution values and how it acts, a process he called reculturing. It is the role of the chief executive to analyze the influence of norms, tacit beliefs, and other cultural properties on behaviour to determine what needs to be addressed to effect change. To move an institution toward cultivating an ever improving ethos of student success, it is essential to address aspects of its culture that are antithetical to the culture of improved student success (Kuh, et al., 2005). In other words, look for, and tackle first, the cultural and systemic challenges to student success. Some examples of these challenges may include a lack of communication and duplication of efforts across administrative units, or a severe mismatch between stated retention goals and the policies that the institution has in place regarding student academic standing. An objective assessment of an institution's readiness to embrace a student success imperative is a sound place to start. In the section that follows, we describe several roles that are specific to the institution's chief executive in order to bring about a culture of student success.

## ASSESSING READINESS FOR A STUDENT SUCCESS CULTURE

When examining institutional culture, a useful starting point is the institution's "readiness" to investigate and improve student success. Often we speak in terms of students' readiness to attend higher education—that is, having developed the knowledge, skills, and behaviours necessary to complete a college-level course of study. Student readiness, which we address below, is of course an important component of their success. From the institutional perspective, however, a culture of student success is focused on making the most of strengths that students bring with them and creating opportunities for students to leverage these strengths. Regardless of students' backgrounds and previous experiences, as Kuh, et al. (2005) noted, what matters most in bringing about positive student outcomes is what students do once they get to campus. Likewise, institutional goals are not only important because of what is gained by achieving them, but how the institution changes as a result of having pursued them. While setting student success goals are essential elements of planning, they are really a statement of the direction the institution hopes to move in.

A revealing question is: Are the institution's retention goals aligned with institutional behaviours, knowledge, and programs? For example, if the institution adopts a goal of improving retention rates over time, yet many departments maintain a culture in which the first year is used to cause "less able" or "less committed" students to "wash out," there is an apparent misalignment between goals and behaviours. While this illustration may seem obvious, there are more subtle examples of institutional readiness for retention. It is important to assess to what degree the institution is ready to identify and attend to high-risk experiences that can be controlled (Black, 2010). There are several foundational questions such as the following that will help reveal the degree to which the institution is ready to improve student success:

- Does the institution have procedures in place to monitor and modify student experiences with processes such as class availability, institutional bureaucracy, and institutional policies that impact student enrolment and progress toward degree?

- Do students receive early academic performance feedback in their classes? How is this early feedback used to promote student achievement?

- Does the institution provide an academic advising model that leads to a comprehensive academic plan and mentoring rather than a mere schedule of courses?

## OFFERING A VISION

In order to change a culture, you must first understand it. This includes investing in the time to talk with campus constituents in order to understand the history, values, and traditions of the institution and how they impact current behaviours and attitudes, identifying and exploring areas of pride and success that are recognized by campus stakeholders, and learning how the institution is recognized by members of other institutions and incoming students. Executive leaders may find that there are a number of components to the institution's culture that must be respected in order to successfully bring about change, and they may find there are components that can be leveraged to bring about change. Additionally, such an effort allows leadership to evaluate the current situation. It may in fact reveal student-centred culture that can be improved upon, or at least identify pockets of success across campus that can be integrated and used as the basis for expanded efforts.

As executive leaders, you are engaged in the process of understanding, articulating, and changing the culture through your daily decision-making. Hence, if you do not have a far-sighted and systematic approach in mind when it comes to creating a culture of student success, it may lead to wasted resources, an unclear set of priorities, and faculty and staff that receive mixed messages as to their role in supporting students. Institutional leadership is in a position to alter the way people look at their own institution. You can raise a topic like building a culture of student success, and create an environment in which stakeholders discuss how to achieve it in such a way as to create a shared sense of ownership and understanding. The key to making the process work is to be as concrete and as collective as possible. Concreteness demands that the process articulate the specifics of behaviours that campus stakeholders can engage in that promotes student success, and collectiveness demands that leadership create a number of mechanisms through which members of the campus community come together to discuss how student success may be achieved.

Institutional leadership should, above all, recognize that their own personal rhetoric and behaviour are among the most powerful influences on campus culture. Leaders seeking to build or sustain a campus culture centred on student success need to regularly examine their own day-to-day behaviour, ensuring that they are consistent in making visible strategic decisions and investments to sustain efforts toward creating a culture of student success. You also should remember that the symbolic, cultural dimensions of your decisions are just as important as its direct operational consequences—the decisions you make will indicate to campus stakeholders the emerging values and direction of the changing campus culture.

## CELEBRATING INDIVIDUAL EFFORTS

One of the key responsibilities of the institutional leader is to recognize the efforts of its members in creating the culture for student success and establish a system that recognizes achievements and provides rewards for programs, offices, and individuals. Nido Qubein (2010), president of High Point University, has noted "You can't make incremental change and transform a culture. You need big results or they won't see or appreciate the changes. If it takes too long to see change, they will give up before they even get started." When positive outcomes are achieved, they need to be publicized. The contributions of staff to student success should be recognized, and programs that have been distinguished by their support to students should be rewarded. Stakeholders in the campus community need to see that the work they are doing is making a difference, and it needs to be emphasized as often as possible. An important role of the retention champion is overseeing and monitoring this system to assure that achievements are recognized and that individual efforts are rewarded.

Marcus Buckingham notes that "if you measure it and reward it, people will try to excel in it" (1999, p. 187). For a retention plan to succeed, buy-in from all stakeholders is essential. While most faculty and staff will generally support the notion of student success, to sustain long-term impact there must be a system in place to recognize and reward the work of individuals in supporting the institution's retention and student success goals. Without such a system in place, campus stakeholders will perceive their work as not valued, and their enthusiasm will wane. The reward system should be specific, and tied to measurable outcomes that reflect institutional goals. Similarly, Black (2010) has noted that the conditions for student success cannot exist unless there is broad-based buy-in, which often is linked to concrete, tangible rewards to campus stakeholders. If campus leadership is not willing to invest in human and organizational capacity in a concrete way, either through financial incentives, recognition, or other methods for recognizing campus community members' contributions to an emerging culture of student success, the effort will not be sustained.

## SETTING PRIORITIES

Since there are many potential innovations that could support and extend the culture for student success, setting priorities is an important task for the institutional leader. Your retention champion should lead efforts to determine what the specific conditions for success are for the population of students that your institution serves, and ensure those conditions are created. While the retention champion can help develop and execute the programs and policies that lead to a culture of success, it is ultimately up to the executive leadership to identify student success mission and priorities. When focusing on specific interventions, it is easy to get caught up into thinking about student success at the "tactical" level and become fixated on short-term gains, while a focus on creating and promoting a campus-wide culture of success brings us to the "strategic" level (Dolence, 1997; Black, 2001).

As we start to examine institutional cultures, it is crucial that we ask ourselves the right questions. Often we fixate on the questions "why do students leave?"; "what are the characteristics of students who are likely to leave?"; "what interventions do we need to provide so that they will choose not to leave?" While these are useful questions, they reflect short-term tactical thinking and do not get at strategic issues. They narrowly focus on the search for how to intervene so that students who are likely to leave have a reduced probability of doing so, rather than building a campus culture that is focused on long-term, sustainable student achievement. For understanding the culture of an institution, however, a far more important question is "why do students stay?" To really comprehend student success at your particular institution, you need to uncover what it is that leads students, some of them under the most adverse and challenging circumstances, to successfully become a part of the campus community and persist to graduation. Such questions point to who is the best fit for your institution, and offers insight into what is working on your campus and for whom. Perhaps equally important, exploring this question can help uncover the barriers to student success that exist on your campus, and identify how successful students overcome them, so that the impact of these barriers may be eliminated either through institutional changes or through teaching incoming student-tested strategies for negotiating them.

The operationalization of priorities can be facilitated by the retention champion through collaboration with campus stakeholders. Part of the role of the retention champion is to lead in the development of an integrated retention plan through a series of forums with campus stakeholders. Such a plan would involve a number of the components to a culture of student success that we have already described:

- A student retention mission statement—a statement, typically arrived at through collaboration with representative campus stakeholders, that indicates the institution's commitment to student success and offers an explanation of how student success is defined on your campus.

- A set of campus-wide priorities—this often includes a number of goals, including recruitment goals, persistence goals, and student learning outcomes. These goals should be informed by retention and student academic achievement data from previous years, and should be developed with a thorough understanding of the students your institution typically enrols. In addition to measures of student achievement, these goals should reflect retention and academic success targets for academic programs, as well as measures of impact for student services such as financial aid, academic advising, and student activities.

- Measureable outcomes and methods of evaluation—the retention plan should include specific methods of evaluating impact and outcomes, sources of data, and a realistic timeline for implementation of retention efforts and when to conduct assessment. Ideally, a comprehensive evaluation model is adopted and a full-time research analyst is responsible for overseeing this process.

- A plan for integrating retention goals with existing programs and services—retention goals should leverage programs and services that are already in place. The plan should examine available data to identify what student services are most needed at different points in a student's academic career. For example, it is generally considered good practice to frontload student interaction with your best teachers and advisors during the first year of enrolment, when they are in the greatest need of support in their transition to college. On the other hand, career services and internship experiences may be most valuable closer to the end of their academic experience.

- Resource requirements and potential sources of funding—stakeholders will not believe their planning efforts are worthwhile if they are not assured of funding from the outset.

- Responsible units and individuals—the plan should describe the roles and responsibilities of members of the campus community in improving student success. Action points, timelines, and accountability should be specific.

- Systems for recognizing and rewarding success—the reward system should be specific, and tied to measurable outcomes that reflect institutional goals.

The development of the plan is an area in which involvement and buy-in of campus stakeholders can be developed and sustained. This approach fulfills the need of campus constituencies to believe that the planning process is authentic and that they have a personal stake in the process and outcomes, and that the entire campus is working toward common goals.

# CONCLUSION

Institutions that are serious about improving student outcomes need a comprehensive, integrated approach to student retention that empowers faculty, staff, and administrators with the skills and resources necessary to address student warning signs as they surface. More importantly, by ensuring the conditions for student success are in place campus-wide, an institution can prevent attrition before the situation reaches a tipping point. A culture of student success helps make the most of strengths that students bring with them and create opportunities for students to leverage these strengths. Regardless of student backgrounds and previous experiences, as Kuh et al. (2005) noted, what matters most in bringing about positive student outcomes is what student do once they get to campus. Likewise, institutional goals are not important because of what is gained by achieving them, but how the institution changes as a result of having pursued them. While setting student success goals are essential, they are really a statement of the direction in which the institution hopes to move. Executive leaders are in a unique position in that they can set goals that—if supported through a labour-intensive effort of implementing new organizational structures, providing appropriate services, training staff, and investing in data collection and analysis—can bring about a culture of student success.

## FOOTNOTES

[2] Numerous resources exist to describe and explain the use of PLM. For example, W.K. Kellogg Foundation: Logic Model Development Guide www.wkkf.org/knowledge-center/resources/2010/W-K-Kellogg-Foundation-Evaluation-Handbook.aspx

[3] AUCC calculates a decline from $21,000 per FTE in 1980 to $15,000 in 2007, using constant dollars.

## REFERENCES

American Association of State Colleges and Universities. (2007). *Hispanic student success.* Retrieved August 2, 2010, from http://www.aascu.org/media/publications/hispanic_success.htm.

AUCC (2007). *Trends in higher education, Vols. 1–3.* Ottawa: Association of Universities and Colleges of Canada. Available at www.aucc.ca.

Black, J. (2010, May). *Creating a retention culture.* [White paper]. Retrieved August 2, 2010, from http://www.semworks.net/white-papers.php.

Black, J. (Ed.). (2001). *The strategic enrollment management revolution.* Washington, DC: American Association of Collegiate Registrars and Admissions Officers.

Buckingham, M., & Coffman, C. (1999). *First, break all the rules.* New York: Simon & Schuster.

Carey, K. (2005). *One step from the finish line.* Retrieved August 9, 2010, from http://www2.edtrust.org/NR/rdonlyres/10D6E141-08E4-42D7-B7E5-773A281BCDB7/0/onestep_.pdf.

# CHAPTER SEVEN
## LEVERAGING TECHNOLOGY TO POWER STUDENT RECRUITMENT AND RETENTION

**BY PHILIP J. BLISS**

In the introductory chapter of this book, it was noted that "often technology is viewed as a proverbial black hole." It does appear that one of the few certainties in life is that the cost of technology is going to rise, but how often is this increase in cost really measured against a true return on investment?

Technology in higher education is in the process of immense change. Technologies are becoming increasingly collaborative and are changing not simply the delivery of learning (e-textbooks) but the way it is being taught. Technology in higher education in the future will support what Tapscott and Williams term the "Global Network for Higher Learning." In their new book *Macrowikinomics* (2010), they assert that,

> If universities open up and embrace collaborative learning and collaborative knowledge production, they have a chance of surviving and even thriving in the networked, global economy.

To be fair, such things as content management systems, customer relationship management systems, student portal or enterprise resource planning systems are often simply not measured very effectively after the implementation phase to determine return on investment (ROI). The more compelling need for technology investment in the next decade may have a somewhat different focus from the past twenty years. In a recent article it was noted that,

> Universities that cannot meet the demands of today's society and technologically driven constituents will quickly find themselves left behind and suffering from decreased enrolment and, consequently, decreased federal and state funding (Fathi & Wilson, 2009).

Like many other areas of society, with the adaption of social computing and the emergence of a new collaborative or conversational paradigm in personal and now business technology, customer-driven technology solutions will be at the forefront of investment. This chapter will focus primarily on the marketing and delivery-focused strategic technology issues that need to be considered over the next decade. We will discuss the recruitment and retention areas of higher education and how and what technology can best be deployed to enhance enrolment management objectives. In a time of aggressive competitive marketing for students, a decline in the traditional applicant pool, and increasing problems occurring with student retention, technology is not a solution in itself, but it is definitely a key enabler for well-thought-through enrolment processes to be applied.

Cost efficiencies are vital when making technology decisions, but if this becomes the foundation of the decision, then from a strategic point of view you are on dangerous ground. In the 2009 IBM Global CEO Study, The New Voice of the CEO, IBM researchers talked to more than 2,500 CEOs from over seventy-five countries and fifteen industries. The key strategic issues for technology in business are:

- driving technology innovation to make it a reality;

- increasing the ROI in information technology (IT); and

- expanding the business impact of IT.

A surprising number of education CEOs told the study that they felt "ill-equipped to cope with this drastically different world." Seventy-nine percent of them expected the level of complexity to grow significantly over the next five years, yet only 45 percent felt they could deal with the complexity successfully. In short, education CEOs face a "complexity gap" that seems to pose bigger challenges than any they have had to deal with in the near past. The combined insights of 1,541 interviews came up with the following priorities for IT in Education:

| Embody creative leadership | Reinvent customer relationships | Build operating dexterity |
|---|---|---|
| • Embrace ambiguity | • Honor your customers above all else | • Simplify whenever possible |
| • Take risk that disrupt legacy business models | • Use two-way communications to sync with customers | • Manage systemic complexity |
| • Leapfrog beyond "tried-and-true" management styles | • Profit from the information explosion | • Promote a mindset of being fast and flexible |
| | | • Be "glocal" |

In the same study, education CEOs were found to differ significantly from other sector CEOs with only 19 percent versus 48 percent from the overall sample focusing on simplifying their products and operations to manage complexity more effectively. Education CEOs also were much less concerned with having to act rapidly and simplifying their products and processes to better manage complexity.

## STRATEGIC TECHNOLOGY OVERVIEW

The eleventh annual 2010 EDUCAUSE Current Issues Survey shows some very familiar themes among the top-ten IT issues of strategic importance to technology leaders. What is interesting, however, is that strategic planning is an issue of renewed importance, highlighting the renewed need for a focus on strategic business issues and how technology can help deliver these. The following eleven items (#6 was a tie) were recorded as the most important issues to IT in higher education in 2009:

1. Funding IT

2. Administrative/ERP/Information Systems

3. Security

4. Teaching and Learning with Technology

5. Identity/Access Management

6. Disaster Recovery/Business Continuity

6. Governance, Organization, and Leadership

7. Agility, Adaptability, and Responsiveness

8. Learning Management Systems

9. Strategic Planning

10. Infrastructure/Cyber Infrastructure

While all of the above issues are very important, three significant external factors seem to be missing from the list: mobile distribution, outsourcing, and cloud computing, although in reality these factors influence every item on the list. Although these are external resource issues, and as such may not be part of the internal strategic focus, these factors will have the most significant strategic and organizational effect on technology within schools in the next decade. With increasing emphasis globally being given to the emerging "on-demand" workforce that outsourcing provides, this option is likely to be taken up more and more as budgets become increasingly restrictive. Moving to an increasingly outsourced labour model and adopting a cloud computing IT structure may be the two most important strategic technology issues to consider over the next three to five years—especially for the small to medium-sized schools.

Outsourcing has been around for many years, and it generally trends upward when high operating and capital costs become prohibitive and when reduced complexity and rapid deployment are needed. This is certainly why it is gaining increased importance. Outsourcing is certainly not a panacea to reduce costs; however, as revenues become tighter, it can potentially offer an ability to decrease costs in some areas of IT . . . and maybe Web services as well.

An example of the effectiveness and maybe the future of outsourcing in higher education can be found in the public sector in the U.K. where the U.K. National Health Service has created a joint venture to provide payroll, finance, and accounting services from India, reportedly reducing operating costs by as much as 30 percent. Outsourcing requires strong internal management controls and equally accomplished negotiating skills—but it does seem to offer the cost savings that will be a necessary part of the future in higher education.

Cloud computing refers to accessing software and a variety of other services from the "cloud." "Cloud computing is Internet-based computing, whereby shared resources, software, and information are provided to computers and other devices on demand, like the electricity grid" (Wikipedia, 2010).

According to Nicholas Carr, the strategic importance of information technology is diminishing as it becomes standardized and less expensive (2004). He argues that the cloud computing paradigm shift is similar to the displacement of electricity generators by electricity grids early in the twentieth century.

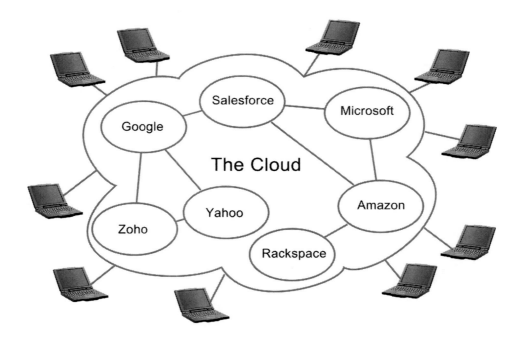

The above illustration (Wikipedia, 2010) provides an example of how the cloud structure impacts all areas of the technology infrastructure, front end, storage, back office, e-mail, and other virtual service offerings.

Cloud computing is the new technology glue. Ramping up your cloud computing structure may be the most important strategic technology issue to consider over the next three to five years. It might be considered both a threat and an opportunity, but it is definitely a challenge that has to be managed. Dan Farber, the Editor in Chief of CNET News, puts it best when he describes the new era of cloud computing:

> We are at the beginning of the age of planetary computing. Billions of people will be wirelessly interconnected, and the only way to achieve that kind of massive scale usage is by massive scale, brutally efficient cloud-based (2008).

From a high-level technical perspective, the two most significant components of cloud computing architecture are known as the front end and the back end. The front end is the part seen by the client, i.e., the computer user. This includes the client's network (or computer) and the applications used to access the cloud via a user interfaces such as a Web browser. The back end of the cloud computing architecture is the "cloud" itself, comprising various data and infrastructure intensive application.

The following benefits can be derived from the cloud computing:

- **Reduced Cost:** cloud technology is paid for incrementally, saving organizations money and not requiring up-front capital expenditure.

- **Increased Storage:** organizations can store more data less expensively than on private computer systems and they do not have to provide increased server capacity and support on site.

- **Highly Automated:** internal IT personnel spend less time keeping software up to date and supporting increasing banks of servers in their data facilities.

- **Flexibility:** flexibility is a key benefit, allowing for on-demand access to such things as the network and storage.

- **More Mobility:** employees can access information wherever they are, rather than having to remain at their desks. However this benefit also highlights the security issues that cloud computing throws up for the organization.

- **Allows IT to Shift Focus:** with IT no longer having to worry about constant server updates and other time-consuming computing support issues, they are free to be more creative and innovate new solutions to increase the efficiencies of the organization

Even now the origins of cloud computing are changing. With the arrival of social or collaborative computing the new Cloud 2.0 is beginning to look like the diagram below.

**Fundamental Shift in Cloud Computing**

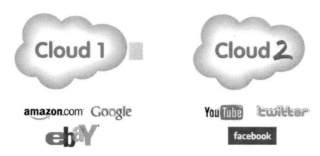

As you can see, the cloud now encompasses social media technologies. By now we all realize the impact of Facebook, Twitter, LinkedIn, blogs, and other collaborative or social media trends. The reality is that most of us are still uncertain how best to leverage these technologies to benefit the organization. With the maturing of social media applications we will see it become less of a gimmick and more of a utility or platform that supports collaboration in many ways. A superb example of this in the Web recruitment area can be found at http://www.rit.edu/emcs/admissions/accepted-student-homepage.

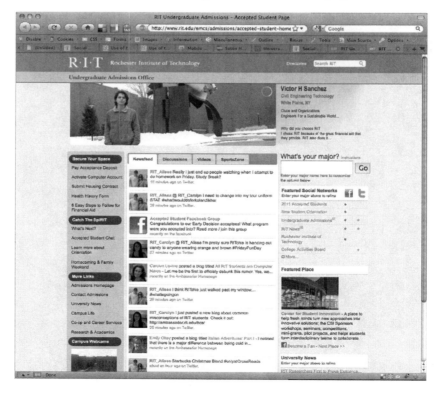

Here we see collaboration computing front and centre on the school's home page. In the words of a true visionary on cloud computing:

> The key apps we use in productivity, collaboration, communication, entertainment, education, and even health, will all be rewritten to take advantage of the new capabilities. This will result in a new generation that looks more like Facebook on the iPad than Yahoo on the PC. Our industry is changing. We all need to step up to meet this change head-on or we will leave an incredible opportunity behind. (Benioff, 2010).

With the dominance of smartphones and now the iPad and soon a host of competitive slate-based devices, the means of accessing and delivering information is changing radically so you need be ready to address these trends. Using the iPad as an example is covered in more depth later in the chapter. This throws up key issues—not the least of which is what will happen to bookstore revenue if all textbooks are delivered digitally?

As a result of improved online delivery and "consumer" convenience, schools quickly have to come to grips with the emerging consumer-driven delivery model that competes with the bricks and mortar institutional model that exists today. For traditional schools, possibly the single most important strategic technology issue to consider over the next two to three years is the delivery of learning. With median household income up by a factor of 6.5 in the past 40 years and the cost of attending a public college up by a factor of 15 for in-province students and 24 for out-of-province students (Schumpeter, 2010), something has to give in the institutional model with today's economic reality.

When you equate the fact the college fees have for decades risen faster than a family's ability to pay them, with the arrival of new, highly efficient, collaborative technologies it is evident that online collaborative technologies have to play a key role in decreasing student expenses in the future. On a strategic level, universities and colleges need to meet the demands of the new technologically driven, mobile student constituents or fall behind and suffer decreased enrolment.

To conclude this overview, it is safe to say that success in the future will distil down to sound management and innovation of the Cloud. The new technology equation looks something like this:

### Facebook + iPad + Cloud Computing = Future

And that Future in the equation looks like a digital sheet of paper, where it is less about typing or clicking and it is more about touching. It is less about textbooks, and it is more about downloadable, interactive text readers that have animation and integrated video. And successful applications will even have a quick link (maybe video) to the teacher or administrator for instant feedback on sections that a student does not understand! It is not about the limits of local disk storage, it is about almost infinite data storage and access via the Cloud. To deal with the future, new applications and processes will need to be developed (and yes that means more budgets) but if schools are to maintain their enrolment, reputation, and revenues they will have to adapt to a customer or student-driven business model that encompasses more flexibility in course delivery and new online teaching models.

In the remainder of this chapter, we will illustrate how strategic technology decisions might expand the reach and effectiveness of an institution's message and increase student satisfaction. The rest of this discussion is broken down into the following two sections:

- Recruitment: can technology improve or get in the way of attracting a student?
- Retention: how much is technology a critical success factor for the student to succeed?

When correct strategies and resources are in place, the technology solutions, if well implemented and supported, can provide better services and communications with an improved ROI that might increasingly be measured as student recruitment and retention.


## RECRUITMENT: HOW TECHNOLOGY IMPACTS THE DECISION-MAKING PROCESS OF A STUDENT

Today, when you think of recruiting new students, you initially think of how new prospects find and view your school on the Web. It is the primary platform where prospective students and parents discover the potential of a school for the first time, and it is where they initiate and, increasingly, complete their application process. Recent data from the PEW Internet and American Life Project revealed that 93 percent of 18- to 29-year-olds in the United States use the Internet (Rainie, 2010). According to Academica's own 2009 WebTrends Survey, prospective students spent an average of 25 hours online per week, with 60 percent connecting to the Internet through a high-speed wireless connection.

The online communicative purposes cited most often by prospective students for using the Internet are checking their e-mail (97 percent), social network sites (75 percent) and instant messaging (72 percent). In terms of entertainment, video streaming Web sites draw the most attention from prospective students (86 percent), followed by downloading music and videos (66 percent) and listening to streaming audio (54 percent).

PEW also finds that young American adults are heavy users of social media: 72 percent of online 18- to 29-year-olds use social networking Web sites (Lenhart, et al., 2010) and 90 percent use video- sharing Web sites, such as YouTube (Madden, 2009).

The Internet has firmly established itself as the key communications tool for higher education institutions looking to attract prospective applicants. Indeed, Academica Group's 2009 University and College Applicant Survey (UCAS™) found that 87 percent of higher education applicants visit institutional Web sites when considering enrolment. Our 2008 Acceptance Declined Survey™ revealed that an institution's Web site is one of the top ten factors influencing an applicant's decision to decline an acceptance offer.

Blue Hue Education also revealed in a recent study (with Noel-Levitz, James Tower, OmniUpdate, and the National Research Center for College & University Admissions) that 70 percent of applicants prefer to complete university and college applications online, 60 percent prefer to communicate with students online, sev70enty percent prefer to communicate with faculty online, and 34 percent want to receive answers to their questions online. These results illustrate how vital it is for institutions to understand the importance of their Web site as a vehicle for strategic recruitment and marketing.

The questions you need to ask today before even thinking about the technology are:

- just how effective is our Web site for our "customers";
- who "owns" the Web strategy and does it reflect our overall enrolment objectives;
- who manages the technology of the Web site and is it well resourced;
- is our Web site able to work effectively with mobile devices; and
- are we leveraging social media technologies to positively impact recruitment?

In one of Academica's recent white papers, Admissions 3.0: successfully connecting and converting students online, it is interesting that at no time did we really consider technology as a part of the review. Instead, we focused on how a number of admissions Web sites in Canada and the U.S. provided or failed to provide usable and useful solutions to students thinking of enrolling. The conclusion we came to follows:

The current state of university and college admissions sites illustrates the need for vast improvement. In order to be truly effective, institutions should focus on providing relevant content in an intuitive manner and using conventions that are focused on the applicant rather than the institution. Admissions sites should maintain consistency with program and department pages, as well as with the institutional home page in order to encourage trust in the information, generate return visits, and establish a dialogue between the institution and prospective students. An institution's social media and rich media presence needs to be tightly integrated into the admissions process and context, and video should be embedded directly on the site.

What we also concluded from this review was that many sites were effectively broken for most prospective student and parent visitors. Many of the application processes we reviewed were lacking in usability logic, ease of access and the contextual data needed to assist the applicants as they progress through their online discovery. In many cases the student application processes were distributed across a number of sites, without providing continuous contextual information. Although this might make sense from an institutional level, for the prospective student and parent it just causes confusion, loss of interest, and loss of conversion.

This kind of disconnect is what we term inside-out thinking. Many higher education sites suffer from this. Inside-out thinking is where the Web site reflects the language and bureaucracy of the school and not the thinking and needs of the external constituent that is visiting the school online for the first time. Overcoming this problem seems easy but adopting outside-in thinking and providing plain and simple language and navigation, in our experience, is sometimes a radical shift for the school. However, if this can be achieved, recruitment from the Web site will improve. This approach and the continuing strategic importance of the Web for recruitment (and all of these rules also apply to internal Web sites and online retention techniques for current students).

In Gerry McGovern's new book, *The Stranger's Long Neck,* he refers to the Web site as the "long neck" of any organization, and he introduces a new rule that reinforces the importance of your main Web site and admissions site (or are these really the same)? McGovern states that:

*The 25:5 rule states that at least 25 percent of demand is for 5 percent of tasks; that 5 percent of content is read by 25 percent of people. The 25:5 rule is a type of distillation of the 80:20 rule (McGovern, 2010). Viewed in graphical form this creates a Long Neck. Admissions Web sites are the Long Neck of any school.*

LONG NECK: 5% of your website delivers 25% of your value. Do you know which 5%?

Increasingly, technology itself is not the issue on school Web sites. The apparent lack of cohesion and logic in many admissions processes clearly shows the need for schools to be more strategic, more unified, more innovative, and less complex at an organizational level. To the outsider or "stranger," at too many of the sites we reviewed, the experience was not simple and the process was highly internalized. These disconnects on the admissions sites we reviewed are symbolic of the organizational disconnects that exist in academic organizations today.

Broken or confusing admissions processes often reflected the island-like status of many faculty, program, or school sub-sites. It is absolutely imperative that while, internally, schools or faculties are recognized as "business" units of the organization, on an external level, the prospective student/parent motivation and direction remains surrounded by an overall branded Web presence that is accessible and innovative. This can be achieved by making online processes and interactions unified and keeping language and tasks in navigation to a minimum. External visitors should find it easy to apply and not face a confusing and overly elaborate process.

In the recent IBM study already mentioned—in most areas the challenges and approaches of higher education mirrored the business world IT issues—education CEOs were found not to place much emphasis on plans for simplification. In my experience, many institutions today are simply not structured to provide the level of simplification that the recruitment and course selection processes need and as a result their technology infrastructures also suffer from similar confusion.

In a 2008 U.K. study by JISC, The Use of Technology to Support Admissions to Higher Education, the following recommendations were made in regard to the online applications process.

- Provide information early
- Respond appropriately
- Always respond
- Get the evidence
- Communicate efficiently and effectively
- Know your feedback system works

These sensible recommendations were defined when considering the recruiting process. Although the U.K. does have a centralized admissions process for students, many of the findings listed below ring true for North American schools.

**Provide information early (and keep providing it in the context of the user's progress).** Web technology today means that you are now able to "follow" your site visitor and provide related contextual information as they navigate the site, and encourage them take action, or interact, when the time is right.

**Respond appropriately and always respond.** This is of tremendous importance and the key to online conversion is to get your online visitor to ask you to respond. When it comes to the application process on many higher education Web sites, we are reminded of the early days of e-commerce. In those early days the drop-off prior to transacting was enormous. This was overcome in the long run, because technology began to support dynamic contextual information. Now, with technology keeping contextual banners and links like "apply now," "related courses," or "take a campus tour" visible as your visitor progresses through the site, applications will increase. It is this interactive or collaborative aspect of technology that makes it able to respond strategically and improve recruitment conversion and prospective student relationships.

**Get the evidence . . . Communicate efficiently and effectively . . . Know your feedback system works.** The technologies at play in this new picture are new generation content management systems (CMS) that ensure you can analyze the path and results of your recruiting efforts, and on the back-end the critical constituent relationship management system (CRM) that may be the key data backbone of your prospective, current, and graduate student relationship and development processes.

## RETENTION: HOW TECHNOLOGY IS A CRITICAL ENABLER OF STUDENT SUCCESS

A good example of how to use technology to retain students is the Virtual Campus initiative by Career Education Corp. Chosen as the 2009 Computerworld Honours award recipient in the Education and Academia category, Virtual Campus lets students attend classes; visit a library; meet with instructors, tutors and other students; access financial aid and other administrative services; and participate in clubs all online. They can also take part in social activities through areas like a Virtual Commons and can even attend virtual graduation ceremonies. Instructors can interact with students and one another, and they can access course development systems.

Virtual Campus is a distance education initiative that absolutely addresses the growing strategic importance of delivering education in the format that is best for the student. The development of campus portals that integrate Learning Management Systems (LMS) and encourage a sense of community, along with providing the day-to-day information that your constituents require is an increasingly important element for student retention. The early days of failed initiatives and massive expenses on student portals were not all in vain. Moving forward, portals will be less about technology and more about communication, delivery, and interaction.

Today's students have a culture of communication that is both immediate and constant. Institutions need to adjust to managing this or suffer the consequences, which is often higher dropout rates. A simple example of utilizing technology to solve strategic issues is in the logic that Georgia Gwinnett College employed when it decided to offer cell phones to its more than 300 full- and part-time faculty members and encouraged them to respond to any calls or texts from students. According to Lonnie D. Harvel, Georgia Gwinnett's vice-president for instructional technology, "a cost analysis demonstrates that the program saves more money than it costs," (2010). Harvel goes on to say that the benefits are "only valid if the institution is intent on expending resources on student engagement." As Tom Mundie, dean of the School of Science and Technology commented, "engagement, after all, is a two-way street; faculty are expected to be responsive to the needs of students, just as students are expected to be responsive to the expectations of their professors." So it would appear that encouraging engagement is a key success factor in the drive for student retention.

The most effective digital platforms have shifted from "disruptive" to "productive" by providing a service or utility . . . [They] fundamentally change the approach from "how we reach our customers" to "how we make their lives better" (Martin and Todorov, 2010).

Staying in this mobility vein, consider the latest mobile/wireless trend, the Apple iPad. Although it still does not have a phone (but with Skype and Google Voice does it need one?), the iPad is shaking the very foundation of information delivery and interaction. The iPad revolution is happening in the midst of a generational shift in technology that will see the decline of the PC as we know it and the rise of mobile Web and the Cloud. A proliferation of smart mobile devices (iPad, Android, BlackBerry, and other smartphones) connecting to the Cloud is an inevitable conclusion. The final debate on standards is ongoing (or has Apple already won?), but without a doubt Google, Apple, and Amazon are the early drivers and may be the winners—although we can expect some new names.

The chart below shows that after only a few months, iPad usage has moved closer to traditional PCs—and this is only the first version of the iPad! According to some higher education commentators the jury is still out on iPad acceptance; however, we do not think they are going by the numbers or realize that the current iPad is in its first generation.

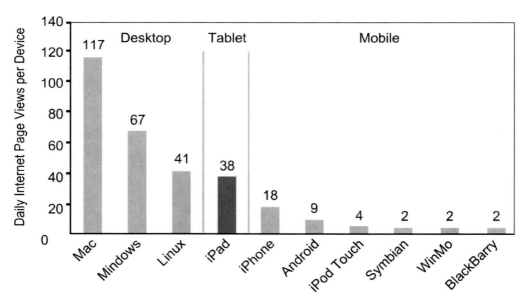

## iPad Internet usage closer to traditional PCs

Source: **Company data, comScore, Gartner, Net Applications, Morgan Stanley Research**

Source: **Business Insider**

## Global iPad Shipments (Thousands of Units)

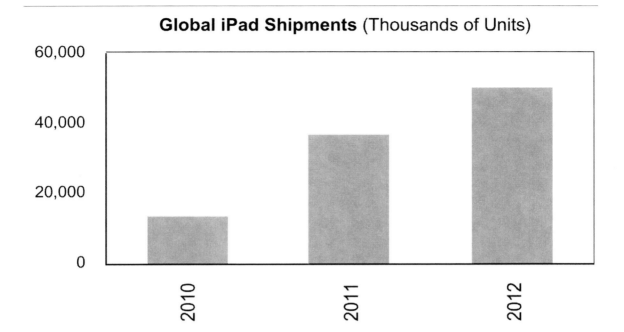

In July 2010, iSuppli predicted Apple will ship 12.9 million iPads in 2010 and that shipments will rise to 36.5 million in 2011 and 50.4 million in 2012. With these kinds of numbers in play, it is evident that tablet-based delivery of information will become the standard in the very near future; therefore, expect significant changes in the use of textbooks, delivery of lectures, peer collaboration, and research. Everything becomes more immediate and portable.

The overarching trend seems to be clear. Higher education needs to find ways to deliver information to these kinds of devices as soon as possible to improve its relationship with future and current students. Naturally, any technology enabler still requires users who to want to learn, and no device can do that, but we are living in changing times and the iPad is exactly the kind of disruptive technology that provides challenges to the existing information structure. We would argue that rather than being disruptive, the "luxury model" that represents the prevailing higher education infrastructure is unlikely to survive what is turning into a prolonged economic downturn. Parents are much less willing to take on debt than they were and much more willing to look abroad for better deals or to encourage their kids to find educational achievement in more innovative ways.

This year, APOL (University of Phoenix) has an enrolment of 478,000 students with a budget of $4.8 billion. This year, the University of Florida has an enrolment of 50,000 students with a budget of $4.9 billion. APOL employs 49,800 teachers and staff with a ratio of nine students for each staff member. Meanwhile, the University of Florida, with more than

900 buildings on a 2,000-plus-acre campus and a staff of 16,000 has a ratio of three students for each staff member. And while the University of Florida continues to raise its rates and beg the legislature for more money because its budget runs more red ink than Chairman Mao's *Little Red Book*; APOL expects to make an $830 million profit (http://newsok.com/university-of-phoenix-stocks-may-soon-soar/article/3503062).

The Internet also poses a growing threat to what Bill Gates calls "place-based colleges." Online, you can listen to the world's best lecturers for next to nothing—yet because of the cost of delivery the business of online education is very good. To a degree many of America's universities have lost their way badly in the era of easy money. If they do not find it again, they may go the way of General Motors; therefore, on the retention front, like the recruitment area, it is the delivery of information that represents the greatest need for strategic and innovative approaches.

In the fall of 2010, all first year undergraduate students at Seton Hill in Pennsylvania will receive a 13-inch MacBook Pro laptop and an iPad. Students will have complete access to these mobile technologies for classes as well as at all times for personal use. After two years, Seton Hill will replace the laptop with a new one—one that students can take with them when they graduate! With this technology at their fingertips, students can create a just-in-time learning environment, stay in touch with professors, advisors, and classmates, research any topic at any time, engage in hybrid and fully online courses, and access a whole host of Seton Hill technology services. In doing so, students will be learning the technological skills they'll need in the twenty-first century workforce.

Seton Hill faculty members (who will be equipped with the same mobile technologies as the students) have been trained to use the best of modern technology to expand learning opportunities. In this way, Seton Hill is training students of all learning styles and abilities to be better researchers, better at compiling and organizing data, and better at publishing and presenting information—better, in fact, at becoming lifelong learners who can easily adapt to new situations and new technologies in their lives and careers. (http://www.setonhill.edu/techadvantage/)

To conclude, it is fair to say that over the next five to ten years, higher education can expect an even faster and more competitive adoption of technologies that will facilitate the creation and adoption of new methods of distributing information, learning and collaboration online, from the public Web site, from learning systems, and from student information systems. On his www.m-trends.org blog, Rudey de Waele compiled a list of mobile trends from numerous contributors. The five we have listed here represent a final perspective that hopefully reinforces some of the thoughts we have offered here and also may provide more direction on strategic technology trends in the next three to five years.

1. Over 50 percent of the world's households will carry a mobile device, i.e., 3G+ (what will it mean for collaboration and new e-learning apps?)

2. Mobile Internet will surpass the wireline Internet in global REACH (distance learning will become a true mobile trend).

3. Thanks to Bluetooth and wireless display technology, the mobile phone will literally be the only computer people own (so whether it is iPad or not, new learning apps will have to be developed to retain students).

4. All urban areas offer free (or funded by taxpayer) Wimax connectivity. Landlines are gone and with them go our current limitations with connectivity—bandwidth will not be an issue).

5. Mobile overtakes the PC as the largest marketing channel, offering the best results and tracking in the history of marketing (current PC applications will change dramatically on a functional and platform level).

**REFERENCES**

Benioff, Marc  (2010, March). *Hello, iPad. Hello, Cloud 2.*, TechCrunch. Accessed at http://techcrunch.com/

Blue Hue Education. *Scrolling towards enrollment: Web site content and the e-expectations of college-bound seniors.* Retrieved April 9, 2010, from http://www.bluehueeducation.com/pdfs/9_ScrollTowardEnrollment.pdf

Carr, N. G. (2004). *Does IT matter? Information technology and the corrosion of competitive advantage.* Boston, MA: Harvard Business School Publishing.

de Waele, R. (2010). *Change and innovation in the new mobile economy.* Retrieved from http://www.m-trends.org

Farber, D. (2008, June). *CNET News.* Accessed at http://news.cnet.com/

Fathi, M. & Wilson, L. (2009). *Strategic planning in colleges and universities, The business renaissance quarterly: Enhancing the quality of life at work,* 4 (1).

IBM Global CEO Study: *Capitalizing on complexity (2010).* Full report available at: www.ibm.com/capitalizingoncomplexity

Ingerman, B. & Yang, C. (2010). *EDUCAUSE: The top ten IT issues.*

JISC (2008). *The use of technology to support admissions to higher education.* Retrieved from http://www.jisc.ac.uk/whatwedo/programmes/elearningcapital/admissions.aspx

Kolowich, S. (2010). *Can you hear me now? Inside highered.* Retrieved from http://www.insidehighered.com/layout/set/popup/news/2010/08/19/cellphones

Lenhart, A., Purcell, K., Smith, A. and Zickuhr, K. (2010). *Social media and young adults, The PEW Internet and American Life Project.* Retrieved March 25, 2010, from http://www.pewinternet.org/Reports/2010/Social-Media-and-Young-Adults.aspx

Madden, M. (2009). *The audience for online video sharing shoots up. The PEW Internet and American life project.* Retrieved March 25, 2010, from http://www.pewinternet.org/Reports/2009/13--The-Audience-for-Online-VideoSharing-Sites-Shoots-Up.aspx

Martin, K. & Todorov, I. (2010). *Blitz, engine digital.* Accessed at http://blog.enginedigital.com/tag/2010/

McGovern, G. (2010). *The stranger's long neck: How to deliver what your customers really want online.* London: A&C Black.

Rainie, L. (2010). *Internet, broadband and cell phone statistics. The PEW Internet and American life project.* Retrieved March 25, 2010, from http://www.pewinternet.org/Reports/2010/Internet-broadband-and-cell-phone-statistics.aspx

Schumpeter. (2010, September). *Declining by degree: Will America's universities go the way of its car companies? The Economist.* Retrieved from http://www.economist.com/node/16941775?story_id=16941775

Tapscott, D. & Williams, A. (2010) *Macrowikinomics: Rebooting business and the world.* New York: Penguin Group.

# CHAPTER EIGHT
## ORGANIZATIONAL CAPACITY FOR SEM

### BY LYNDA WALLACE-HULECKI

In a previous chapter by this author on reframing SEM from the academic lens, the first of two primary challenges in creating a high performance enrolment organization was discussed—fostering a campus-wide SEM ethos that is rooted within the academic context. In this chapter, the second primary challenge is addressed—building a high performance enrolment organization at the operational level.

This chapter is structured in two parts. Part I begins with a brief introduction on the importance of performance management within today's higher education context and a simple framework to clarify the interrelated concepts of organizational performance and capacity, followed by a discussion of the characteristics commonly associated with high performing organizations with particular attention to higher education. Drawing from the concepts and frameworks presented, Part I culminates with a portrait of the defining features and characteristics associated with a high performing "enrolment" organization. Part II presents a brief overview of the common barriers to achieving optimal organizational performance, followed by a model and guidelines for building organizational capacity to create the conditions for optimal SEM performance.

## PART I

# DEFINING HIGH PERFORMANCE WITHIN THE CONTEXT OF HIGHER EDUCATION AND SEM

### INTRODUCTION

Higher education is not immune to the forces of environmental conditions or to changes in the marketplace. Since the mid-1990s, following a dramatic reduction in the level of federal-provincial government transfer payments in Canada, the higher education system has been under strain. With the advent of rising costs and declining funding within a social policy context of "access to education," Canada's public colleges and universities have been perpetually challenged to increase enrolment while simultaneously reducing reliance on public funding and responding to rising expectations of students and their parents who have borne much of the financial impact. Throughout this period and to the present, many institutions have been challenged to "evolve, adapt, or desist" in response (Swail, 2002, pp. 15–16), and to reconsider traditional models across all aspects of operation. Issues of postsecondary access, quality, funding and affordability, and accountability have been at the forefront of policy review and have led to higher education reforms across the provinces. These events have had reverberating effects on individual institutions and on the role of institutional leaders of those organizations.

With the ever-present challenges of managing the nexus between student enrolment, financial imperatives, and academic missions, it is not surprising that the concept of SEM emerged in Canada and took hold as a professional field of practice over this same period of time. Not unlike the private sector, public and nonprofit organizations that want to survive, prosper, and do good, must respond to the changing environmental context (Bryson, 2004). In times of rapid change, research suggests that "incremental" changes, such as organizational restructuring, reducing costs, or downsizing the workforce, are seldom sufficient. Rather, there is a need to make "transformational" changes, which means changing the way we approach and respond to the changing environmental context (Horton, 2003).

Over the past three decades, the literature has exploded with new strands of research in order to understand the dynamics associated with "high performing" organizations. Studies have abounded in an effort to define the characteristics associated with organizational excellence, and to understand the relationship between organizational performance and the conditions associated with performance improvement, such as leadership styles, change-management approaches, applications of systems theory and strategic management, service orientation, quality improvement processes, performance measurement, to name a few. Much of this research has been grounded in the practices of the private sector. However, in recent years there has been growing attention given to these concepts within the public and nonprofit sectors, and notably within higher education for the reasons elucidated above.

A discussion of the characteristics of a high-performing organization within the context of SEM must first be grounded in an understanding of the concepts underlying organizational performance, which is undeniably broad and complex in nature; therefore, it is important to begin this chapter with a simple framework to clarify the concepts and language that frame the discussion of building a high performing enrolment organization.

## OVERVIEW OF THE INTER-RELATED CONCEPTS OF ORGANIZATIONAL PERFORMANCE AND CAPACITY

A simple, yet empirically grounded framework for understanding the complexities of organizational performance has been developed by the International Development Research Centre (IDRC) and Universalia Management Group based upon extensive research in a range of organizations (nonprofit and private) throughout the world (Lusthaus, Adrien, Anderson, & Carden, 1999). In the schematic representation of the IDRC/Universalia model presented in Figure 1 below, organizational performance and capacity are shown as interrelated concepts. The framework defines performance in relation to four primary elements:

1. **Effectiveness**—an organization's ability to fulfill its functional goals relative to its mission

2. **Efficiency**—an organization's ability to realize value for the money expended

3. **Relevance**—an organization's ability to align its mission, goals, programs, and activities with the evolving needs of its key stakeholders and constituents

4. **Financial viability**—an organization's ability to raise the funds required to meets its functional requirements in the short, medium, and longer term

The framework implies that certain contextual forces drive an organization's performance, and include:

- Organizational motivation—an organization's history, mission, culture, and incentive/reward systems;

- Organizational capacity—an organization's ability to use its resources (people, financial, physical, infrastructure, information, technology) to learn and change in realization of its goals through the application of management systems and practices (e.g., strategic leadership, change management, governance structures, etc.);

- External environment—the enabling environment in which an organization operates (e.g., economic, political, socio-cultural, demographic, technological) that impact the organization's ability to perform effectively and realize its goals

*Figure 1:* *Schematic Representation of the IDRC/Universalia Model*

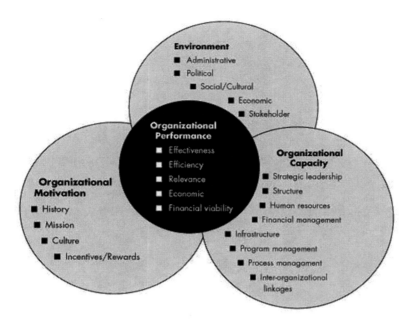

**Source:** *From Organizational Assessment: A Framework for Improving Performance, by C. Lusthaus, M-H Adrien, G. Anderson, F. Carden, & G. Montalván (2002, p. 10). International Development Research Centre and Inter-American Development Bank. Reproduced with permission.*

In application, the IDRC/Universalia framework defines an organization to be a "good performer" when it balances effectiveness (i.e., the ability to achieve its goals), efficiency (i.e., results relative to resources invested), and relevance to stakeholders over time (implying an ability to innovate) in keeping with its mission, while remaining financially viable (Lusthaus, Adrien, Anderson, Carden, & Montalván, 2002, pp. 11–12). By extension, the measurement of organizational performance in relation to each of the four elements is a function of its mission. For example, organizations within the public and nonprofit sectors tend to define and measure their performance in relation to "creating public value" that advances the public interest and common good at a reasonable cost; whereas, for-profit organizations tend to define their performance more in relation to maximizing net revenues (Moore, 1995, 2000 cited in Bryson, 2004, p. 8).

In considering the capacity of an organization to improve its performance, it follows that it is the ability of an organization to adapt old capabilities (i.e., resources, infrastructure) to new environmental threats and opportunities, as well as to create new capabilities in consideration of environmental forces of change. Strategic planning, organizational assessment, and change management processes are often the vehicles by which capacity development strategies are identified and executed.

## CRITERIA COMMONLY ASSOCIATED WITH HIGH PERFORMING ORGANIZATIONS

A strong body of research has emerged in recent years related to the defining characteristics of "high performing" organizations and the conditions associated with organizational capacity for change. The latter topic is considered by some to be a nascent field of research of growing interest to today's organizational leaders (Judge & Blocker, 2008). While much of the current research emanates from studies in the private sector, many useful insights and perspectives can be drawn that are of relevance to the public and nonprofit sectors, and specifically to this discussion pertaining to higher education. For purposes of illustration, the following examples have been drawn from contemporary authors of popular books on organizational performance and leadership.

- **Ken Blanchard,** author of the best selling series *Leading at a Higher Level* (2010), purported that in high-performing organizations, everyone's energy is focused on being: 1) a provider of choice, 2) an employer of choice, and 3) the investment of choice. He associated high-performing organizations with **FLEXIBILITY, NIMBLENESS, AND RESPONSIVE SYSTEMS** that can demonstrate results consistently over time. Blanchard drew from the extensive research of Drs. Carew, Kandarian, Parisi-Carew, and Stoner on defining and identifying the characteristics of high performing organizations (HPOs). These researchers defined HPOs as "enterprises that over time continue to produce outstanding results with the highest level of **HUMAN SATISFACTION** and commitment to success" (p. 9). According to this line of research, six elements of strength were commonly exhibited by HPO organizations:

**S** = SHARED INFORMATION AND OPEN COMMUNICATION
**C** = COMPELLING VISION
**O** = ONGOING LEARNING
**R** = RELENTLESS FOCUS ON CUSTOMER RESULTS
**E** = ENERGIZING SYSTEMS AND STRUCTURES
**S** = SHARED POWER AND HIGH INVOLVEMENT

At the core of the HPO SCORES™ model is the ability to build a **VISIONARY ORGA-NIZATION** that endures beyond the leader (p. 13), whereby participatory and collaborative **LEADERSHIP PRACTICES** and values permeate the organization. According to the authors, in HPO organizations, attention is given to the **DEVELOPMENT OF HUMAN CAPITAL** and to the **FOSTERING OF A LEARNING ORGANIZATION**—a term popularized by Peter Senge in his 1990 book *The Fifth Discipline*. A learning organization in this context refers generally to an organization's investment in the learning and development of both its people, as well as in the continuous improvement of its programs, services, and processes, and to the application of the knowledge gained to new situations.

- **Jim Collins** is perhaps best known for his popular book, *Good to Great* (2001). The pivot point in his research is what he termed the "Hedgehog Concept"—the essence of which is to attain piercing clarity about how to produce the best long-term results, and then to exercise **RELENTLESS DISCIPLINE** in focusing the organization on three things: 1) What you are deeply passionate about, 2) What you can be the best in the world at, and 3) How can you develop a sustainable resource engine to deliver superior performance relative to your mission. Collins suggested that in good-to-great companies, a "culture of discipline" existed that when combined with an ethic of **ENTREPRENEURSHIP** led to magical alchemy of great performance (p. 13). In his monograph, *Good to Great and the Social Sectors: Why Business Thinking Is Not the Answer* (2005), Collins rejected the idea that the primary path to greatness in the social sector is to become "more like a business." His argument stemmed from the standpoint that most businesses are mediocre, so why would you want to emulate them? The challenge particular to the social sector, he argued, is that executive leaders must rely on people who are often underpaid (or unpaid as is the case with volunteers) relative to the private sector. Collins advanced the perspective that it is not how (or how much) you pay, but who you have on the bus. From his informed perspective, people are not your most important asset. **THE RIGHT PEOPLE IN THE RIGHT SEATS** are.

- **Bolman & Deal** in their 1997 highly acclaimed book, *Reframing Organizations: Artistry, Choice, and Leadership,* presented a four-frame model for diagnosing an organization's situational context to assist change leaders in conceptualizing different approaches to leadership. The model is based on four frames from which to reimagine the reality of a situation (i.e., structural, human resource, political, and cultural). Pivotal to their model is A THOUGHTFUL, EXPLICIT PHILOSOPHY OF HOW TO TREAT PEOPLE (p. 122).

- **Robert Quinn** conceptualized a new model of leadership, not as behaviours and techniques, but as a state of being. In his book, *Building the Bridge as You Walk On It: A Guide for Leading Change* (2004), Quinn theorized that organizational excellence tends not to be a function of "imitation," but rather a function of **ORIGINATION**. He posited that transformative leaders know how to enter a creative personal state of leadership that becomes infectious and gives rise to a creative collective state of leadership that permeates all levels of operation of an organization.

- Empirical studies conducted in the early 1990s by Cameron and his colleagues (Cameron, Freeman, & Mishra, 1991; Cameron, 1992; Cameron, 1995) in more than 100 organizations that had engaged in Total Quality Management (TQM) and downsizing as strategies for enhancing effectiveness, produced unequivocal results. When TQM, downsizing, and other change initiatives were implemented independent of a culture change, they were unsuccessful (Cameron and Quinn, 1999, 2006). While the literature suggests that in most organizations, culture evolves over time by default, and that there is no "right" culture associated with high-performing organizations, some have postulated that there is one common feature among high performing organizations—**THE CULTURE "SERVES THEIR PEOPLE, CUSTOMERS, AND STAKEHOLDERS EQUALLY"** (Blanchard, 2010). Therefore, understanding the predominant culture value orientations within an organization is a critical element in motivating change and improved performance (Lusthaus et al., 2002, p. 87). Culture reflects fundamental values and implicit assumptions about how an organization functions (Cameron and Quinn, 1999, 2006). There is abundant literature that substantiates the symbiotic relationship between employee satisfaction and customer satisfaction. Highly regarded scholars and researchers such as Tom Peters, Ron Zemsky, Peter Drucker, Jack Zenger (and Zenger-Miller executives) among others have all reached the same conclusion. People are the institution's capacity to produce results. How you deploy them, support them, develop them, treat them, and lead them largely determines how well your students (among other key constituents) are served and, in turn, how well your organization performs (Clemmer, 1992).

Admittedly, the selected resources represent a very few within a literature pool that is rich and extensive; however, two general observations can be drawn from these notable works that are of significance here:

1. Strategic leadership, visioning, culture management, and investment in people are repeatedly emphasized as fundamental conditions for high performance; and

2. There is striking similarity between the general themes ascribed throughout the above-referenced literature that emanates from the private sector and the categories associated with "performance excellence" that are encapsulated within the Malcolm Baldrige Education Criteria for Performance Excellence presented in Table 1 below.

## PERFORMANCE EXCELLENCE IN HIGHER EDUCATION

The Malcolm Baldrige Education Criteria for Performance Excellence (MBECPE) is among the best known published frameworks to measure, assess, and improve quality and performance specific to the education sector. Since the late 1980s, the standards associated with the MBECPE have been increasingly used within higher education as a tool for measuring performance and planning in an uncertain environment. The Malcolm Baldrige assessment framework is intended to assist educational institutions with an integrated approach to performance management that results in delivery of ever-improving value to students and stakeholders, and that contributes to education quality and organizational stability, overall organizational effectiveness and capabilities, and organizational and personal learning.

*Table 1:* Malcolm Baldrige Education Criteria for Performance Excellence

| CATEGORIES OF PERFORMANCE | CORE VALUES AND CONCEPTS |
|---|---|
| 1. Leadership<br>2. Strategic planning<br>3. Customer management<br>4. Knowledge management<br>5. Workforce engagement<br>6. Process management<br>7. Results orientation | • Visionary leadership<br>• Learning-centred education<br>• Organizational and personal learning<br>• Valuing workforce members and partners<br>• Agility<br>• Focus on the future<br>• Managing for innovation<br>• Management by fact<br>• Societal responsibility<br>• Focus on results and creating value<br>• Systems perspective |

Source: 2009–10 Baldrige National Quality Program Education Criteria for Performance Excellence (pp. 1, 51, 57). Available at: http://www.baldrige.nist.gov/PDF_files/2009_2010_Education_Criteria.pdf

An abridged description of the 2009–10 MBECPE model is presented below. This description serves as the contextual background and organizing construct for discussion of the defining characteristics of a high performing "enrolment" organization within the context of SEM.

1. **Leadership**—and the **actions of senior leaders** are highlighted as critical to guiding and sustaining an organization, stimulating innovation, building knowledge and capabilities, and to setting organizational vision, values, and performance expectations. The importance of the **organization's governance system** is emphasized as a critical role of leadership in fulfilling its legal, ethical, and societal responsibilities, and in supporting its key communities.

2. **Strategic planning**—addresses how strategies and action plans are developed, how the plans are deployed and aligned with adequate resources, how plans are changed if circumstances require a change, and how accomplishments are measured and sustained. Performance excellence is associated with the capability of an organization to both develop and execute plans.

3. **Customer management**—recognizes the importance of how an organization seeks to engage students and stakeholders, with a focus on meeting student and stakeholder needs, building relationships, and building loyalty to the organization and its programs, offerings, and services.

4. **Knowledge management**—speaks to the importance of the quality, availability, and use of key information in driving improvement in student and operational performance and in stimulating innovation and strategy.

5. **Workforce engagement**—acknowledges the importance of key workforce practices in creating and maintaining a high-performance work environment with a strong focus on students and learning, where faculty staff are engaged and empowered.

6. **Process management**—considers how an organization's work systems, core competencies, and work process decisions create value for students and other key stakeholders and improve the organization's educational **effectiveness, efficiency** of operations, and **agility** in adapting quickly, flexibly, and effectively to changing requirements.

7. **Results orientation**—refers to the importance of an organization's key student learning outcomes, with the aim of demonstrating the effectiveness of educational programs and services in achieving value that leads to student and stakeholder satisfaction and engagement.

Embedded within the above-referenced seven performance criteria are a set of interrelated core values and concepts that derive from the literature on high-performing organizations and include:

- **Visionary leadership** in creating a student-focused, learning-oriented climate;

- **Learning-centred education** that involves ongoing monitoring of the changing and emerging needs of students and stakeholders and the factors that drive student learning, satisfaction, and persistence; and the appropriate translation of these needs into curricula and developmental experiences;

- **Organizational and personal learning** through the continuous improvement of existing programs and services to effect meaningful change and innovation; as well as through education and training opportunities for all staff and faculty (including volunteers) to enhance personal learning and skill development;

- **Valuing workforce members and partners** by creating workplace conditions that engender faculty and staff commitment, engagement, satisfaction, development, and well-being;

- **Agility** in the organization's capacity for fast and flexible response to the evolving needs of students, stakeholders, and society;

- **Focus on the future** through a forward looking and anticipatory approach to institutional planning and assessment;

- **Managing for innovation** that is ingrained within the learning culture of the organization to improve programs, services, processes, operations, and business model, if appropriate, in creating new value for stakeholders;

- **Management by fact** that is informed by a comprehensive and integrated performance measurement and analysis system that supports decisions related to student learning, performance improvement, and change management;

- **Societal responsibility** whereby institutional leaders serve as role models in focusing the organization on ethics and on the protection of public health, safety, and the environment;

- **Focus on results** and creating value for students and key stakeholders with the aim of building loyalty;

- **Systems perspective** that involves a holistic and integrated approach to planning by which all resources of the organization are consistently focused on goals for performance improvement and on meeting the needs of students and stakeholders.

The Malcolm Baldrige performance criteria, values, and concepts align closely with the fundamental tenets underlying effective SEM planning and practices, which are discussed in more detail below. The importance of **strategic leadership, visioning, culture management, and investment in people**, within a cultural context that is **student-focused and learning-oriented** are central to the defining features and characteristics of a high-performing enrolment organization.

## APPLICATION OF HIGH PERFORMANCE CRITERIA TO STRATEGIC ENROLMENT MANAGEMENT

The concepts and best practices associated with SEM have been described as an "eclectic patchwork of the best practices found in business and industry" that have been adapted to the academic context (Black, 2003). Backdating to the early 1990s, SEM was described as a process associated with **strategic planning and performance measurement** (Hossler & Bean, 1990; Dolence, 1993, 1997), and more recently as a **sophisticated management function** linked to resource management and accountability (Black, 2008c; Bontrager, 2004; Hossler, 2008; Norris, Baer, Leonard, Pugliese, & Lefrere, 2008; Kisling & Riggs, 2004). Throughout the literature, SEM has been referred to as a process of **culture change** (Kemer, Baldrige, and Green, 1982; Hossler and Bean, 1990; Henderson, 2001), and as a tool by which an organization of learning is transformed into a **learning organization** (Dolence, 1993, 1997; Senge, 1990).

An illustration of the relationship of SEM to performance management can be drawn from the work of George Kuh, who has conducted extensive research on the conditions that foster student engagement and success. Kuh is particularly known for his empirically-based research pertaining to the National Survey of Student Engagement (NSSE)—a study specifically designed to assess the extent to which students are engaged in "good educational practices" and what they gain from their educational experience. He is also reputed for his work on the Documenting Effective Educational Practices (DEEP, 2005) project—a study designed to discover and describe what strong-performing four-year colleges and universities do to foster student success—broadly defined to encompass reasonable levels of student engagement, satisfaction, and educational attainment.

Kuh (2006) observed that some large public universities have "beaten the odds" of their size, and multiple missions of teaching, research, and service to create the conditions for student success; and concluded that aspiring to anything less is a recipe for mediocrity. On the strength of his research, Kuh maintained that successful DEEP schools created a culture over time of **SHARED RESPONSIBILITY FOR EDUCATIONAL QUALITY AND STUDENT SUCCESS**—a topic discussed in a previous chapter in this book. Such processes required **FOCUSED LEADERSHIP** and **SYSTEMATIC REVIEWS** of policy and practice to test prevailing assumptions about student aspirations, motivations, as well as preferred learning styles, teaching approaches, and institutional practices, and the contribution of all of these to desired outcomes. In order to cultivate an ethic of "positive restlessness" that values student success, Kuh asserted that at the core is the need to address aspects of **INSTITUTIONAL CULTURE,** including whether reward systems and the criteria for distributing resources encourage or discourage people to work toward desired ends (Kuh & Whitt, 1988, In Kuh, 2006).

Drawing from the Malcolm Baldrige model of performance excellence in higher education, and following from best practices and research by thought leaders in the field of SEM (including this author's research), a portrait of the defining features and characteristics for a high performing enrolment organization has been developed and is presented in Table 2 below. **Eight primary features** and associated characteristics of a high-performing enrolment organization are presented that align closely with the Malcolm Baldrige model, as shown below:

| PRIMARY FEATURES OF HIGH PERFORMANCE IN SEM | MALCOLM BALDRIGE PERFORMANCE CATEGORIES |
|---|---|
| 1. Bold and disciplined leadership | Leadership |
| 2. A visionary enterprise | Strategic Planning |
| 3. Enabling structures & governance model | Governance—a sub-set of Leadership |
| 4. A campus-wide focus on students and student success | Customer Focus |
| 5. Knowledge management and people driven strategy | Knowledge Management |
| 6. Shared responsibility for performance improvement | Workforce Focus |
| 7. Service-oriented systems and practices | Process Management |
| 8. Effective use of strategic enrolment intelligence | Results Orientation |

A SEM capacity-building model and guidelines for creating the conditions for optimal SEM performance associated with these eight features are presented in Part II of this chapter, which follows.

*Table 2:* *Portrait of a High-performing Enrolment Organization*

| FEATURES | DEFINING CHARACTERISTICS |
|---|---|
| 1. BOLD AND DISCIPLINED LEADERSHIP | **Leadership** is demonstrated at all levels of the organization to:<br>• Strategically innovate<br>• Embrace and mobilize change<br>• Recalibrate resource allocation for optimal deployment, where "optimal" is defined within the academic context |
| 2. A VISIONARY ENTERPRISE | **SEM planning** leads to the development of a clear and compelling vision for the "ideal" experience the institution seeks to deliver to all students that:<br>• Is rooted in the academic context<br>• Is passionately embraced by campus constituents<br>• Is distinctive from that of competitors<br>• Leverages the organization's core competencies and resources<br>• Is future-oriented and aligned with changing environmental conditions<br>• Balances academic mission with student enrolment and financial imperatives |
| 3. ENABLING STRUCTURES & GOVERNANCE MODEL | **Organizational structures and governance** enable strategic thinking, dexterity in acting, and organizational learning through:<br>• Participatory approaches to management and decision-making<br>• Cross-divisional communication and collaboration |
| 4. A CAMPUS-WIDE FOCUS ON STUDENTS AND STUDENT SUCCESS | **Student and stakeholder focus** in policies, systems, and processes are:<br>• Student and stakeholder centred<br>• Learning-oriented<br>• Geared to building student and stakeholder loyalty and affinity<br>• Aligned with a holistic approach to student learning and development |

| FEATURES | DEFINING CHARACTERISTICS |
|---|---|
| **5. KNOWLEDGE MANAGEMENT AND PEOPLE DRIVE STRATEGY** | **Knowledge management** and people drive strategy development and implementation, whereby:<br>• Strategic decisions are tied to attracting, retaining, and developing the "right" people<br>• Individual and organizational learning are among the highest priorities |
| **6. SHARED RESPONSIBILITY FOR PERFORMANCE IMPROVEMENT** | **Knowledge management** and people drive strategy develop Workforce focus is demonstrated by a work environment that creates the conditions for:<br>• Empowered and engaged faculty and staff<br>• Teamwork and collaboration<br>• Individual and a collective focus on continuous quality improvement, where organizational "quality" is defined by the relevance of programs and services in meeting stakeholder needs<br>• Individual and organizational learning, which are tied to performance management, reward systems, and accountability with consequences |
| **7. SERVICE-ORIENTED SYSTEMS & PRACTICES** | **Process management** is service-oriented in nature with the aim of:<br>• Creating value for students and other key stakeholders through seamless service delivery (inside and outside the classroom)<br>• Improving organizational effectiveness, efficiency of operations, and agility in adapting to change |
| **8. EFFECTIVE USE OF STRATEGIC ENROLMENT INTELLIGENCE** | **Results orientation** is demonstrated by the systematic use of research and data as:<br>• Actionable intelligence—the right information to the right people at the right time to inform operational performance<br>• Strategic intelligence—to inform planning, development, innovation, and renewal of programs and services<br>• Enablers of organizational effectiveness—whereby return-on-investment is demonstrated on strategic initiatives<br>• Enablers of strategic dexterity and high-agility decision-making and action! |

# A MODEL AND GUIDELINES FOR BUILDING ORGANIZATIONAL CAPACITY FOR SEM

Jim Clemmer wrote in his book, *Firing on All Cylinders: The Service/Quality System for High-Powered Corporate Performance* (2nd ed.) that "[O]nly a tiny fraction of executives are prepared to pay the price of improved performance—although many are interested" (1992, p. 339). He argued that performance improvement requires commitment of the management team, an "assault" on deeply rooted customs and procedures, redeployment of resources with a focus on those you serve, and staying power during the period of cultural transition—in short, the commitment and bold leadership of the executive to stay the course of change during turbulent times. Part II of this chapter begins with a review of common barriers to achieving high organizational performance, and is followed by a presentation of a SEM capacity-building model and guidelines for building organizational capacity conditions for optimal SEM performance.

## COMMON BARRIERS TO ACHIEVING OPTIMAL ORGANIZATIONAL PERFORMANCE

As previously discussed, organizational capacity pertains to the ability of an organization to use its resources in order to learn and change in realization of its goals. An organization's capacity to improve its performance is a function of its leadership (doing the right thing), management (doing this right), and the application of sound strategic planning and management concepts that leads to strategic thinking, acting, and learning (Bryson, 2004). Clemmer's assertion that few executives are "willing to pay the price" is not surprising when one considers the substantive barriers to high performance that may be encountered. Drawing from the research of Bolman and Deal (1997) among others, typical barriers may include:

- Political issues (e.g., power and control agenda, interdepartmental conflict)

- Human resource issues (e.g., inadequate staffing levels or staff competencies/skills, lack of investment in organizational learning, lack of employee incentives tied to accountability)

- Structural issues (e.g., inefficient and/or outdated business processes, inaccurate or inaccessible information, inadequate or poorly utilized technology, poor communications particularly across functional and organizational boundaries, organizational structures that inhibit seamless service delivery)

- Symbolic issues (e.g., lack of strategic leadership, a culture that is not aligned with change)

To effectively anticipate and respond to the dramatic changes that have and will likely continue to affect higher education, today's institutional leaders must be adept at effectively deploying strategic planning and management concepts in assessing the institution's current performance relative to its mission, mandate, and stakeholder values; identifying environmental factors that present opportunities and threats to its future well-being; and promoting strategic thinking, action and learning (Bryson, 2004). These same concepts underlie effective SEM planning processes.

## A SEM CAPACITY-BUILDING MODEL

While many institutions have invested in strategic planning and in the development of enrolment plans to enhance student recruitment, marketing, and retention practices, many suffer from an inability to execute the plans (Black, 2008a, Copeland, 2009). At a leadership symposium this author attended a few years ago, a prominent and accomplished Canadian university president was the keynote speaker. At the end of the speech, the president was asked "What one piece of advice would you offer others based upon your leadership experience?" In response, the president indicated without hesitation, "I would have started by getting the right team of people into the right positions from day one." Interestingly, this is the same finding that Collins found from his good-to-great research. That is, invest first in the who (i.e., the right people in the right seats), and then define the what and how to get there.

The wisdom shared here applies at all levels of operation in high performing organizations, and  has been adopted as the underlying tenets of the SEM capacity-building model for a high performing enrolment organization advocated by this author and depicted in Figure 2 below. As shown in Figure 2, the SEM capacity-building model involves three core elements:

(1) **START WITH THE "WHO"**—Build an enrolment leadership team with the right people in the right seats to lead the way in creating the workplace conditions associated with a high performance organization.

**(2) DEFINE THE "WHAT"**—Foster strategic thinking, action, and learning through a SEM visioning and change management process by which a clear, single purpose for the "ideal" student experience is articulated and passionately embraced by campus constituents.

**(3) LEAD THE WAY TO THE "HOW"**—Invest in creating the conditions for success of your greatest asset—your people. This investment involves building the organizational capacity conditions as defined by policies, systems, structures, as well as your performance management and reward systems that motivate your people around a central purpose, empower them to assume shared responsibility for enrolment performance outcomes, and support them in achieving their highest potential in realization of the vision for change.

# Figure 2: SEM Capacity-Building Model for a High Performing Enrolment Organization

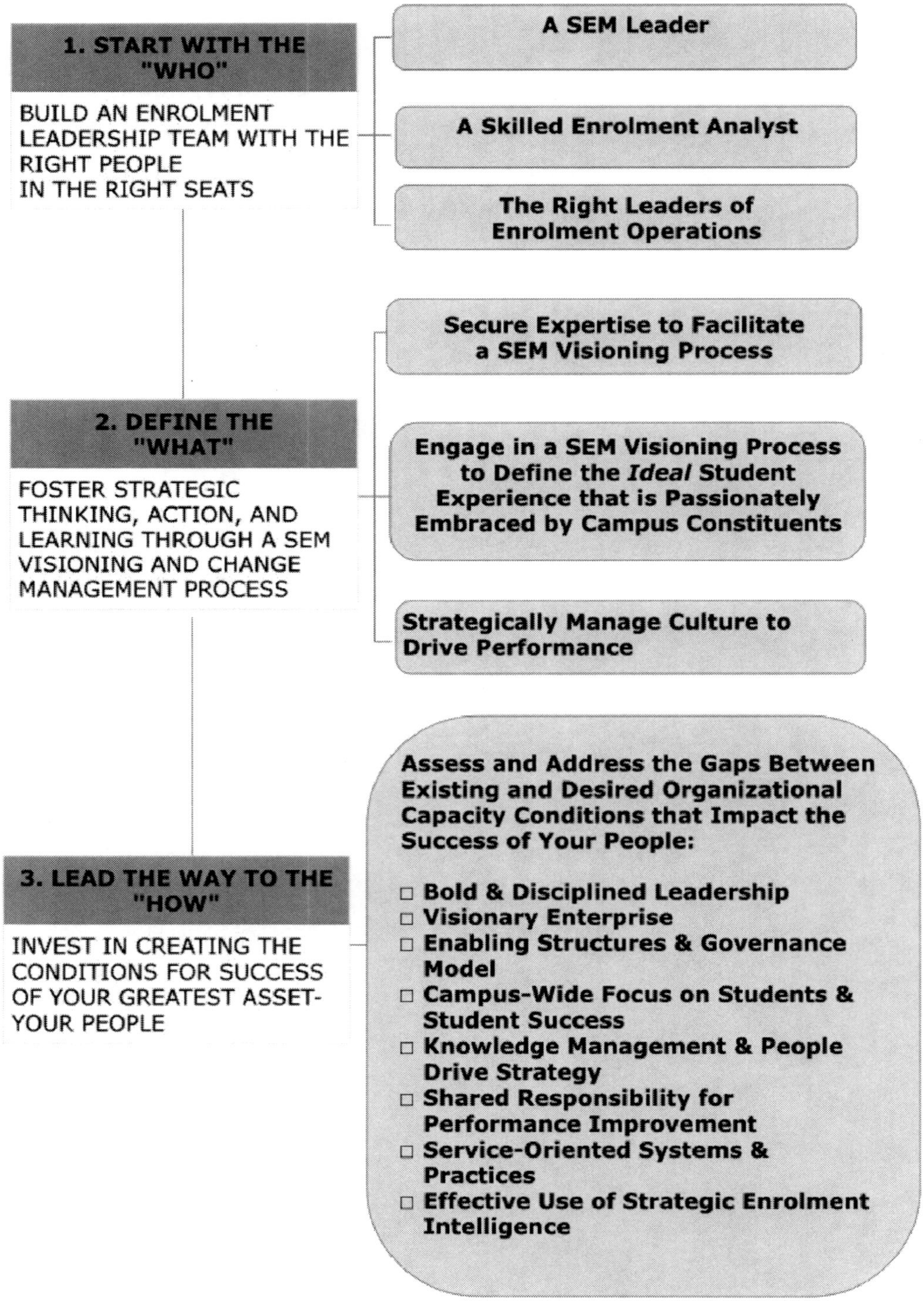

**1. START WITH THE "WHO"**

BUILD AN ENROLMENT LEADERSHIP TEAM WITH THE RIGHT PEOPLE IN THE RIGHT SEATS

- A SEM Leader
- A Skilled Enrolment Analyst
- The Right Leaders of Enrolment Operations

**2. DEFINE THE "WHAT"**

FOSTER STRATEGIC THINKING, ACTION, AND LEARNING THROUGH A SEM VISIONING AND CHANGE MANAGEMENT PROCESS

- Secure Expertise to Facilitate a SEM Visioning Process
- Engage in a SEM Visioning Process to Define the *Ideal* Student Experience that is Passionately Embraced by Campus Constituents
- Strategically Manage Culture to Drive Performance

**3. LEAD THE WAY TO THE "HOW"**

INVEST IN CREATING THE CONDITIONS FOR SUCCESS OF YOUR GREATEST ASSET-YOUR PEOPLE

Assess and Address the Gaps Between Existing and Desired Organizational Capacity Conditions that Impact the Success of Your People:

- ☐ Bold & Disciplined Leadership
- ☐ Visionary Enterprise
- ☐ Enabling Structures & Governance Model
- ☐ Campus-Wide Focus on Students & Student Success
- ☐ Knowledge Management & People Drive Strategy
- ☐ Shared Responsibility for Performance Improvement
- ☐ Service-Oriented Systems & Practices
- ☐ Effective Use of Strategic Enrolment Intelligence

## SEM CAPACITY-BUILDING GUIDELINES

Guidelines for implementing the SEM capacity-building model described in Figure 2 are presented below. The guidelines address the "who," the "what," and the "how" elements of the model. With regard to the "how," capacity building guidelines are offered in relation to each of the features of a high performing enrolment organization presented in Table 2. In combination, the model and guidelines provide a foundation to guide your journey in building organizational capacity for a high performing enrolment organization.

## 1. THE "WHO"— BUILD AN ENROLMENT LEADERSHIP TEAM

Central to all SEM initiatives are strategies that require change in the core enrolment management business functions typically associated with marketing, recruitment, financial aid, admissions, registrarial services, student services, and retention (e.g., student orientation, advising, first-year experience, counseling, career services). Successful change efforts require management of barriers to implementation. The effective management of barriers goes well beyond the responsibility of those who occupy formal leadership roles. In high performing organizations, the key is the empowerment of others, from the receptionist to the designated enrolment leader, in order that each individual can release their knowledge, experience, and motivation in contributing to the realization of the vision (Blanchard, 2010).

Leadership is a process that inspires and mobilizes others to take collective action in pursuit of a common purpose (Bryson, 2004). Leadership is needed throughout the organization to achieve optimal results that can be sustained over time. Within a workplace environment where people are empowered, individuals are driven by a sense of pride in performing their responsibilities and take ownership of the results achieved. Three keys are often associated with empowerment in the workplace: 1) information is shared freely to build trust, organizational learning, and responsibility, 2) there is clarity of performance boundaries, expectations, and accountabilities associated with the vision, and 3) cross-functional and self-directed teams work collectively to realize results (Blanchard, 2010). However, to foster empowerment within the workplace, strong leadership is required from those who hold formal leadership roles and are accountable for effecting change; therefore, your initial focus should be on identifying the very best people to occupy formal leadership roles associated with the following three fundamental capacity conditions for a high performing enrolment organization:

1. A Dedicated Enrolment Leader

2. A Skilled Enrolment Analyst

3. The Right Leaders of Enrolment Operations

## Capacity Condition 1—A SEM Leader

The importance of designating an enrolment champion to a position of influence was discussed in detail in the chapter on reframing SEM from the academic lens. The critical attributes of the individual as well as options to fill the void if such an individual is not readily available were also presented; however, beyond securing the right person in the role, you must ensure the conditions for the individual's success are in place. On the strength of experience, this author ardently believes that to be successful, the designated enrolment leader requires the following support conditions:

- An internal mentor from among the academic deans who is well-attuned to the academic culture and institutional politics of "how things get done";

- An external professional SEM mentor in cases when the incumbent is new to the field or is a less-experienced professional;

- A seat at the dean's council or equivalent advisory council to the provost/vice-president academic;

- A seat at the budget and resource planning decision table; and

- A dedicated enrolment analyst to support the enrolment planning process.

The latter support condition is unarguably a fundamental condition to effective SEM practice and constitutes capacity condition #2.

## Capacity Condition 2—A Skilled Enrolment Analyst

For SEM planning to be strategic, it must be guided by research and data. In its absence, an investment in the SEM planning process and implementation strategies are likely to provide only tactical and short-term benefits (Black, 2008a). Insights gleaned from the systematic collection and analysis of enrolment performance measurement information and market research are prerequisites to creating a highly functional enrolment management organization that is strategic and market-oriented. In the least, one skilled enrolment analyst must be in place to support the enrolment leader. This is a fundamental capacity condition that may require a recalibration of how human resources are allocated. The responsibilities of this position may include:

- Track and report enrolment trends associated with enrolment operations (e.g., student inquiries, applications, admits/declined offers, enrolment yields, student attrition and persistence rates, etc.)
- Conduct strategic research and analyses (e.g., retention studies, return on investment analyses)
- Produce financial aid leveraging models and yield analyses
- Conduct market research and analyses, student surveys, and student flow studies
- Undertake environmental scanning to monitor changes in external conditions and the competitive marketplace

However, generating the information and research intelligence meets only half of the capacity condition. The other half of the equation resides in the appropriate use of the research and data in strategic decision-making and in the allocation of institutional resources—a responsibility and accountability that must be engrained in organizational performance management systems—a topic to be addressed in more detail under Capacity Conditions 10 and 11 below.

## Capacity Condition 3—The Right Leaders of Enrolment Operations

The process of introducing transformative change that shifts the culture of an organization requires both a willingness and ability to change (Kotter, 1995 and Owen, 2001). Unless your management team is in synch with the new direction, embarking on the change effort will only lead to cynicism (Clemmer, 1992). Therefore, choose your leadership team within enrolment operations wisely. Determining who should be on your leadership team (and who should not be) requires bold decisions and informed judgment about the character and attributes of people. In keeping with the features of a high- performing enrolment organization, these individuals should be purpose-centred, people-focused, strategic thinkers, innovators, and managed risk-takers. In selecting people to assume leadership positions, consideration should be given to their ethical conduct, work ethic, dedication to fulfilling commitment, basic intelligence, values, political acumen, among other desired leadership attributes. As change leaders, these individuals must possess the ability to engender open and trusting relationships and also be willing to commit to deep change and embrace uncertainty. From personal experience, this author recommends that the following criteria be weighted heavily in determining who should lead your enrolment services operations:

- Passion for excellence
- Service-orientation
- Professional ethics
- Ability to leverage information and data in strategic decisions
- Systems perspective on how their unit contributes to the success of the institution
- Management style in creating optimal workplace conditions for employee success
- Leadership philosophy on their role in developing leadership potential in others

The latter point is deserving of specific attention here. In an organization that is focused on the development of human capacity—your people—attention must be given to building leadership potential in others through effective mentorship and through more formal leadership programs. Preparing the "next generation of leaders" is considered by some to be fundamental to the role of those who occupy leadership positions (Quinn, 2004); therefore, consider carefully who occupies formal leadership roles in your enrolment services operations. The following three guiding principles may prove useful in governing this process:

**a**. When hiring into a vacant or new position and you are in doubt, don't hire. Find another way to fill the void until the right candidate can be found. Options to address the interim situation might include negotiating a temporary assignment of an experienced staff member from within the unit or from another unit, securing a consultant to fill the position on an interim basis, or engaging an experienced retired employee on a temporary assignment. Be creative. There is always a solution.

**b**. When an existing incumbent is considered not to be the best fit for the position they occupy, do not avoid making a decision. Seek a creative solution to redeploy the individual to a role that better suits his/her talents or to transition the individual to a new career opportunity.

**c**. Consider every position vacancy an opportunity to rethink and redefine the role, responsibilities, and skill requirements in keeping with the vision and changing environment.

Your actions in selecting your leadership team will send symbolic messages throughout the organization regarding your commitment to purpose, your support of people, and your leadership style. The importance of working with your human resource specialist to ensure integrity of process cannot be overstated.

## 2. THE "WHAT"—FOSTER STRATEGIC THINKING, ACTION, AND LEARNING THROUGH A SEM VISIONING AND CHANGE MANAGEMENT PROCESS

For leadership to be effective there must be a clearly articulated vision that is passionately embraced throughout your organization and that actively guides everyday decision-making. A student focus helps to anchor an enrolment management effort to a common purpose that most in higher education can embrace. The focus in articulating the vision needs to be on creating student loyalty and affinity to the institution with every interaction students have, as each interaction shapes the perception of those you serve (Black, 2008c). Through building student loyalty, you will be making a long-term investment in the future of the institution. However, if the culture does not change, your efforts will be futile. Therefore, the process of defining the vision for the student experience must be an inclusive, campus-wide process that engages and builds buy-in early on to increase the probability of the acceptance of change. An inclusive visioning process will engender trust and foster collaboration. Staff and faculty need to know that their perspectives matter and that they are valued. If well executed, there is incredible power of organizational visioning in inspiring excitement and commitment to a significant shared purpose (Blanchard, 2010). Many change experts agree that a strong, focused culture starts with a compelling vision (Blanchard, 2010; Clemmer, 1992). However, the process by which to create a compelling vision that is shared throughout the enterprise can be elusive. To address this capacity imperative, strong consideration should be given to the use of competent external experts to help navigate the "potholes, dead ends, and bogs on the perilous road" (Clemmer, 1992, p. 342).

### Capacity Condition 4—Secure Expertise to Facilitate a SEM Visioning Process

Often, it is helpful to secure the expertise of professional experts to facilitate the visioning process. If selecting an external expert to your institution, it is essential that you select an individual or firm that is the right fit to your organization and to working as a partner with you in the process. The following guidelines have been adapted from Clemmer (1992) to a SEM context, and may prove useful in this process:

- The firm uses an "open system" (a focus on the external environment and the inter-play between the internal and external forces of change) approach to planning that is adaptable to your organization's culture and context;

- The firm's planning framework balances the need for advancing both strategic and tactical strategies in tandem;

- Knowledge transfer is built into the consultancy process so that your organization can learn and develop the capacity for self-sufficiency;

- The firm has a breadth of professional services and capabilities from which to draw that are aligned with your organization's capacity needs, such as expertise in strategic planning and change management, strategic research, staff development programs and workshops, among other areas;

- The firm is networked within the field and has knowledge of and access to best practices and benchmarking data;

- The firm has a proven reputation for service quality and excellence;

- The firm uses a well-proven consultancy model and methods;

- The firm's consultancy approach fosters institutional ownership and engagement in the development and execution of strategies; and

- The firm works in partnership with you to develop and implement actionable and practical strategies that are grounded in good practice concepts and theories.

### Capacity Condition 5—Engage in a SEM Visioning Process

Ideally, a vision for the student experience should be a campus-wide initiative. With that said, "[V]ision is the responsibility of every leader at every level of an organization" (Blanchard, 2010, p. 27). The power of visioning is in the process of engaging your constituents in shaping the direction, and then in supporting people in achieving the desired ideal state of service to students. If effectively and expertly led, the SEM visioning process should result in the articulation of a vision for the "ideal" student experience, including an assessment of what features characterize the desired state as compared to the existing state. More specifically, the following elements should be addressed and clarified in the visioning process in order to create the foundation for defining the "HOW":

- Values-based principles that will guide strategic decisions related to the various dimensions of delivering on the student experience, such as the learning/teaching environment, student learning supports, student life environment, infrastructure conditions (e.g., teaching capacity, study space, technology, etc.), to name a few

- Key messages you desire to convey regarding your promise that is aligned with the values of each constituent group

- Student-centred service values that can be translated into behavioural expectations for performance management and accountability within the workplace

- Core organizational competencies that define the strengths of the organization on which to build

- Performance gaps that exist between the current state and desired state that will serve to focus the development of enrolment strategies

- Change management issues and obstacles

- Performance indicators, metrics, and measures that define what success looks like under the "ideal" state

- Strategic research questions that must be addressed to inform strategy development and implementation

## Capacity Condition 6—Strategically Manage Culture to Drive Performance

"If culture change is to be successful, everyone—from executive leaders, managers, supervisors, team leads, frontline staff—should be held accountable for achieving performance and living organizational values" in how they perform their respective roles (Blanchard, 2010, p. 249). A high-performing enrolment enterprise possesses an organization culture where student enrolment, student learning, and student success are viewed as shared responsibilities; where student relationships are cultivated from the initial point of inquiry throughout the student life cycle; and where knowledge sharing and accurate information are valued. In such a culture, it is everyone's job to ensure students are provided with the information they need to make sound and timely decisions. All employees take pride in maintaining data integrity, reducing student runaround, and preventing errors that cause student problems. The underlying premise of culture change is that you begin with an understanding of the existing culture in relation to two questions:

1. Do you understand the predominant values and beliefs that underlie how decisions are made in your organization?

2. Does the existing culture serve your organization?

Recognizing that the process of assessing culture is not an exact science, there are a number of tools that have been empirically tested, validated, and applied within the academic context, and that can offer valuable insights. For example, the Organizational Cultural Assessment Instrument (OCAI) developed by Cameron and Quinn (1999, 2006) is a six-item questionnaire that has been found to be useful in diagnosing the desire for change and discrepancies between the current and preferred culture values associated with change (refer to http://www.ocai-online.com/about-OCAI).

Regardless of the tool or methods you choose to use, what is important is that you ascertain an understanding of prevailing versus desired organizational values associated with the change effort. In this context, the basis of analysis can be at the institutional level and/or at the unit level where unique subcultures exist. Once known, you can determine what leadership styles, management roles, human resource management philosophy, service standards, quality management program, and effectiveness criteria may contribute to organizational performance improvement (Cameron and Quinn, 2002). Following from an understanding of the prevailing versus desired organizational values, the symbolic decisions and actions advanced by institutional leaders, if effectively and consistently managed, have the power to galvanize a change initiative.

## 3. "THE HOW" INVEST IN CREATING THE CONDITIONS FOR SUCCESS OF YOUR GREATEST ASSET—YOUR PEOPLE

Focusing on the critical gaps between the desired and the existing capacity conditions is what sets apart high performing organizations from those that are constantly dealing with the crisis of the day or are responding to enrolment challenges in a panic-driven mode (Black, 2008b). To successfully deliver the ideal student experience, you must focus on creating the conditions for the success of your greatest asset—your people. Determination of which gaps in capacity conditions offer the greatest potential return on investment in relation to the realization of your vision emanates from the SEM visioning process. While it is natural to focus on enhancing the conditions that already exist and on developing new capacities where none exist, there also must be a willingness to examine: a) what capacities in the form of people, processes, and systems should be discontinued, b) what resources should be real-located, and c) what staffing and organizational patterns must be changed in order to ensure the successful execution of your vision for change. Your openness to exploring new possibilities and letting go of the old will determine the impact of the SEM visioning process.

Fundamental capacity conditions associated with the features of a high performing enrolment organization as profiled in Table 2 are presented below. The capacity conditions are keyed to each of the eight defining features of a high performing enrolment organization. Each of the capacity conditions is described in relation to the core tenets underlying effective SEM practice, which are encapsulated within the defining characteristics described in Table 2. It should be noted that each of these capacity conditions is deserving of a level of discussion that goes well beyond what can be justly served within the scope of this chapter; therefore, it is anticipated that these topics will formulate the basis of future white papers and/or book chapters.

## Capacity Condition 7—"Bold and Disciplined Leadership" and "A Visionary Enterprise"

Given the interrelatedness of the role of leadership in SEM visioning and strategic planning, the capacity conditions associated with these two features of a high performing enrolment organization are discussed in combination here. The elusive nature of the terms "leadership" and "management" have generated considerable controversy in the literature regarding their meaning and the associated functions of "leaders" versus "managers." Some have offered the distinction that "managers do things right, and leaders do the right thing" (Bennis and Nanus, 1985 In Bohlman and Deal, 1997). By extension, the concept of management has often been associated with maintaining the peak performance of an organization in its present state, while leadership has been associated with developing the organization to sustain peak performance into the future. Others have argued that all managers should be encouraged to be leaders, and that "leadership" is "management" practiced well (Mintzberg, 2009). Regardless of the nuances of the vernacular, few would argue that both functions are required to successfully navigate today's rapidly changing environmental conditions.

Within the context of SEM, enrolment strategies have the highest potential of impacting institutional goals when those occupying leadership roles know the institution and those you serve, know the competition, know how to get things done on the campus, and know the environmental factors that may impact enrolment outcomes—that is, they have a systems planning perspective. Institutional leaders serve a critical role in inspiring and encouraging workforce engagement in strategic thinking, learning and acting, thereby creating a learning-oriented organization that is open to strategic innovation and change. The process of managing change requires sound planning and a great deal of flexibility and listening on the part of those in leadership roles; therefore, leadership development and change management programs are essential. Key capacity conditions include:

■ Leadership and management development programs are in place that address the following competency and skill areas (adapted from Lufthaus et al., 2002):

- Leadership skills in relation to collaboration (e.g., facilitation, coaching, and fostering dialogue), innovation (e.g., visioning, championing, and diffusing), integration (e.g., organizing, improving, and bridging), and production (e.g., targeting, improving, and measuring)

- Change management concepts and techniques

- Strategic planning concepts and techniques

- SEM planning concepts and techniques

- Niche management concepts to understand the fundamentals of managing distinctive competencies

■ Beyond formal training programs, strategies must be in place to sustain strategic intelligence that is gained through professional networks and strategic alliances, as well as to ensure the currency of institutional leaders is maintained on evolving trends and issues occurring within relevant professional fields of practice. Too often the resources associated with travel and attendance at conferences are eliminated during times of financial exigency. Institutional leaders at all levels and across all functions must foster healthy relationships with other education providers, government at all levels, research and funding agencies, professional associations, and the like. Organizational capacity and performance can effectively be leveraged through such means as maintaining active involvement in professional associations and networking groups, engaging in inter-institutional collaborations and joint ventures, to name a few.

## Capacity Condition 8—Enabling Structures and Governance Model

In its application, organizational structures deal with both how to allocate work and how to coordinate work across different roles and units. Coordination and control are achieved in two primary ways: 1) hierarchically—through top-down assigned authority, rules and policies, and planning and control systems (e.g., performance management systems), and 2) laterally—through meetings, task forces, coordinating roles, matrix structures, and networks. Formal structures both enhance and constrain what organizations can accomplish, and change over time as the capacity needs of the organization change. The literature suggests that organizations operating within more stable environmental contexts tend to create more vertical structures, while organizations operating within rapidly changing contexts tend to create more flexible, lateral structures (Bolman and Deal, 1997). The process of enrolment management and the mandate of enrolment managers by definition bring the institution into alignment with its changing environmental context through processes that yield campus-wide cooperation and coordination. With that said, designing a workable structure that leads to optimal organizational performance must take into account the capacity needs of the organization as it looks to the future—that is, its size, age, core processes, environment, culture, strategy and goals, technology, resources, and workforce characteristics. Therefore, there is no single structure that creates the ideal organizational conditions for SEM. However, the structures should serve to support cross-functional and cross-divisional coordination and collaboration to optimize resource use and maintain consistency in strategic focus. Key capacity conditions in Organizational Structures include:

- The structures that support student recruitment foster coordination and collaboration with institutional marketing, student communications, admissions, orientation, enrolment services, as well as with the academic units.

- The structures that support student retention and success permit proactive interventions in identifying and supporting students at risk, starting in the student recruitment process and throughout the student enrolment life cycle.

In relation to the governance model and decision-making processes, high-performing enrolment organizations align all of their institutional resources with the achievement of a single common purpose while maintaining financial vitality. In a SEM change process, which is grounded in the principles of shared responsibility for performance improvement, the business model and funding decisions serve as important levers. Of critical importance is the need for an enabling governance model through which agility in strategic decision-making can be achieved to support innovation and change and to advance institutional competitiveness. Key capacity conditions include:

- Governance structures enable "nimble, flexible, and responsive" decision-making, whereby academic program innovation and development are responsive to evolving constituent needs and emergent strategic opportunities that enhance institutional competitiveness.

- The business model of the institution appropriately balances the need for entrepreneurism with incentives for collaboration and coordination across divisional boundaries.

## Capacity Condition 9—A Campus-Wide Focus on Students and Student Success

Having the right programs and services in the right markets, delivered in a manner that is conducive to the needs and preferences of those served in those markets is mission critical; therefore, high- performing enrolment organizations engage in integrated planning with a focus on the needs of students, and on creating a student experience that engenders student loyalty and affinity to the institution. Therefore, mechanisms must be in place to ensure that the learning and development needs of students are understood and incorporated in an integrated manner in the design and delivery of academic programs and services. To this end, a holistic approach to student learning and development is required by which student affairs and enrolment professionals partner with the academic community in the education process. Key capacity conditions include:

- Mechanisms are in place to obtain and use continuous feedback from students and other key constituents with the aim of building a more student- and stakeholder-focused culture and identifying opportunities for innovation.

- A holistic approach to student learning and development underlies the student experience.

- Academic and enrolment planning processes are integrated and linked to resource allocation and budgetary decisions.

## Capacity Condition 10—Knowledge Management and People Driving Strategy

High-performing organizations attract, retain, and grow faculty, staff, and administrators who are a best-fit with the institution, its culture, and development directions. Strategic decisions and actions are driven by ensuring the right people are in the right positions to lead and execute the strategy. In creating a student-focused and learning-oriented culture, investments must be made to ensure that faculty, staff, and administrators have the information, skills, competencies, and tools they need to: a) remain sensitive to changing and emerging student/ stakeholder needs and the factors that drive student learning, satisfaction, and persistence; b) translate student/stakeholder needs into appropriate changes in curricula and developmental experiences; and c) critically assess student/stakeholder needs and effectively ensure that those needs are met through the provision of accurate information, timely decisions, and services of the highest quality. When service providers (academic and administrative) place the needs of students ahead of their own, they perform job tasks and make decisions within a student-centred context. This mindset combined with a "customer care" attitude can be a powerful force in providing high-performing enrolment services. An investment in individual learning and knowledge management systems that support organizational learning are key elements in ensuring effective service delivery as well as the continuous improvement of programs and services. While the return on investment that can be realized from employee training and development is well documented, this is an area where many organizations fail to invest (Bolman and Deal, 1997). Key capacity conditions include:

- Faculty and staff learning and development systems are aligned with the changing profile of today's learners (e.g., cultural and diversity awareness, technology orientation, student development principles), and the skills/competencies they require to maintain currency and relevancy in the performance of their responsibilities.

- A student-centred service orientation is embedded within hiring, staff and faculty orientation, learning and development strategies, and performance management systems.

- Staff learning and development are tied to performance management systems.

- Technology-enabled knowledge management systems are in place to support organizational learning, and the delivery of consistent and accurate information to students.

## Capacity Condition 11—Shared Responsibility for Performance Improvement

In high-performing organizations, employees (faculty, staff, and administrators) are engaged and empowered to respond to students' educational needs, to improve processes, and to improve student learning and the organization's performance results. High levels of employee engagement have a significant, positive impact on organizational performance and student/stakeholder satisfaction. Employee engagement is enhanced when the desired organizational culture values are aligned with the personal values of individuals and reinforced within hiring, performance management, and reward systems. Therefore, a workforce environment conducive to high performance within the context of SEM reinforces organizational values associated with a student-centred and learning-oriented ethos that is demonstrated through teamwork and collaboration, knowledge sharing, a focus on continuous quality improvement, a "caring" service orientation, and the highest standards of professionalism and performance. Key capacity conditions include:

- Shared responsibility for enrolment performance improvement is embodied within clearly defined position descriptions, performance expectations, and accountability and reward systems.

- Teamwork, collaboration, and knowledge sharing within and across organizational boundaries are incorporated into regular work processes.

- Performance management, reward, and accountability systems reinforce a student-centred and learning-oriented ethos.

## Capacity Condition 12—Service-Oriented Systems and Practices

Within a SEM context, organizational "quality" is defined by the relevance of programs and services to the needs of target student segments. High-performing enrolment organizations focus on improving their capabilities through continuous improvement of their programs and services. In a student-focused environment, the primary goal is to make the processes of the institution as intuitive and invisible as possible for students. To accomplish this goal, processes must be viewed through the students' eyes and add value to the student experience. Typically, students do not view student services through our hierarchical organizational structures, but rather as a means to an end. Consequently, organizational boundaries need to be made invisible and processes that cross those boundaries should be seamless. In addition, both formative evaluation to innovate and reinvent and summative evaluation to gauge return on investment and achievement of goals are needed to guide enrolment management efforts. What is learned from these processes must be translated and adopted into routine operations as an accountability linked to employee performance. Key capacity conditions include:

- Mechanisms to support cross-functional planning are in place in order to identify critical student needs, bottlenecks, and/or gaps in program and service delivery.

- Mechanisms to support systematic improvements in business processes are in place that ensure:

  - Student runaround is eliminated.

  - The blend of high tech and high touch are appropriate to user needs.

  - Information is relevant, accurate, and communicated in a timely manner.

  - Services are convenient, accessible, and intuitive in keeping with the user needs.

  - Student learning and development strategies are aligned with the needs of target student segments.

  - Mission critical student related systems are in place (e.g., degree audit, academic scheduling systems, online course management systems).

  - Staff productivity is maximized by reducing manually intensive, low-value work through enabling technologies (e.g., document imaging).

- Systematic evaluation processes (both formative and summative) support the continuous improvement of academic programs and services for students.

## Capacity Condition 13—Effective Use of Strategic Enrolment Intelligence

SEM is inherently goal-driven and results-oriented. While many institutions operate with the goal of increasing enrolment, few have the ability to define optimum enrolment capacity in order to maximize net revenues and achieve financial imperatives. To thrive into the future, you must have the actionable intelligence that allows your institution to focus on the right strategic issues, and to strategically deploy your resources where the highest potential return on investment exists. The successful execution of the "right" strategies is determined in large measure by the degree to which the institution develops, shares, and uses information to inform action related to immediate situations or to a forecasted challenge or opportunity. Therefore, organizational policies, systems and structures must be in place that support the collection and management of the right data, the translation of data into information, and the communication of information to those who require it. In doing so, technology becomes the vehicle that high performing enrolment organizations leverage to work smarter and more efficiently. Key capacity conditions include:

- There is a robust enrolment performance measurement and reporting system to support both tactical and strategic enrolment decisions and assessment of return on investment of strategies implemented.

- Technology is leveraged in support of functions associated with:

  - Student and stakeholder relationship management

  - Knowledge management to support organizational learning

  - Workforce engagement and productivity

  - Process management in the delivery of seamless, effective, efficient, and nimble services

  - Information and data management as sources of actionable and strategic intelligence

## SUMMARY

To create the capacity conditions for success, high performing enrolment organizations start by assembling a leadership team of the "right" people in the "right" seats; by infusing strategic thinking, acting, and learning into the organization through a process of "organizational visioning"; and by investing in people to create the conditions for their success in realization of the vision. It is the synergy created by firing on all cylinders that creates the organizational conditions for high performance and success (Clemmer, 1992). Therefore, the aforementioned capacity conditions are not mutually exclusive. Bold and disciplined leadership is required at all levels of the organization to define the vision for change, and lead the way in creating the conditions for optimal enrolment performance. While the road ahead may appear to be formidable, now more than ever before, higher education needs leaders among leaders who can "unleash the power and potential of people and organizations for the greater good" (Blanchard, 2010).

## REFERENCES

Baldrige National Quality Program: *Education Criteria for Performance Excellence.* Web site. Available @ http://www.baldrige.nist.gov/Education_Criteria.htm

Black, J. (2003, October). *Defining enrollment management: The symbolic frame.* [White paper]. Retrieved from http://www.semworks.net/about-us/resources/jim-black-publications.php

Black, J. (2008a, January). *The art and science of enrollment planning.* [White paper]. Retrieved from http://www.semworks.net/white-papers.php

Black, J. (2008b, May). *Enrollment management: A systems approach.* [White paper]. Retrieved from http://www.semworks.net/white-papers.php

Black, J. (2008c, May). *Perfecting enrollment strategy.* [White paper]. Retrieved from http://www.semworks.net/white-papers.php

Blanchard, K. (2010). *Leading at a higher level.* New Jersey: Blanchard Management Corporation Publishing.

Bryson, J. (2004). *Strategic planning for public and nonprofit organizations: A guide to strengthening and sustaining organizational achievement* (3rd ed.). San Francisco: Jossey-Bass.

Bolman, L. & Deal, T. (1997). *Reframing organizations: Artistry, choice and leadership* (2nd ed.). San Francisco: Jossey-Bass.

Bontrager, B. (2004). *Enrollment management: An introduction to concepts and structures.* College and University Journal, 79 (3), 11–16.

Cameron, K. S., & Quinn, R. E. (1999, 2006). *Diagnosing and changing organizational culture: Based on the competing values framework.* Revised Edition. Jossey-Bass, San Francisco, CA. OCAI Instrument available at http://www.ocai-online.com/about-OCAI .

Clemmer, J. (1992). *Firing on all cylinders: The service/quality system for high-powered corporate performance* (2nd ed). Toronto: Macmillan Canada, a Division of Canada Publishing Corporation.

Collins, J. (2001). *Good to great.* New York, NY: HarperCollins Publishing Inc.

Collins, J. (2005). *Good to great and the social sectors.* New York, NY: HarperCollins Publishing Inc.

Copeland, T. (2009). *The recruitment and outreach scorecard: moving from a tactically driven to a strategy driven enrollment office.* College and University Journal, 84 (3), 35–39. Retrieved August 21, 2009, from http://www.enrollmentmarketing.org/research/College-University-Recruitment-Outreach-Scorecard-Tim-Copeland.pdf

Dennison, D., and Gallagher, P. (1986). *Canada's community colleges, a critical analysis.* Vancouver: University of British Columbia Press.

Dolence, M. G. (1993, 1997). *Strategic enrollment management: A primer for campus administrators.* Second edition. Washington, D.C.: American Association of Collegiate Registrars and Admissions Officers.

Henderson, S. E. (2001, November). *On the brink of a profession: A history of enrollment management in higher education.* In Black, J. (Ed.). (2001). The strategic enrollment management revolution, 3–36. Washington, DC: American Association of Collegiate Registrars and Admissions Officers.

Horton, D.; Alexaki, A.; Bennett-Lartey, S.; Brice, K. N; Campilan, D.; Carden, F.; de Souza Silva, J.; Duong, L. T.; Khadar, I.; Maestrey Boza, A.; Kayes Muniruzzaman, I., Perez, J.; Somarriba Chang, M.; Vernooy, R.; & Watts, J. (2003). *Evaluating capacity development: experiences from research and development organizations around the world.* The Netherlands: International Service for National Agricultural Research (ISNAR); Canada: International Development Research Centre (IDRC), the Netherlands: ACP-EU Technical Centre for Agricultural and Rural Cooperation (CTA). Available at http://www.idrc.ca/en/ev-31556-201-1-DO_TOPIC.html

Hossler, D., Bean, J. P., & Associates. (1990). *The strategic planning of college enrollments*. San Francisco: Jossey-Bass.

Hossler, D. (2008). The public landscape: *Financing higher education in America*. In Bontrager, B. (Ed.). SEM and institutional success: integrating enrollment, finance and student success, 2–13. Washington, DC: American Association of Collegiate Registrars and Admissions Officers.

Judge, W. & Elenkov, D. (2005). *Organizational capacity for change and environmental performance: an empirical assessment of Bulgarian firms*. Journal of Business Research, 58 (7) 893–901.

Judge, W. & Blocker, C. (2008). *Organizational capacity for change and strategic ambidexterity: Flying the plane while rewiring it*. European Journal of Marketing, 42 (9/10) 915–926.

Kemer, F., Baldrige, J. V., & Green, K. (1982). *Strategies for effective enrollment management*. Washington, DC: American Association of State Colleges and Universities.

Kisling, R. & Riggs, R. (2004, April). *Moving toward a SEM plan: Part II*. AACRAO SEM Source Newsletter.

Kotter, J. P. (1995, March-April). *Leading change: Why transformation efforts fail*. Harvard Business Review, 73, 59–67.

Kuh, G. D., & Whitt, E. J. (1988). *The invisible tapestry: Culture in American colleges and universities,* ASHE-ERIC Higher Education Report, 17[1]. San Francisco, CA: Jossey-Bass.

Kuh, Kinzie, Schuh, Whitt, & Associates. 2005. *Student success incollege: creating conditions that matter*. San Francisco: Jossey-Bass, Inc.

Kuh, G. D. (2006). *Making students matter*. In J.C. Burke (Ed.), *Fixing the fragmented university: Decentralization with Direction*, 235–264). Bolton, MA: Jossey-Bass.

Lusthaus, C., Adrien M-H., Anderson,G., Carden, F., & Montalván, G. (2002). *Organizational assessment: A framework for improving performance*. Published jointly by the International Development Research Centre and Inter-American Development Bank.

Lusthaus, C., Adrien M-H., Anderson,G., & Carden, F. (1999). *Enhancing organizational performance: A toolkit for self-assessment*. Published by the International Development Research Centre.

Mintzberg, H. (2009, August). *The best leadership is good management*. Bloomberg Business Week. Retrieved from www.businessweek.com/magazine/content/09_33/b4143068890733.htm

Norris, D.M. & Leonard, J. (2008, March). *What every campus leader needs to know about analytics*. [White paper]. Retrieved from www.istrategysolutions.com/documents/AnalyticsWhitePaper.pdf

Norris, D.M. (2008, September). *Metrics and analytics in SEM*. White paper. Retrieved July 24, 2010, from http://www.semworks.net/papers/wp_Metrics-and-Analytics-in-SEM.php

Norris, D., Baer, L., Leonard, J., Pugliese, L. & Lefrere, P. (2008, January/February). *Action analytics: Measuring and improving performance that matters in higher education*. EDUCAUSE Review, 43 (1) 42–67. Retrieved from http://www.educause.edu/EDUCAUSE+Review/EDUCAUSEReviewMagazineVolume43/ActionAnalyticsMeasuringandImp/162422

Owen, Rita, R. (2001). *SEM as a driver for institutional change*. In J. Black (Ed.), The strategic enrollment management revolution, 111–128. Washington, DC: American Association of Collegiate Registrars and Admissions Officers.

Quinn, R. (2004). *Building the bridge as you walk on it: A guide to leading change*. Jossey-Bass, John Wiley & Sons, Inc.

Shanahan, T. and Jones, G. (2007). *Shifting roles and approaches: Government coordination of postsecondary education in Canada from 1995 to 2006*. Journal of Higher Education Research and Development. 26 (1), 31–43.

Senge, P. (1990). *The fifth discipline: The art and practice of the learning organization*. New York: Doubleday.

Swail, W. S. (2002, July/August). *Higher education and the new demographics: questions for policy*. Change, 15–23. Retrieved from www.educationalpolicy.org/pdf/higherED_demographics02.pdf

# CONCLUSION

# CHAPTER NINE
## REPUTATION, RECRUITMENT, AND RETENTION IMPERATIVES

**BY JIM BLACK**

A considerable portion of this book is devoted to strategic issues such as the use of actionable intelligence, change management, institutional culture, and building organizational capacity. However, we would be remiss not to share insights into the role of executive leaders in guiding the tactical side of the enrolment enterprise. In particular, this chapter will identify imperatives in three areas: reputation, recruitment, and retention. For each, five imperatives will be explored: 1) goal-driven, integrated plans; 2) adequate resource deployment to support plans; 3) assessment; 4) strategy-related metrics; and 5) accountability. The conclusion is centred on translating the theory espoused in earlier chapters into leadership action related to these imperatives.

To be clear, we are not recommending draconian oversight of day-to-day operations. When leaders wade too far into the weeds, they are prone to lose sight of the strategic. This is a fatal misstep. Consequently, the author is advocating for visionary, inspirational leadership. Your support of tactical efforts will aid in the attainment of institutional enrolment goals if your leadership is laser focused on the right things: articulating a clear direction, asking thought-provoking questions, ensuring the antecedents for success are present, motivating the troops, holding people accountable for quality execution and timely deliverables, recognizing contributions to enrolment goals in meaningful ways, evaluating ROI to inform strategy, and demonstrating the courage to stay the course even when internal and external pressures beg for immediate, panic-driven responses. Truthfully, there is no substitute for strong leadership. In large measure, your institution's enrolment vitality is dependent upon your leadership.

## REPUTATIONAL LEADERSHIP IMPERATIVES

According to Sevier (1998), an institution's "image is everything." Perhaps this is hyperbole, but you are cautioned not to dismiss this claim summarily. The reputation your institution possesses in the PSE landscape matters, particularly as it is weighed against the reputations of your primary competitors.

Decades of research with college and university entering first-year students reveals that academic reputation appears to be the top factor in selecting a first choice institution (Higher Education Research Institute, 2007). However, an alternate conclusion is found in the extensive research of Canadian college and university applicants conducted by Academica Group. Steele (2008, May) observed that academic reputation is one of the top two decision factors considered by students pursuing "elite" institutions—the other being high admission averages. Results from Academica's University and College Applicant Study (UCAS™) reveal that the top decision factors vary by perceived reputation of an institution. For instance, at "commodity" schools (mostly two-year colleges), affordability factors along with proximity to home are the primary decision drivers, not academic reputation.

Using the naming conventions adopted by Academica, schools that are perceived as elite, outcome, nurturing, campus, or commodity institutions have different categorical reputational attributes. The point here is that regardless of your reputational category, your institution will benefit from being the "best of breed" (the best within a reputational category) and by engaging in differential positioning among competitors in other reputational classifications.

**To achieve these positioning objectives, leadership support is required in the following reputational imperatives:**

- **A goal-driven, integrated branding plan.** In order to be goal-driven, an institution must first come to grips with its current reputational position and then determine the desired position for the future—the goals. To begin this process, unearth existing reputational data that define the decision factors for students selecting your institution as well as for the competitor institutions they choose. Next, identify reputational data and research gaps. And then, conduct the necessary research internally or outsource the research to a firm such as Academica. When the needed benchmark data are collected, analyze reputational findings and utilize the analysis to develop your institution's integrated brand platform—the compass for the strategies in the plan. The brand platform should include elements such as a succinct positioning statement, a brand rationale, brand attributes, proof points that support the brand position, as well as messaging and supporting visual identity elements. Throughout this process, you are encouraged to engage the campus community in the development of goals and the subsequent plan.

- **Human and financial resources adequate to support goal attainment.** Our marketing and communication audits at North American colleges and universities have exposed significant variance in funding and staffing at institutions with similar missions, enrolments, and reputational goals. This variance is almost always directly correlated to an institution's ability to achieve its reputational objectives. Therefore, you must accurately gauge the resource requirements of your branding plan—dollars sufficient to have a sustained presence in the market, adequate staffing levels with the right composition of needed skill sets among marketing personnel, and enabling technologies. This requires an extensive assessment of organizational capacity around the marketing enterprise. The assessment should be holistic—searching for duplication of effort as well as possible synergies. Regardless of the exact resources required, you are strongly encouraged to appoint a brand champion, an individual with the expertise to facilitate strategy development and deployment and who has the political acumen necessary to foster brand adoption and compliance.

- **Assessment of the quantity and quality of marketing activities designed to promote the reputational image.** As the plan is implemented, the institution needs to assess the degree to which constituent awareness and perception are shifting from those indentified in the benchmark data toward established reputational goals. Replicating prior image and applicant studies will demonstrate the effectiveness of your branding efforts. Other assessments can provide indirect evidence of your effectiveness: monitoring the number and quality of inquiries and applicants over time; comparing win rates with competitors (the percentage of admits who select your institution over a competitor when offered admission to both); and studies that reveal the level of congruence between your marketing claims and the actual experiences of your students.

- **Strategy-related metrics.** Confirm that metrics have been defined, related data are being captured, and metric analysis is informing future strategies. Senior leadership must create a culture of evidence in order to ensure the research and data are used appropriately in the strategy decision-making and prioritization process.

- **Accountability mechanisms.** Actively support campus-wide brand adoption and compliance with established brand guidelines. For example, consider requiring all marketing materials produced internally to be vetted through a central marketing unit, and ensure that any outsourced marketing projects must be awarded to an approved agency of record (AOR) that has agreed to adhere to the brand guidelines. Your Procurement Department can control the use of the approved AOR when institutional funds are being expended.

Through our consultancies, we have witnessed many reputational positioning efforts get derailed or become diluted to the point of being ineffective. The fallout from a failed positioning endeavour is substantial internally and externally and as such, is extremely difficult to overcome. Your leadership is required to prevent this cataclysmic outcome. More importantly, your leadership is essential to creating a "game changing" institutional position.

## RECRUITMENT LEADERSHIP IMPERATIVES

Most undergraduate recruitment operations remain bound to the traditional mode of recruitment—travel to high schools and in some cases, to two-year colleges. Even worse, graduate recruitment operations tend to passively wait for interested students to self-identify. The recruitment process parallels the prospective student life cycle and as such, includes the prospect, inquiry, application, admission, and enrolment stages of the life cycle (commonly referred to as the enrolment funnel). Travel outreach primarily is designed to move prospects (any potential student) to inquiries (students who express an interest in the institution). This strategy seldom addresses the other stages of the life cycle.

Applying a horticultural analogy, recruitment outreach through travel and other means are "seed planting" activities. Perhaps, the most important and most neglected facet of recruitment is "crop cultivation" or more aptly named, "relationship management." The purpose of this recruitment stage is to aggressively cultivate interest. Unfortunately, we often find minimal interaction with prospective students between the inquiry and admit stages. The final stage of our horticultural analogy is the "harvest." The vast majority of recruitment operations we assess do a reasonably good job of facilitating the admit conversion to enrolment stage. They keep students focused on elements needed to complete the enrolment process and assist them as needed in navigating processes and the institution. With that said, recruitment efforts at this stage are habitually, and sometimes singularly, focused on process to the exclusion of continued selling of institutional benefits, connecting students with other incoming and returning students, fostering critical relationships with faculty and advisors, and "closing the deal."

While recruitment solutions will be different for each college or university based on institutional mission, market position, competitors, available resources, capacity, the profile of students served, and a host of other factors, there are five basic principles that can be applied universally. First, as implied earlier, students are influenced by relationships. A major focus of any recruitment strategy should be on cultivating a relationship between the prospective student and the institution (e.g., with current students, faculty, staff, alumni). Second, students want to be treated as individuals. The customization of communications, so that it is personalized, timely, and relevant to an individual is of paramount importance. Regardless of the medium through which the message is delivered, a customized message is always more powerful than one that is generic. Third, communications should be delivered through multiple channels (e.g., promotional advertising, direct mail, social media, and digital media) by multiple people (e.g., the chancellor, recruiter, faculty, and the parents of current students) with a single voice. Repetition is necessary to expand interest in the school and move a prospective student to action (e.g., visit the campus, apply for admission, attend orientation, register for classes, and pay the bill). Fourth, every interaction with a prospective student is a "moment of truth" (Carlson, 1987) for the institution. As such, each interaction should be carefully orchestrated to ensure the desired outcome. For example, the campus visit, for most institutions, is the pivotal "moment of truth" when students decide if a school is right for them or not. Seldom can they articulate the reasons other than to say, "It just feels right." This suggests, at least for most traditional-aged undergraduates, the decision is more emotional than intellectual. Following this premise, campus visits should be engineered to deliver emotional appeal rather than voluminous facts that are not retained beyond the parking lot. And fifth, a slow response to a student inquiry or request is the proverbial kiss of death. A slow response signals to the student that the institution does not care. Nothing else the institution can do will matter.

As an executive leader, you are encouraged to ensure that recruitment efforts are appropriately distributed across the prospective student life cycle and focused on the right things. Equally as important, you should evaluate the existence and quality of the following:

- A goal-driven, integrated recruitment plan. Recruitment goals should be aligned with and support institutional enrolment goals. In this context, an integrated recruitment plan includes EVERY recruitment activity engaged by the institution (inclusive of those implemented by academic departments), not just those that are implemented centrally. Such coordination and planning will reduce duplication of effort, ensure potential synergies are maximized, and most importantly, cause centralized and decentralized recruitment interactions with prospective students to appear as if they are orchestrated and coming from the same institution.

- Human and financial resources adequate to support goal attainment. Recruitment efforts that are under resourced tend to be poorly executed. As stated previously, execution, not strategies per se, represents your institution's competitive advantage. Your role is to ensure that the necessary antecedents are in place to execute your recruitment plan better than competitors can. This includes, but is not limited to, having the right level and mix of staff, adequate funding, information structures, and needed technologies.

- Assessment of the quantity and quality of interactions with prospective students. This is an area where you may want to contract with an objective third party. Experienced consultants know what to look for in such an assessment—number of touch points at each stage of the enrolment funnel, quality and relevance of touch points, effectiveness of touch points, etc.

- Strategy-related metrics. Confirm that metrics have been defined, related data are being captured, and metric analysis is informing future strategies. Senior leadership must create a culture of evidence in order to ensure the research and data are used appropriately in the strategy decision-making and prioritization process.

- Accountability mechanisms. For recruitment efforts, create a venue for routine reporting to senior leadership on progress toward goals and metric attainment. You are cautioned not to rely solely on applicant and admission numbers as barometers of effectiveness. These measures alone produce false positive as well as false negative indicators. We have observed several recruitment operations where enrolment numbers suggest that recruitment efforts are "hitting on all cylinders" only to find a dysfunctional organization. The converse is also true.

## RETENTION LEADERSHIP IMPERATIVES

In prior chapters, authors have discussed the need for a culture of student success along with the role of leaders in creating and sustaining such a culture. While the culture is the heart of any retention initiative, it must be undergirded with the right conditions for student success to occur. The retention literature is replete with examples of success conditions such as:

- clear communication regarding institutional expectations, values, policies, and procedures (Berger, 2001–02; Braxton & McClendon, 2001–02; Kuh, 2001–02);

- an engaging student experience inside and outside the classroom (Kuh, 2001–02; Keeler, 2004);

- informed faculty and staff regarding reasons for student attrition and knowledge of campus resources available to support student retention (Hossler, Bean, & Associates, 1990);

- accessible support services (e.g., learning skills development, tutoring, and counseling) that enhance the probability of student success (Tinto, 1993);

- advising that is more about exploring career and life interests and setting related educational goals than course scheduling (Light, 2001; Damminger, 2007);

- transitional assistance provided to students as they matriculate into the institution (Gardner & Jewler, 1985; Tinto, 1993);

- effective teaching and learning practices such as collaborative and active learning (Boyer,1990; Kuh, 2001, May/June; Nilson, 2010);

- a reward structure that recognizes faculty who foster retention through their teaching practices (Braxton & McClendon, 2001–02);

- curriculum tied to students' lives outside the classroom (Kuh, 2001–02);

- and early warning systems designed to identify students experiencing difficulty, so that appropriate interventions can occur (Tinto, 1993; Light, 2001).

**The pertinent question here is how do leaders contribute to establishing and sustaining these conditions for student success on a campus. Related retention imperatives are presented below:**

- **A goal-driven, integrated retention plan.** Retention goals should be aligned with and support institutional enrolment goals. An integrated retention plan pulls together loosely coupled services, programs, and success conditions in an orchestrated fashion, so that these elements work in harmony to enhance the potential for student success to occur. It is imperative that student affairs and academic units work collaboratively to this end.

- **Human and financial resources adequate to support goal attainment.** Generally speaking, our consultants find that colleges and universities have a tendency to under resource success initiatives, particularly in comparison with institutional investments in marketing and recruitment. Consider the revenue savings every time you retain a student. The positive ROI for retention efforts is compelling.

- **Assessment of the quantity and quality of interactions with current students.** Again, you may want to consider utilizing external reviewers for this purpose. Both the quantity and quality of interactions are directly correlated to retention. Regarding the former, it is common to find exemplary services that are underutilized or have minimal impact on retention because they are limited to one or two interactions with students. For the latter, many retention programs are not evaluated for effectiveness routinely. As a campus leader, you should insist on annual evaluations and redeploy resources from less effective initiatives to those with more potential to support retention goals.

- **Strategy-related metrics.** Confirm that metrics have been defined, related data are being captured, and metric analysis is informing future strategies. Senior leadership must create a culture of evidence in order to ensure the research and data are used appropriately in the strategy decision-making and prioritization process.

- **Accountability mechanisms.** Accountability is challenging due to the broadly accepted mantra, "retention is everyone's business," which oft translates into there is no one to hold accountable for related outcomes. Consequently, you need to assign ownership for overall retention outcomes as well as for ensuring each of the conditions for success is in place. Accountability can be assigned to a retention champion, the chief enrolment officer, academic deans, as well as to academic and administrative units. Linking funding to the retention and enrolment outcomes will demonstrate that the institution values and expects contributions to student success.

## FINAL THOUGTHS ON LEADERSHIP

One of the early contemporary writers on leadership theory, Max DePree (1989), described leadership as "more an art, a belief, a condition of the heart, than a set of things to do." Though much of this book is dedicated to practical ways in which campus leaders can support strategic enrolment efforts, this author subscribes to DePree's perspective on leadership. Taskmasters are seldom effective in an academic environment. A much more sophisticated array of skills than task management is required to navigate the leadership terrain within the ivy-covered walls of the academy.

Stephen Covey's (1989) seminal book on leadership, The *Seven Habits of Highly Effective People,* references soft skills of an effective leader: being proactive, beginning with the end in mind, discerning urgent priorities from important priorities, searching for win-wins, seeking to understand before being understood, and recognizing the importance of continuous improvement. A multitude of other leadership experts advocate for characteristics such as being grounded in reality, possessing strong convictions, creating shared values, co-opting others into your vision, enabling others to act, modeling desired behaviours, leaving a legacy, developing learning organizations, and being a servant leader—just to name a few (Senge, 1991; Kouzes & Posner, 1995; Hesselbein, 1996; Greenleaf, 2002). If the reader is interested in leadership as it relates to the domain of enrolment management, there are two noteworthy publications you should consider: *Becoming a Leader in Enrollment Services* (Swanson & Weese, 1997) and *Navigating Change in the New Millennium: Enrollment Leadership Strategies* (Black, 1999). Reading these works may provide additional insights into how best to incorporate leadership theory into the world of enrolment management.

Regardless of the characteristics you possess or aspire to, recognize that leadership in the academy is often a "slippery slope." The rules of engagement are frequently vague or nonexistent, and there are natural tensions that exist between an academic culture and enrolment objectives. Examples of the latter are presented here: 1) By nature, academic cultures promote autonomy, yet SEM is intrinsically intertwined with the common good of the institution. 2) As stated in Chapter Seven, academic organizations are highly decentralized. At times, decentralized structures present impediments to a core objective of SEM—integration. 3) Because colleges and universities often possess rich traditions and rituals, they are inclined to revel in maintaining a modicum of sameness. When pressed to an extreme, this phenomenon results in people and the organization clinging to the status quo. SEM, on the other hand, lives in the midst of constant change. In fact, change is a prerequisite for successful SEM. 4) Academic cultures are founded on intellectual inquiry and cognitive dissonance, which can be at odds with the SEM objective of seeking broad-based buy-in and involvement. 5) Lastly, academic organizations tend to be faculty- or administration-centred while SEM is always student-centred.

Be conscious of these tensions as you wade into leading the SEM effort at your institution. Though daunting, these challenges are not insurmountable for the politically savvy leader. Set your sights on the enrolment goals of the institution and remain committed to stay the course. You will prevail.

## REFERENCES

Berger, J. B. (2001–2002). *Understanding the organizational nature of student persistence: Empirically-based recommendations for practice.* Journal of College Student Retention, 3 (1), 3–21. New York: Baywood Publishing Company.

Black, J. (1999). *Navigating change in the new millennium: Enrollment leadership strategies.* Washington, DC: American Association of Collegiate Registrars and Admissions Officers.

Boyer, E. L. (1990). *Scholarship reconsidered: Priorities for the professorate.* San Francisco: John Wiley & Sons, Inc.

Braxton, J. & McClendon, S. (2001–2002). *The fostering of social integration and retention through institutional practice.* Journal of College Student Retention: Research, Theory, and Practice, 3 (1). New York: Baywood Publishing Company.

Carlson, J. (1987). *Moment of truth.* New York: Harper & Row Publishing, Inc.

Covey, S. R. (1989). *The 7 habits of highly effective people.* New York: Simon & Schuster, Inc.

Damminger, J. K. (2007). *Self-assessment: Relevance and value in first-year advising.* In M. S. Hunter, B. McCalla-Wriggins, & E. R. White (Eds.), Academic advising: New insights for teaching and learning in the first year. 59–69. Columbia, SC: University of South Carolina, National Resource Center for The First-Year Experience and Students in Transition.

Greenleaf, R. K. (2002). *Servant leadership: A journey into the nature of legitimate power & greatness* (3rd ed.). Mahwah, NJ: Paulist Press.

Hesselbein, F. (1996). *The "how to be" leader.* In F. Hesselbein, M. Goldsmith, & R. Beckhard (Eds.), *The leader of the future.* 121–124. San Francisco: Jossey-Bass.

Higher Education Research Institute (2007). *The American freshman.* Los Angeles, CA: UCLA Graduate School of Education and Information Studies. Retrieved from http://www.heri.ucla.edu/cirpoverview.php.

Hossler, D., Bean, J. P., & Associates. (1990). *The strategic planning of college enrollments.* San Francisco: Jossey-Bass.

Keeler, R. P. (2004). *Learning reconsidered: A campus-wide focus on the student experience.* Washington, DC: National Association of Student Personnel Administrators & American College Personnel Association.

Kouzes, J. M. & Posner, B. Z. (1995). *The leadership challenge.* San Francisco: Jossey-Bass.

Kouzes, J. M. & Posner, B. Z. (1996). *Seven lessons for leading the voyage to the future.* In F. Hesselbein, M. Goldsmith, & R. Beckhard (Eds.), *The leader of the future.* 99–110. San Francisco: Jossey-Bass.

Kuh, G. D. (2001, May/June). *Assessing what really matters to student learning.* Washington, DC: Change.

Kuh, G. D. (2001–2002). *Organizational culture and student persistence: Prospects and puzzles.* Journal of College Student Retention, 3 (1), 23–29. New York: Baywood Publishing Company.

Light, R. J. (2001). *Making the most of college: Students speak their minds.* Cambridge: Harvard University Press.

Nilson, L. B. (2010). *Teaching at its best: A resource-based resource for college instructors* (3rd ed.). San Francisco: John Wiley & Sons, Inc.

Senge, P. (1990). *The fifth discipline: The art and practice of the learning organization*. New York: Doubleday.

Sevier, R. A. (1998). *Integrated marketing for colleges, universities, and schools*. Hiawatha, Iowa: Strategy Publishing. Washington, DC: Council for Advancement and Support of Education.

Steele, K. (2008, May). *Classifying universities: Institutional brands from the market's perspective*. London, Ontario: Academica Group. Retrieved from http://www.academicagroup.com/sites/academicagroup.com/files/ClassifyingU-2008.pdf.

Swanson, R. M. & Weese, F. A. (1997). *Becoming a leader in enrollment services*. Washington, DC: American Association of Collegiate Registrars and Admissions Officers.

Tinto, V. (1993). *Leaving college: Rethinking the causes and cures of student attrition* (2nd ed.). Chicago: The University of Chicago Press.

# INDEX